STATUTORY INST

1981 No. 859

ROAD TRAFFIC

The Traffic Signs Regulations and General Directions 1981

Made – – – –	10*th June* 1981
Laid before Parliament	23*rd July* 1981
Coming into Operation	13*th August* 1981

LONDON
HER MAJESTY'S STATIONERY OFFICE: 1981

STATUTORY INSTRUMENTS

1981 No. 859

ROAD TRAFFIC

The Traffic Signs Regulations and General Directions 1981

Made - - -	10*th June* 1981
Laid before Parliament	23*rd July* 1981
Coming into Operation	13*th August* 1981

ARRANGEMENT

PART I—TRAFFIC SIGNS REGULATIONS

SECTION I

Preliminary

	Regulation
Citation	1
Revocation	2
Savings	3
Interpretation	4, 5

SECTION II

Miscellaneous General Provisions

Authorisations by the Secretary of State	6
Application of section 22 of the Road Traffic Act 1972 to signs and disqualification for offences	7
Variations in dimensions	8

SECTION III

Traffic Signs shown in Schedule 1

Signs to be of the sizes, colours and types shown in diagrams...	9
Sign shown in diagram 610 and its significance	9A
Signs shown in diagrams 601.1, 602, 602.1 and 649.1 and their significance	10, 11

[DET 35332]

Permitted variants 12
Dimensions 13
Proportions and form of letters and numerals 14
Illumination of signs by steady lighting 15, 16
Illumination of signs shown in diagrams 560 and 561 by reflectors etc. 17
Illumination of signs by reflecting material 18, 19

SECTION IV

Traffic Signs shown in Schedule 2

Road markings 20
Particular road markings 21–23
Colour of road markings 24
Use on road markings of reflecting material and studs with reflectors 25
Height of road markings and size of studs 26

SECTION V

Miscellaneous Traffic Signs

Certain temporary signs 27
Flashing beacons and flags 28
Cones and cylinders 29
Refuge indicator lamps 30
Light signals for control of vehicular traffic 31, 32
Portable light signals for control of vehicular traffic 33
Significance of light signals 34
Light signals for pedestrians 35
Light signals for lane control of vehicular traffic 36
School crossing patrol signs and warning lights 37
Light signals for motorways 38, 39
Road danger lamps 40

SCHEDULES

Page
1. Part I —Warning signs 37–58
Part II —Regulatory signs 59–75
Part III—Directional informatory signs 76–107
Part IV—Other informatory signs 108–132
Part V —Directional and other informatory signs on motorways 133–140
2. Markings on the road 141–168

3. Size and colour of arrow in light signals for control of vehicular traffic and methods of incorporation of the arrow in those signals 169–171
4. Size, colour and type of light signals for pedestrians ... 172–174
5. Size, colour and type of light signals for lane control of vehicular traffic 175
6. Size, colour and type of temporary indications on motorways 176–180
7. Proportion and form of letters, numerals and other characters 181–193
8. Exercise of powers 194

PART II—GENERAL DIRECTIONS

PART III—GENERAL CITATION AND COMMENCEMENT

The Secretary of State for Transport, the Secretary of State for Scotland and the Secretary of State for Wales make these Regulations and give these Directions in exercise of the powers conferred by sections 25, 54 and 55 of the Road Traffic Regulation Act 1967(**a**) and by the provision in column 5 of Part I of Schedule 4 to the Road Traffic Act 1972(**b**) which relates to section 22 of that Act, and now vested in them (**c**), and of all other enabling powers, and after consultation with representative organisations in accordance with section 107(2) of the said Act of 1967 and section 199(2) of the said Act of 1972 (the said powers being exercised by the said Secretaries of State either jointly or separately as respects England, Scotland and Wales in the manner set out in Schedule 8 to these Regulations).

PART I—TRAFFIC SIGNS REGULATIONS
SECTION 1

Preliminary

Citation

1. These Regulations may be cited as the Traffic Signs Regulations 1981.

Revocation

2. The Traffic Signs Regulations 1975(**d**) are hereby revoked, and the said Regulations of 1975 are hereinafter in these Regulations referred to as "the Regulations of 1975".

Savings

3.—(1) Any traffic sign, which immediately before the coming into operation of these Regulations is in being, if it is a sign shown in any of the diagrams Nos. 564.2 to 564.4 in Schedule 1 to the Regulations of 1975 or is a sign for which there is provision in Regulation 27(1)(*a*)(iv) of those Regulations and if it then complies with the provisions relating thereto by virtue of those

(**a**) 1967 c.76.
(**b**) 1972 c. 20.
(**c**) S.I. 1981/238 (as respects the powers of the Secretary of State for Transport).
(**d**) S.I. 1975/1536.

Regulations, shall so long as it continues to comply with the said provisions as though the same had not been revoked be treated as if prescribed by these Regulations until 31st December 1985.

(2) Any traffic sign, which immediately before the coming into operation of these Regulations is situated on or near any road, if it is a sign prescribed, or to be treated as if prescribed by the Regulations of 1975 and if it then complies with the provisions relating thereto by virtue of those Regulations, shall so long as it continues to comply with the said provisions as though the same had not been revoked, be treated as if prescribed by these Regulations, any provisions thereof to the contrary notwithstanding;

Provided that this paragraph shall cease to have any effect—

(i) on and after 1st January 1983 in relation to any sign shown in diagram No. 601 in Schedule 1 to the Traffic Signs Regulations 1964 (**a**) (hereinafter in these Regulations referred to as "the Regulations of 1964") and to any sign shown in diagram No. 1035 in Schedule 2 to the Regulations of 1975 as varied by the substitution of the words "turn left", "ahead" or "turn right",

(ii) on and after 1st January 1984 in relation to any sign shown in diagram No. 1002, in Schedule 2 to the Regulations of 1975, and

(iii) on and after 1st January 1990 in relation to any sign shown in any of the diagrams Nos. 622.1, 626, 628, 639.1, 640.2, 649, 719.3, 806.2, 808.2 and 819 in Schedule 1 to the Regulations of 1975.

Interpretation

4.—(1) In these Regulations the following expressions have the meanings hereby respectively assigned to them:—

"the Act" means the Road Traffic Regulation Act 1967;

"chief officer of police", in relation to England and Wales, has the same meaning as in the Police Act 1964(**b**), and, in relation to Scotland, the same meaning as in the Police (Scotland) Act 1967(**c**),

"enactment" includes any instrument made under an Act;

"goods vehicle" means a motor vehicle constructed or adapted for use for the carriage of goods or a trailer so constructed or adapted;

"hours of darkness" means the time between half-an-hour after sunset and half-an-hour before sunrise;

"maximum gross weight" means—

(i) in relation to a goods vehicle equipped with a Ministry plate in accordance with regulation 148 of the Motor Vehicles (Construction and Use) Regulations 1978(**d**), the weight not to be exceeded in Great Britain by that vehicle and shown in column (2) of the plate opposite to the words "GROSS WEIGHT" appearing in column (1) thereof,

(ii) in relation to a goods vehicle not so equipped as aforesaid, but equipped with the appropriate plate required to be affixed in accordance with paragraph (2) of Regulation 42 of the said Regulations of 1978, the maximum gross weight appearing on that plate as part of the particulars which

---

(**a**) S.I. 1964/1857.
(**b**) 1964 c. 48.
(**c**) 1967 c. 77.
(**d**) S.I. 1978/1017; an amending instrument S.I. 1978/1235 is relevant to the references to Regulation 42 in items (ii) and (iii) above but no other amendments are relevant here.

it is required to contain under the relevant provisions of the said Regulation, and

(iii) in relation to a motor vehicle (in this paragraph called "the drawing vehicle") constructed to form part of an articulated vehicle as defined by regulation 3(1) of the said Regulations of 1978, the train weight as defined by regulation 146 of those Regulations and of which particulars are shown in column (2) of the said Ministry plate opposite to the words "TRAIN WEIGHT" appearing in column (1) thereof or, if the drawing vehicle is not equipped with a Ministry plate, the maximum train weight for the purposes of paragraph (4)(*a*)(i) of the said Regulation 42 of which particulars are contained on a plate affixed to the drawing vehicle in accordance with paragraph (2) of that regulation.

"motorway" means a special road—

(*a*) which in England or Wales (save as otherwise provided by or under regulations made under, or having effect as if made under section 13 of the Act) can only be used by traffic of Class I or II of the classes of traffic set out in Schedule 4 to the Highways Act 1980(**a**), or

(*b*) which in Scotland can only be used by traffic of Class I or Class II of the classes of traffic set out in Schedule 2 to the Special Roads Act 1949(**b**);

"primary route" means a route, not being a route formed by any part of a motorway, formed—

(*a*) by a length of trunk road,

(*b*) by a length of trunk road together with another road, not being a trunk road, or

(*c*) by a length of road, not being a trunk road,

being a route as respects which the Secretary of State—

in the case at (*a*) is of the opinion, and in the cases at (*b*) and (*c*) after consultation with the highway authority for the road, not being a trunk road, is of the opinion that it provides the most satisfactory route for through traffic between two or more places of traffic importance;

"non-primary route" means a route, not being a primary route or a motorway or part of a primary route or a motorway;

"scheduled express carriage" means an express carriage operated in accordance with a time-table, and includes a vehicle operating a service in accordance with a time-table contained in an authorisation issued under Council Regulation (EEC) No. 516/72(**c**) (shuttle services by means of coach and bus between Member States) or under Council Regulation (EEC) No. 517/72(**d**) (regular and special regular services by the said means) both of 28th February 1972;

"school bus" means a vehicle constructed or adapted to carry 12 or more passengers and being used to carry persons to or from school as defined by section 114(1) of the Education Act 1944(**e**) and, in Scotland, as defined by section 145 of the Education (Scotland) Act 1962(**f**);

(**a**) 1980 c. 66.
(**b**) 1949 c. 32. Schedule 2 was amended by S.I. 1971/1211.
(**c**) O.J. No. L67, 20.3. 1972, p. 13 (S.E. 1972 (I), p. 137).
(**d**) O.J. No. L67, 20.3. 1972, p. 19 (S.E. 1972 (I), p. 143).
(**e**) 1944 c. 31.
(**f**) 1962 c. 47.

"stud" means a prefabricated device fixed or embedded as a mark in the carriageway;

"temporary statutory provision" means a provision having effect under section 12 of the Act (temporary prohibition or restriction of traffic on roads) or section 9 of the Act (which relates to experimental traffic schemes) as those sections are amended by Part IX of the Transport Act 1968 or contained in sections 57 (traffic signs for giving effect to local traffic regulations), 58 (emergency traffic signs) or 60 (traffic signs in connection with experimental traffic schemes in London) of the Act;

"Wales" and "England" have the meanings respectively assigned to them by section 269 of the Local Government Act 1972(**a**);

"works bus" means a vehicle constructed or adapted to carry 12 or more passengers which has been provided by an employer for the purpose of carrying persons employed by him or on his behalf to or from their place of employment and being used for such a purpose.

(2) Nothing in these Regulations shall have effect so as to authorise any persons not otherwise authorised to do so to place on or near the road any object or device for warning traffic of a temporary obstruction.

5.—(1) References in these Regulations to a numbered Regulation or Schedule shall, unless the reference is to a regulation of, or a schedule to, specified regulations, be construed as references to the Regulation or Schedule bearing that number in these Regulations.

(2) References in any of these Regulations to a numbered paragraph shall, unless the reference is to a paragraph of a specified Regulation, be construed as references to the paragraph bearing that number in the first mentioned Regulation.

(3) Any reference in these Regulations to a diagram by a number is a reference to the diagram of that number in any of the Schedules to these Regulations.

(4) Any reference in these Regulations to any sign shown in a diagram being a diagram in Schedule 1, Schedule 2, Schedule 5 or Schedule 6 shall be construed as including a reference to any such sign varied in accordance with the provisions of these Regulations except where otherwise expressly provided.

SECTION II

Miscellaneous General Provisions

Authorisations by the Secretary of State

6. Nothing in these Regulations shall be taken to limit the powers of the Secretary of State under section 54 of the Act to authorise the erection or retention of traffic signs of a character not prescribed by these Regulations.

(**a**) 1972 c. 70.

Application of section 22 of the Road Traffic Act 1972 to signs and disqualification for offences

7.—(1) Section 22 of the Road Traffic Act 1972 shall apply—

(*a*) to signs of the type shown in any of the diagrams 601.1, 602, 603, 606, 610, 616 and 649.1 and to the sign of the type shown in diagram 602 when used in combination with that shown in diagram 602.1,

(*b*) to the red signal when shown by the light signals prescribed by Regulation 31, by Regulation 31 as varied by Regulation 32, or by Regulation 33,

(*c*) to the road marking shown in diagram 1013.1 insofar as that marking conveys the requirements specified in Regulation 23(2),

(*d*) until the 31st December 1982 inclusive of that date, to any sign which in accordance with Regulation 3(2) is treated as if prescribed by these Regulations until that date, if it is a sign of the type shown in the diagram numbered 601 in Schedule 1 to the Regulations of 1964,

(*e*) until the 31st December 1989 inclusive of that date, to any sign which in accordance with Regulation 3(2) is treated as if prescribed by these Regulations until that date, if it is a sign of the type shown in the diagram numbered 649 in Schedule 1 to the Regulations of 1975, and

(*f*) to any sign which in accordance with Regulation 3(2) is treated as if prescribed by these Regulations, if it is a road marking of the type shown in the diagram numbered 1013 in Schedule 2 to the Regulations of 1964 insofar as that marking conveys the requirements specified in Regulation 23(2) thereof.

(2) The signs specified hereby for the purposes of the paragraph appearing in column 5 of Part I of Schedule 4 to the said Act of 1972 in relation to section 22 thereof, are:—

(*a*) the sign shown in the diagram numbered 601.1,

(*b*) the sign shown in the diagram numbered 649.1,

(*c*) the red signal when shown by light signals prescribed by Regulation 31, by Regulation 31 as varied by Regulation 32, or by Regulation 33,

(*d*) the road marking shown in the diagram numbered 1013.1 insofar as that marking conveys the requirements specified in Regulation 23(2),

(*e*) until the 31st December 1982 inclusive of that date, the sign shown in the diagram numbered 601 in Schedule 1 to the regulations of 1964, which in accordance with Regulation 3(2) is treated as if prescribed by these Regulations until that date,

(*f*) until the 31st December 1989 inclusive of that date, the sign shown in the diagram numbered 649 in Schedule 1 to the Regulations of 1975 which in accordance with Regulation 3(2) is treated as if prescribed by these Regulations until that date, and

(*g*) the road marking shown in the diagram numbered 1013 in Schedule 2 to the Regulations of 1964 insofar as it conveys the requirements specified in Regulation 23(2) thereof which marking is in accordance with Regulation 3(2) treated as if prescribed by these Regulations.

Variations in dimensions

8.—(1) Any variation in a dimension (other than a dimension as to the height of a letter or expressed as being the maximum or, as the case may be, minimum) specified in any of the diagrams in Schedule 1 or Schedules

3 to 6 shall be treated as permitted by these Regulations if the variation—

(*a*) in the case of a dimension so specified as 300 millimetres or as over 300 millimetres, does not exceed 5% of that dimension,

(*b*) in the case of a dimension so specified as 50 millimetres or as over 50 millimetres but as under 300 millimetres, does not exceed 7·5% of that dimension, or

(*c*) in the case of a dimension so specified as under 50 millimetres, does not exceed 10% of that dimension.

(2) Any variation in a dimension as to the height of a letter specified in any of the diagrams in schedule 1 shall be treated as permitted by these Regulations if the variation—

(*a*) in the case of a dimension so specified as 100 millimetres or as over 100 millimentres does not exceed 5% of that dimension, or

(*b*) in the case of a dimension so specified as under 100 millimetres, does not exceed 7·5% of that dimension.

(3) Without prejudice to the next following paragraph, any variation in a dimension (other than a dimension expressed in diagrams 1003.4, 1013.1, 1027.1, 1040 to 1045 or 1055 as being the maximum, or as the case may be, minimum) specified in any of the diagrams in Schedule 2 shall be treated as permitted by these Regulations if the variation—

(*a*) in the case of a dimension so specified as 3 metres or as over 3 metres, does not exceed 15% of that dimension,

(*b*) in the case of a dimension so specified as 300 millimetres or as over 300 millimetres but as under 3 metres, does not exceed 20% of that dimension, or

(*c*) in the case of a dimension so specified as under 300 millimetres, does not exceed 30% of the dimension so specified, and is not less than 20% of the dimension so specified.

(4) Any variation in a dimension as to the angle of hatching specified in any of the diagrams in Schedule 2 except diagrams 1043 to 1045 shall be treated as permitted by these Regulations if the variation does not exceed 5 degrees.

SECTION III

Traffic Signs shown in Schedule 1

Signs to be of the sizes, colours and types shown in diagrams

9. Subject to the provisions of these Regulations, a traffic sign for conveying—

(*a*) to vehicular traffic on roads a warning of the description specified in or under a diagram in Part I of Schedule 1 shall be of the size, colour and type shown in the diagram relating to that warning;

(*b*) to vehicular traffic on roads a requirement, prohibition or restriction specified in or under a diagram in Part II of Schedule 1 (other than a requirement shown in diagram 601.1, 602, 602.1, 610 or 649.1) shall be of the size, colour and type shown in the diagram relating to that requirement, prohibition or restriction;

(*c*) to traffic on a road other than a motorway information of a directional nature of the description specified in or under a diagram in Part III of Schedule 1 shall be of the size, colour and type shown in the diagram relating to that information;

(*d*) to traffic on roads information of the description specified in or under a diagram in Part IV of Schedule 1 shall be of the size, colour and type shown in the diagram relating to that information:

Provided that until 1st January 1992 a traffic sign indicating a stopping place for stage or scheduled express carriages may, notwithstanding that it is not of the size, colour and type shown in any of the diagrams 845 to 852, be of a circular or rectangular shape of not less than 30 square centimetres on which the lettering shall be shown coloured black, dark brown, dark blue or dark red on a white or yellow background, or white or yellow on a red, blue, green, brown or black background if such sign so indicating is situated on or near any road immediately after the coming into operation of these Regulations;

(*e*) to traffic on a motorway information of a directional or other nature specified in or under a diagram in Part V of Schedule 1 shall be of the size, colour and type shown in the diagram relating to that information.

Sign shown in diagram 610 and its significance

9A.—(1) Subject to the provisions of these Regulations, a traffic sign for conveying to vehicular traffic on roads the requirement specified in paragraph (2) or (3) shall be of the size, colour and type shown in diagram 610.

(2) Except as provided in paragraph (3) the requirement conveyed by the sign shown in diagram 610 shall be that vehicular traffic passing the sign must keep to the left of the sign where the arrow is pointed downwards to the left, or to the right of the sign where the arrow is pointed downwards to the right.

(3) On an occasion when a vehicle is being used for fire brigade, ambulance or police purposes and the observance of the requirement specified in paragraph (2) would be likely to hinder the use of that vehicle for the purpose for which it is being used on that occasion, then, instead of that requirement, the requirement conveyed by the traffic sign in question shall be that the vehicle shall not proceed beyond that sign in such a manner or at such a time—

(i) as is likely to cause danger to the driver of any other vehicle proceeding on or from another road or on or from another part of the same road; or

(ii) as is likely to cause danger to non-vehicular traffic proceeding on or from another road or on or from another part of the same road.

Signs shown in diagrams 601.1, 602, 602.1 and 649.1 and their significance

10. Subject to the provisions of these Regulations, a traffic sign for conveying to vehicular traffic on roads the requirements specified in paragraph (1)(*b*) of the next succeeding Regulation shall be of the size, colour and type shown in diagram 601.1, a traffic sign for conveying to such vehicular traffic the requirements specified in paragraph (1)(*c*)(i) of the said Regulation shall be of the size, colour and type shown in diagram 602, a traffic sign for conveying to such vehicular traffic the requirements specified in paragraph (1)(*c*)(ii) of the said Regulation shall comprise a sign of the size, colour and type shown in diagram 602 used in combination with a sign which shall be of the size, colour and type shown in diagram 602.1 and a traffic sign for conveying to such vehicular traffic the requirement specified in paragraph (2)(*b*) of the said Regulation shall be of the size, colour and type shown in diagram 649.1.

11.—(1)(*a*) For the purposes of paragraph (1)—

"minor road" means a road at a road junction on which road there is placed the sign shown in diagram 601.1 or 602;

"major road" means the road at a road junction into which road there emerges vehicular traffic from a minor road.

(*b*) The requirements conveyed by the sign shown in diagram 601.1 shall be that—

(i) every vehicle shall, until 1st January 1984, before entering the major road, stop at the transverse lines shown in diagram 1002 in Schedule 2 to the Regulations of 1975 or, if they are not for the time being visible, at the major road, and shall, whether before on or after that date, before entering the major road, stop at the single transverse line shown in diagram 1002.1, or if that line is not for the time being visible, at the major road; and

(ii) no vehicle shall proceed past the single transverse line shown in diagram 1002.1 or, until 1st January 1984, in the case of the transverse lines shown in the said diagram 1002, past such one of those lines as is nearest to the major road into that road or, if that line or those lines are not for the time being visible, shall enter into that road, in such a manner or at such a time as is likely to cause danger to the driver of any other vehicle on the major road or as to necessitate the driver of any such other vehicle to change its speed or course in order to avoid an accident with the first-mentioned vehicle.

(*c*) The requirements conveyed by the sign shown in diagram 602 shall be—

(i) unless it is used in the combination specified in (ii) of this sub-paragraph, that no vehicle shall proceed past such one of the transverse lines shown in diagram 1003 as is nearest to the major road into that road, or, if those lines are not for the time being visible, shall enter into the major road, in such a manner or at such a time as is likely to cause danger to the driver of any other vehicle on the major road or as to necessitate the driver of any such other vehicle to change its speed or course in order to avoid an accident with the first-mentioned vehicle; but

(ii) whenever the sign shown in diagram 602 is used in combination with that shown in diagram 602.1, that no vehicle shall proceed past such one of the said transverse lines so shown as is nearest to the level crossing by a railway of the road on which is placed the sign shown in diagram 602 when so used as aforesaid, into that crossing, or, if those lines are not for the time being visible, shall enter into the said level crossing in such a manner or at such a time as is likely to cause the driver of any railway vehicle to change its speed in order to avoid collision with the first-mentioned vehicle.

(2)(*a*) For the purposes of paragraph (2)—

"automatic open crossing (R)" means a level crossing without automatic barriers where a road is crossed by a railway and where light signals are so installed as to be operated automatically by the trains approaching the crossing and the operation of the signals is monitored remotely from the crossing;

"automatic half-barrier level crossing" means a level crossing where a road is crossed by a railway and where barriers are installed to descend automatically across part of the road when a train approaches;

"vehicle combination" means a combination of vehicles made up of one or more motor vehicles and one or more trailers all of which are linked together when travelling;

"abnormal transport unit" means—

(i) a motor vehicle or a vehicle combination—

(A) the overall length of which, inclusive of the load (if any) on the vehicle or the combination, exceeds 55 feet;

(B) the overall width of which, inclusive of the load (if any) on the vehicle or the combination, exceeds 9 feet 6 inches; or

(C) the weight of which, inclusive of the load (if any) on the vehicle or the combination, exceeds 32·5 tonnes; or

(ii) a motor vehicle, or a vehicle combination, which in either case is incapable of proceeding, or is unlikely to proceed, over an automatic half-barrier level crossing or an automatic open crossing (R) at a speed exceeding 5 miles per hour; and

"driver", in relation to an abnormal transport unit means where that unit is a single motor vehicle the driver of that vehicle and, where that unit is a vehicle combination the driver of the only or the foremost motor vehicle forming part of that combination.

(*b*) The requirement conveyed by the sign shown in diagram 649.1 shall be that no abnormal transport unit shall proceed onto or over an automatic half-barrier level crossing or an automatic open crossing (R) unless:—

(i) the driver thereof has himself before the unit so proceeds used a telephone placed at or near the crossing for the purpose of obtaining from a person duly authorised by the railway authority permission for that unit so to proceed;

(ii) such permission has been obtained before the unit so proceeds; and

(iii) the unit so proceeds only in accordance with the terms of that permission:

Provided that conditions (ii) and (iii) above shall not apply if—

(A) on the use by the driver of the telephone placed at or near the crossing he receives an indication for not less than two minutes that the telephone at the other end of the telephone line is being called, but no duly authorised person answers it or he receives no indication at all due to a fault or malfunction of the telephone; and

(B) the driver then drives the unit on to the crossing with the reasonable expectation of crossing it within times specified in a railway notice at that telephone as being times between which trains do not normally travel over that crossing.

Permitted variants

12.—(1) Where the circumstances so require, the indications given by the signs shown in the diagrams in Schedule 1 shall or may be varied as hereinafter provided in this paragraph—

(*a*) any indication given by such a sign may be varied in the respect (if any) in which it is shown below the diagram relating to that sign that the indication may be varied;

(*b*) in the signs shown in diagrams 502, 503, 523.1, 524.1, 530, 532.1, 534.1 to 535.1, 556.4, 626.1, 628.1 to 629.2, 712.1, 719.3A and 729.2 the numerals shall be varied to accord with the circumstances except that no fractions of a number shall be used;

(*c*) in the signs shown in diagrams 527, 565.4, 571, 715, 724, 724.2, 728.1 to 729, 730 to 733, 838.2, 911, 915 and 916, the numerals shall be varied to accord with the circumstances, distances being expressed in miles to the nearest mile except that in the case of any of the signs so shown other than a sign shown in diagram 715, 724.2, 732.2 or 911 the fractions $\frac{3}{4}$, $\frac{1}{2}$ and $\frac{1}{4}$ may be used for distances of less than 3 miles;

(*d*) in the sign shown in diagram 572 the numerals shall be varied to accord with the circumstances, distances being expressed in yards to the nearest 50 yards;

(*e*) in the signs shown in diagrams 534.2, 547.3, 556.4, 569.2, 570, 573, 734.8, 746.2, to 753.1, 759, 818.1, 818.2, and 841 to 842.4, the numerals indicating distance shall be varied to accord with the circumstances, distances of less than $\frac{1}{2}$ mile being expressed in yards to the nearest 50 yards, distances of $\frac{1}{2}$ mile or more but less than 3 miles being expressed in miles so long as no fractions other than $\frac{3}{4}$, $\frac{1}{2}$ or $\frac{1}{4}$ are used, and distances of 3 miles or more being expressed in miles to the nearest mile;

(*f*) in the sign shown in any diagram in Schedule 1, any numerals which indicate route numbers shall be so varied as to indicate the route number for the time being appropriate to the route to which the indication refers and when a route number has been superseded by a new route number, any such numerals indicating the old route number may be retained in the said sign so long as those numerals so indicating are cancelled by a red bar to indicate that that route number has been superseded;

(*g*) in the signs shown in diagrams 618, 638 to 641, 646, 660.2, 662, 801.5, 805, 806.1, 806.3 and 807 the legend shall be varied, so far as respects any reference to a period of time, time of day or day of the week, and may be supplemented by a reference to days of the month or months of the year, so as to accord with the prohibition or restriction imposed in relation to vehicular traffic;

(*h*) in the signs shown in diagrams 515, 534.2, 553, 556.4, 567.1, 567.2, 569, 573, 580, 606 (through either 90° or 180° above horizontal), 639, 640, 640.2A, 644, 703.1, 703.2, 705, 714, 718.1, 718.2, 720, 721.1, 723, 724.1, 727, 727.2, 728.1, 730, 732.1, 733.1, 734.2, 734.4, 734.9, 734.10, 741.1, 742.2, 742.4, 754, 755, 756, 757, 810, 842.2, 844, 855, 910.1 and 912, the direction of any arrow or chevron shown therein shall be varied to accord with the circumstances, so however that no chevron shown in diagrams 515 or 569 and no arrow shown in diagram 553, 639, 640, 640.2A, 644, 810, 842.2, 855 or 912 shall point otherwise than horizontally either to the left or to the right, and so that from the signs shown in diagram 639, 640, 757 and 842.2, the arrows may be omitted;

(*i*) in any of the signs shown in diagrams 637, 641, 651, 662, 758, 805, 818.2, 841 and 842.4, an arrow pointing in the appropriate direction horizontally left or right may be included;

(*j*) in the signs shown in diagrams 713, 714, 724.1, 729 to 729.2 and 741 an indication of distance may be expressed to the nearest mile, in the signs shown in diagrams 734.1 to 734.4, 734.6, 736, 736.1, 739 to 739.2 and 756 such an indication as aforesaid may be expressed to the nearest mile for a distance greater than 3 miles, to the nearest $\frac{1}{4}$ mile for a distance less than 3 miles but greater than $\frac{1}{2}$ mile, and to the nearest 50 yards for a distance of 800 yards or less, and in the signs shown in diagrams 724, 728.1, 728.2, 729, 730 to 732.1, 733, 734.8, 749, 759, 841, 842.2 and 842.4 the distance may be omitted;

(*k*) in the signs shown in diagrams 713, 724, 728, 728.2, 728.3, 732, 732.4, 733, 734.1, 734.3, 734.5 to 734.8, 736, 736.1, 737.1, 739, 739.1 to 739.3, 741, 742.1, 742.3, 749, 751, 753, 753.1, 755.1, 756.1, 759, 841.1, 842.1, 842.3, 903.1 and 904.1 the direction in which they point shall be reversed;

(*l*) in the signs shown in diagrams 703.1 to 705, 708 to 711.1, 712.1, 718, 723 and 728.1, where a junction with a motorway is to be indicated, the appropriate panel or panels shall be blue with a white legend and the route number of the motorway shown in characters of the proportion and form shown in Parts I, II and III of Schedule 7; in the signs shown in diagrams 718 to 723 and 728.1 where a non-primary route joins a primary route the primary route number shall be shown in yellow on a green panel; and without prejudice to the foregoing provisions of this sub-paragraph, whenever a motorway route number is indicated on a sign shown in any of the diagrams 701 to 715, 718 to 724.2 and 728, that number shall be shown in white on a blue panel;

(*m*) in the signs shown in diagrams 701 to 716, 718 to 725, 727 to 733.1, 734.8, 737.1, 739, 741 to 744.1, 747 to 759, 818.1, 818.2, 838.1, 841 to 842.4, 903.1 to 911 and 915 to 916.1 the route numbers, place names, route symbols, junction numbers and distances (other than the mileages in diagrams 702, 702.1, 905, 906, 906.2, 908.1 and 908.2) shall, subject to the preceding provisions of this paragraph, be varied, where appropriate and the words "Other routes" or as the case may be, "Ring road" may be substituted for the place name, having regard to the place where any such sign is erected;

(*n*) in the signs shown in diagrams 728 to 732.1, there may be substituted for, or added to the place name the words "Tourist information", "Toilets", "Ladies toilet", "Mens toilet", "Airport", "Station", "Bus Station", "Coach Station", "Country park" or "Public Telephone", or any of the following symbols, that is to say, the aircraft shown in diagram 733, the white on red symbol indicating British Railways and shown in diagram 734.1, the red circle and bar on white indicating London Transport and shown in diagram 734.4, the parking symbol shown in diagram 734.8, the telephone handset shown in diagram 734.6, the disabled person symbol shown in diagram 736.1, the building shown in diagram 747, the building shown in diagram 748, the tent and caravan symbol shown in diagram 750, the youth hostel symbol shown in diagram 752, the picnic site symbol shown in diagram 752.1, the black on white letter "i" shown in diagram 758, or the white on blue letter "H" shown in diagram 827;

(*o*) without prejudice to the next following paragraph, the white lorry symbol shown in diagram 727.2 may be incorporated on a black panel in the signs shown in diagrams 718 to 724.1, 728.1, 728.2 and 729 to 732.1 when those signs are placed on or near a road other than a motorway or a primary route to indicate that the route with which the symbol is associated on the sign is a route suitable for goods vehicles;

(*p*) the aircraft symbol shown in diagram 733 either with or without the name of an airport may be substituted for, or added to, a place name shown on any of the signs shown in diagrams 701 to 714, 718 to 724.1 and 903.1 to 910.1 to indicate the site of an airport.

(2) Where overall dimensions are shown in Schedule 1 for any such sign as is mentioned in the preceding paragraph and where the legend on that

sign may be varied and the sign is varied in accordance with that paragraph, the overall dimensions or the number of lines filled by the legend or both may be varied in so far as is necessary to give effect to that variation.

(3) In the sign shown in diagram 536 the number of bells shall be increased or decreased according to the width of the road over which it is placed, and in each of the signs shown in diagrams 534.1 to 535.1 the safe height shown on the sign shall be varied where necessary so that it is between 1 foot 6 inches and 2 feet less than the height of the lowest part of the overhead wire, of which it gives warning, over the highest part of the surface of the carriageway beneath the said wire.

(4) The signs shown in diagrams 732, 733, 734.8, 736 to 737.1, 739, 741 to 742.4, 743.1, 744.1, 805 (except when varied to convey a condition), 814, 820 to 822, 833 to 836 and 916.1, when erected in Wales may show the information contained on the sign in both the English and Welsh languages:

Provided that—

(*a*) except in the case of the signs shown in diagrams 743.1 and 744.1 names indicating the location of a place shall be those in common usage in the English language;

(*b*) all information shown on any such sign as is mentioned in this paragraph shall be shown in both the English and Welsh languages;

(*c*) one language version of each item of information shall be placed immediately above the other language version of that item; and

(*d*) the same size lettering shall be used for each language version of each item of information.

(5) Where a sign shown in diagrams 743.1, 744.1, 805, 814, 820 to 822 and 833 to 836 is varied in accordance with the last preceding paragraph, the overall dimensions as shown in the said diagrams may be varied in so far as is necessary to give effect to that variation.

(6) Where a sign shown in any diagram in Part III of Schedule 1 other than any of the diagrams 742.1 to 759 indicates a road or a route, and that road or route is temporarily closed, there may be affixed to the sign or to that part of the sign where that road or route is indicated, so as to cancel temporarily the indication, a board coloured red and on which are inscribed in white characters the words "road temporarily closed" or "route temporarily closed".

Dimensions

13.—(1) Where as respects any diagram in Schedule 1 a dimension for the sign shown in the diagram is indicated in one or more sets of brackets against a dimension not indicated in brackets, any dimension indicated in a set of brackets may be treated as an alternative to the dimension not so indicated.

(2) Where a sign shown in any of the diagrams 606 to 614, 616 or 637 to 645 is placed temporarily on a road by a constable or a person acting under the instructions (whether general or specific) of the chief officer of police for the purposes of a temporary statutory provision any dimension specified for the sign in such a diagram may be reduced so long as any dimension shown in the diagram for measurement horizontally is not reduced to less than 200 millimetres.

(3) A sign shown in a diagram in Part III of Schedule 1 other than in diagrams 717, 726, 734.7 and 754 and a sign shown in a diagram in Part

V of that Schedule other than in any of the diagrams 901.1, 910, 912 to 915, and 916.1 to 920 shall be of such dimensions having regard to the character of the road and the speed of the vehicular traffic generally using it as are necessary to accommodate any place name, route symbol, route number, arrow, any indication of distance, or any other indication which in accordance with these Regulations may be shown therein and it is appropriate to show for the purpose for which the sign is placed on a road.

Proportions and form of letters and numerals

14.—(1) Subject to the provisions of paragraphs (2) to (4) of this Regulation, and without prejudice to Regulation 12(1)(*l*) (variant requirements to signs there specified), all letters incorporated in the signs shown in the diagrams in Schedule 1 other than in diagrams 742.1 to 742.4, 828.1 and 849 to 852 shall have the proportions and form shown in either Part I, Part II, Part V or Part VI of Schedule 7, all numerals incorporated in the signs shown in the diagrams in Schedule 1 shall have the proportions and form shown in Part III or Part VII of Schedule 7 and all other characters incorporated in the signs shown in the diagrams in Schedule 1 shall have the proportions and form shown in Part IV or Part VIII of Schedule 7.

(2) Letters and numerals used for the purposes of indicating a route number on the sign shown in diagram 757 and on any sign shown in a diagram in Part V of Schedule 1 shall have the proportions and form shown in Part IX of Schedule 7.

(3) Any arrow to be used in any of the signs shown in diagrams 703.3, 718.3 or 908.2 when those signs are erected over the carriageway on structures on which there is also mounted equipment for displaying the signs shown in diagram 6021 in Schedule 6 shall have the proportion and form of the arrow shown in the last diagram in Part IV of Schedule 7 and any such arrow to be used in any of the signs first above-mentioned when those signs are erected over the carriageway on structures on which no such equipment is also mounted shall have the proportion and form of the arrow shown in the penultimate diagram in the said Part IV.

(4) Subject to and within the limits of any dimension specified as maximum or minimum in diagrams 743.1 and 744.1, any letters, numerals or other characters incorporated in those diagrams may have proportions and form other than the proportions and form shown in any Part of Schedule 7.

Illumination of signs by steady lighting

15.—(1) In this Regulation (except in paragraph (6) as respects the sign shown in diagram 828.1) and in Regulations 16 and 17 the references to lighting shall be construed as references to steady lighting.

(2) Subject to the provisions of paragraph (7), this paragraph applies to the signs shown in diagrams 606, 609 to 616, 617 (except when used with the sign shown in diagram 618), 619, 619.1, 621 to 622.2 and 622.4 in construing the following sub-paragraphs—

(*a*) when the signs shown in diagrams 606 and 612 to 614 are fixed to light signals prescribed by Regulation 31, or by Regulation 31 as varied by Regulation 32, they shall be illuminated by a means of internal lighting at all times except when the light signals to which they are fixed are being maintained or repaired;

(*b*) when the signs shown in diagrams 606, 609 to 611 and 616 are mounted in a bollard fitted with a means of lighting them internally, they shall be illuminated throughout the hours of darkness by that means of internal lighting;

(*c*) without prejudice to the next following sub-paragraph, if a sign specified in sub-paragraph (*a*) above when not so fixed, or a sign specified in sub-paragraph (*b*) above when not so mounted, or any other sign to which this paragraph applies is erected on a road within 50 metres of any lamp lit by electricity which forms part of a system of street-lighting furnished by means of at least three such lamps placed not more than 183 metres apart, that sign shall be illuminated by a means of internal or external lighting either for so long as the said system is illuminated, or throughout the hours of darkness, unless it is erected temporarily for any of the following reasons—

(i) for the purpose of a temporary statutory provision,

(ii) by reason of some emergency, or,

(iii) if that road is a road subject to a speed limit of 30 m.p.h. or under, by reason of the execution of works, or of any obstruction on the road;

(*d*) any sign to which this paragraph applies and is either not so fixed as provided in sub-paragraph (*a*) or is erected in such a manner that it is not illuminated regularly throughout the hours of darkness by a means of internal or external lighting, shall be illuminated by the use of reflecting material in accordance with the provisions of Regulation 18(3) and (4).

(3) Subject to the provisions of paragraph (7), this paragraph applies to any sign shown in diagrams 501, 504.1 to 510, 512, 513, 516, 517, 520 to 524.1, 528 to 532.1, 533, 537, 538, 543, 544 to 544.2, 555, 556, 564, 564.5 to 566, 567.2, 569.2, 569.3, 601.1, 602, 626.1, 628.1 to 632, 642 (if the diameter of that sign is more than 450 millimetres), 649.1, 652 to 654, 701 to 712.1, 714, 718.2, 718.3, 727.2, 818 to 819.2, 837.1 to 838.2, 858 to 858.2, 901.1 to 911, 915 to 916.1, 918.1 and 919.1 in construing the following sub-paragraphs—

(*a*) without prejudice to the next following sub-paragraph, if a sign to which this paragraph applies is erected on a road within 50 metres of any such lamp as is described in sub-paragraph (*c*) of paragraph (2) that sign shall be illuminated by a means of internal or external lighting as is therein provided unless it is erected temporarily for such a reason as is therein specified;

(*b*) any sign to which this paragraph applies which is erected in such a manner that it is not illuminated regularly throughout the hours of darkness by a means of internal or external lighting, shall be illuminated by the use of reflecting material as provided by paragraph (2)(*d*).

(4) Any sign shown in diagrams 515, 539 to 542.2, 545, 548 to 552, 554, 554.1, 557 to 559, 562, 569, 569.1, 569.4, 574, 577, 578, 580, 633 to 635, 642 (if the diameter of that sign is 450 millimetres or less), 646, 647, 655, 713, 715 to 718.1, 719 to 727, 728 to 737.1, 746.2, 754 to 757, 760, 761, 801, 806 to 806.3, 808.1, 808.3, 811 to 812.2, 819.3 to 825, 827, 828.2, 830 to 832.2, 838.3, 838.4, 854 to 856, 861 to 863, 912, 917, 920 and 925 may be illuminated by a means of internal or external lighting, but if not so illuminated throughout the hours of darkness, shall be illuminated by the use of reflecting material in accordance with the provisions of Regulation 18(3) and (4).

(5) The signs shown in diagrams 603, 604 and 814, shall be illuminated throughout the hours of darkness by a means of internal or external lighting.

(6) The sign shown in diagram 828.1 shall be illuminated by an intermittent light flashing at a rate of not less than 54 nor more than 90 flashes per minute during such times only as it is necessary that the sign shall be illuminated for the purpose of indicating the information shown in diagram 828.1.

(7) Where a sign to which any of the foregoing paragraphs applies is placed on or near a road for the purpose of conveying a warning or information from time to time to vehicular traffic, or in connection with a statutory prohibition, restriction or requirement which relates to such traffic but does not apply at all times, that sign shall be illuminated in accordance with such of the foregoing provisions of this Regulation as apply to it but only during such times as, for the said purpose or in the said connection, it is necessary that the sign shall be visible from a reasonable distance to drivers of approaching motor vehicles, any other provision of this Regulation to the contrary notwithstanding.

(8) Subject to the foregoing paragraphs of this Regulation and to Regulation 19, any sign shown in a diagram in Schedule 1 may be illuminated by a means of internal or external lighting and where, subject as aforesaid, the means of lighting any such sign is external, then that means of lighting shall be either fitted to the sign or to the structure on which it is mounted or otherwise specially provided.

16. Where a sign shown in a diagram in Schedule 1 (not being a sign consisting of a plate) is illuminated by a means of lighting in accordance with the provisions of Regulation 15 and a plate shown in a diagram in that Schedule is used in conjunction with that sign, the said plate shall, unless the means of lighting provided for the illumination of the sign adequately illuminates the plate, be illuminated, during such times as the sign is illuminated, by a means of lighting and that means of lighting shall accord with that one of the methods of lighting, namely, internal or external adopted for the illumination of the sign.

Illumination of signs shown in diagrams 560 and 561 by reflectors etc.

17.—(1) The signs shown in diagrams 560 and 561 shall not be illuminated by the fitting of a means of internal or external lighting.

(2)(*a*) If the sign shown in diagram 560 has a diameter of 150 millimetres, that sign shall be illuminated by either of the methods prescribed at (i) and (ii) of sub-paragraph (*c*) below and not otherwise.

(*b*) If the said sign has a diameter of 75 millimetres or more but less than 150 millimetres, that sign shall be illuminated by either of the methods prescribed at (iii) and (iv) of sub-paragraph (*c*) below and not otherwise.

(*c*) The methods referred to in sub-paragraphs (*a*) and (*b*) above are:—

(i) by the use of 14 circular reflectors of the corner cube type, each reflector having a diameter of 22 millimetres,

(ii) by the use of reflecting material extending over the whole surface of the sign,

(iii) by the use of a single circular reflector of the corner cube type extending over the whole surface of the sign,

(iv) by the use of reflectors consisting of bi-convex lenses extending over the whole surface of the sign.

(*d*) If the sign shown in diagram 561 has an area of 180 square centimetres, that sign shall be illuminated by the method prescribed at sub-paragraph (*c*) (ii) above and not otherwise; but if that sign so shown has an area of less than 180 square centimetres and no less than 45 square centimetres, then it shall be illuminated either by the use of a single rectangular reflector of the corner cube type extending over the whole surface of the sign or by the method prescribed at sub-paragraph (*c*)(iv) above but by no other method.

(3) The colour reflected by the sign shown either in diagram 560 or in 561 shall be red when the sign indicates the edge of the left-hand side of the carriageway or an obstruction near that edge and shall be white when the sign indicates the edge of the right-hand side of the carriageway or an obstruction near that edge, unless the sign indicates the edge of the right-hand side of the carriageway of a dual-carriageway road or an obstruction near that edge when the said colour so reflected shall be amber.

Illumination of signs by reflecting material

18.—(1) Nothing in this Regulation shall apply to the signs shown in diagrams 536, 560, 561 and 828.1.

(2) Subject to the provisions of Regulation 15 and paragraph (1) above, any sign shown in a diagram in Schedule 1 may be illuminated by the use of reflecting material in accordance with the following provisions of this Regulation.

(3) Subject to paragraph (4) where reflecting material is used on any sign shown in a diagram in Schedule 1 it shall be of the same colour as that of, and extend throughout, that part of the sign to which it is applied:

Provided that no reflecting material shall be applied to —

(*a*) any part of a sign coloured black, or

(*b*) any part of the sign shown in diagram 605.1 which is coloured fluorescent yellow unless the reflecting material is applied to that part in horizontal strips each such strip being 3 millimetres wide, spaced at intervals of 6 millimetres from each other, the centre of the sign being located at a point in one such interval equidistant from the strips so spaced.

In this paragraph the word "part", in relation to a sign, means any part of the surface of that sign uniformly coloured and bounded by parts of a different colour.

(4)(*a*) Where in accordance with the last paragraph, different colours of reflecting material are used next to one another on the same sign being a traffic sign to which this paragraph applies in accordance with the next following sub-paragraph, a gap of not more than 20 millimetres in width may by left between the different colours of reflecting material.

(*b*) This paragraph applies only to traffic signs which being circular in shape have a diameter of at least 1·2 metres, being triangular in shape have a height of at least 1·2 metres along the perpendicular from apex to base, or being rectangular in shape have a side which is at least 1·2 metres in length.

19. Where a sign shown in a diagram in Schedule 1 (not being a sign consisting of a plate) is illuminated by the use of reflecting material in accordance with the provisions of Regulation 15 and 18 and a plate shown in a diagram in that Schedule, other than a plate shown in diagram 662, is used in conjunction with that sign, the said plate shall be illuminated by the use of reflecting material in accordance with the provisions of Regulation 18(3).

SECTION IV

Traffic Signs shown in Schedule 2

Road markings

20.—(1) Subject to the provisions of these Regulations, a traffic sign consisting of a line or mark on a road (in these Regulations referred to as a "road marking") for conveying to traffic on roads a warning, a requirement or information of the description specified under a diagram (other than diagrams 1003 and 1013.1) in Schedule 2 shall be of the size and type shown in the diagram relating to that warning, requirement or information.

(2) In any diagram in Schedule 2, the dimensions indicated in brackets against dimensions not so indicated may be treated as an alternative to the last mentioned dimensions.

(3) Where the circumstances so require, the indication given by any of the signs shown in the diagrams in Schedule 2 shall or may be varied as hereinafter provided in this paragraph:—

(*a*) any indication given by such a sign may be varied in the respect (if any) in which it is shown below the diagram relating to that sign that the indication may be varied;

(*b*) in the sign shown in diagram 1035 route numbers place names and the direction in which any arrow-head points shall be varied and interchangeable to accord with the circumstances but the words "turn left", "ahead" or "turn right" shall not appear as a part of the said sign.

Particular road markings

21. A road marking for conveying to vehicular traffic the requirement specified in paragraph (2) of the next succeeding Regulation shall be of the size and type shown in diagram 1003.

22.—(1) For the purposes of this Regulation—

"minor road" means a road at a road junction on which road there are placed the transverse lines shown in diagram 1003;

"major road" means the road at a road junction into which road there emerges vehicular traffic from a minor road.

(2) Except as provided by the next following paragraph, the requirement conveyed by the said transverse lines, whether or not they are used in conjunction with the sign shown in diagram 602, shall be that no vehicle shall proceed past such one of those lines as is nearest to the major road into that road in such a manner or at such a time as is likely to cause danger to the driver of any other vehicle on the major road or as to necessitate the driver of any such other vehicle to change its speed or course in order to avoid an accident with the first-mentioned vehicle.

(3) Whenever the said transverse lines are used in conjunction with the sign shown in diagram 602 and that sign is at the same time used in combination with the sign shown in diagram 602.1 at a level crossing where a road is crossed by a railway then the said requirement shall be that no vehicle

shall proceed past such one of those lines as is nearest to the said level crossing in such a manner or at such a time as is likely to cause the driver of any railway vehicle to change its speed to avoid collision with the vehicle first above-mentioned in this paragraph.

23.—(1) A road marking for conveying the requirements specified in the next succeeding paragraph and the warning specified in paragraph (5) shall be of the size and type shown in diagram 1013.1.

(2) The requirements conveyed by the road marking mentioned in the last preceding paragraph shall be that—

(*a*) subject to the provisions of paragraph (3), no vehicle shall stop on any length of road along which the marking has been placed at any point between the two ends of the marking; and

(*b*) subject to the provisions of paragraph (4), every vehicle proceeding on any length of road along which the marking has been so placed that, as viewed in the direction of travel of the vehicle, a continuous line is on the left of a dotted line or of another continuous line, shall be so driven as to keep the first-mentioned continuous line on the right hand or off side of the vehicle.

(3) Nothing in sub-paragraph (*a*) of the last preceding paragraph shall apply—

(*a*) so as to prevent a vehicle stopping on any length of road so long as may be necessary—

(i) to enable a person to board or alight from the vehicle,

(ii) to enable goods to be loaded on to or to be unloaded from the vehicle, or

(iii) to enable the vehicle, if it cannot be used for such purpose without stopping on that length of road, to be used in connection with any building operation or demolition, the removal of any obstruction to traffic, the maintenance, improvement or reconstruction of that length of road, or the laying, erection, alteration or repair in or near to that length of road of any sewer or of any main, pipe or apparatus for the supply of gas, water or electricity, or of any telegraphic line as defined in the Telegraph Act 1878(**a**),

so, however, that no vehicle shall be enabled by virtue of this sub-paragraph to stop for any of the purposes at (i), (ii) or (iii) above on a part of that length of road, not being a lay-by or a road verge, if it is reasonably practicable to stop the vehicle for that purpose on a part of that length of road, being a lay-by or a road verge;

(*b*) to a vehicle used for fire brigade, ambulance or police purposes;

(*c*) to a pedal bicycle not having a sidecar attached thereto, whether additional means of propulsion by mechanical power are attached to the bicycle or not;

(*d*) to a vehicle stopping in any case where the person in control of the vehicle is required by law to stop, or is obliged to do so in order to avoid an accident, or is prevented from proceeding by circumstances outside his control; or

(*e*) to anything done with the permission of a police constable in uniform or in accordance with the direction of a traffic warden.

(**a**) 1878 c. 76.

(4) Nothing in sub-paragraph (*b*) of paragraph (2) shall apply so as to prevent a vehicle crossing or straddling the continuous line first mentioned in that sub-paragraph for the purpose of obtaining access to any other road joining the length of road along which the line is placed or to land or premises situated on or adjacent to the said length of road or if it is necessary to do so —

(*a*) in order to pass a stationary vehicle, or owing to circumstances outside the control of the driver or in order to avoid an accident, or

(*b*) for the purposes of complying with any direction of a police constable in uniform or a traffic warden.

(5) The warning conveyed by the road marking mentioned in paragraph (1) shall be that no vehicle while travelling next to a dotted line placed on the left, as viewed in the direction of travel of the vehicle, of a continuous line should cross or straddle the first mentioned line unless it is seen by the driver of the vehicle to be safe to do so.

Colour of road markings

24.—(1) Except as otherwise provided by this Regulation, the road markings shown in the diagrams in Schedule 2 shall be white.

(2) Road markings shown in diagrams 1016.1 to 1021, 1027.1 and 1043 to 1045 shall be yellow.

(3) In the road markings shown in the diagrams 1025.1 and 1025.3 the line shown therein as coloured yellow and having a width of 200 or 300 millimetres shall be yellow.

(4) The road markings shown in diagrams 1025 and 1025.2 and when displaying the word "Taxis" in diagram 1028.1 shall be yellow in the following but in no other circumstances, that is to say, where those markings are placed in a part of the carriageway which is subject to restrictions on waiting or on waiting, loading and unloading for at least 8 hours during the period from 7 a.m. to 7 p.m. on at least 4 days, none of them being a Sunday, in any week by all vehicles, other than stage and express carriages in the case of the markings shown in diagrams 1025 or 1025.2 and other than hackney carriages in the case of the marking shown in diagram 1028.1.

(5) Road markings shown in diagram 1055 consisting of marks arranged in transverse lines may be either white or silver or light grey in colour.

(6) In this Regulation, "hackney carriage" has the same meaning as in the Vehicles (Excise) Act 1971 (**a**).

Use on road markings of reflecting material and studs with reflectors

25.—(1)(*a*) The road markings shown in diagrams 1011 to 1014 shall be illuminated with reflecting material, and

(*b*) studs incorporating reflectors and spaced so as to form a single line of studs at intervals of not less than 3·6 nor more than 4·4 metres apart shall be fitted between the two lines constituting the marking shown in diagram 1013.1 unless that marking—

(i) is placed on any automatic railway level crossing, or

(ii) is placed on a length of the road falling within a distance of 90 metres measured from the transverse stop line provided in association with any such crossing and in conformity with diagram 1001, or

(iii) is so placed that the continuous lines shown in diagram 1013.1 are more than 175 millimetres apart and are separated by an area of cross-hatching so shown.

(**a**) 1971 c. 10.

(*c*) Where the marking shown in diagram 1013.1 is placed as described in any of the cases in sub-paragraph (*b*) (i) to (iii) above, then such studs as aforesaid and so spaced as aforesaid shall be fitted either within the width of each of the said two lines or between them.

In this paragraph the expression "automatic railway level crossing" means an automatic half-barrier level crossing, and an automatic open crossing (R) as both those crossings are defined for the purposes of Regulation 11(2) and includes a level crossing which is the same as an automatic open crossing (R) except that the operation of the light signals is monitored at or near the crossing by the driver of the train instead of remotely from the crossing.

(2) Subject to the foregoing provisions of this Regulation, any road marking may be illuminated with reflecting material and studs incorporating reflectors may be fitted to the markings shown in diagrams 1003.4 to 1012.1, 1025.2, 1025.3 and 1040 to 1042 in such a manner that any such stud shall not be fitted to any mark coloured white and forming part of any of the markings so shown as aforesaid but shall be applied to the surface of the carriageway in the gap between any two such marks:

Provided that in the case of the markings shown in diagram 1011 or 1012.1 the said studs shall, if fitted, be applied to the surface of the carriageway at the side of and adjacent to the line shown in the diagram.

(3) Reflectors incorporated in studs shall be white except that in the case of reflectors fitted to the markings shown in diagrams 1009 to 1012.1, 1025.2, 1025.3, 1041 and 1042 they may be—

(*a*) red where the near side edge of a carriageway is indicated to drivers of approaching motor vehicles, or when fitted to the markings shown in diagrams 1041 and 1042 to indicate the offside edge of a carriageway,

(*b*) amber to indicate the offside edge of a carriageway which is contiguous to a central reservation or which carries traffic in one direction only, and

(*c*) green when fitted to the markings shown in diagrams 1009, 1010, 1025.2 and 1025.3 where the edge of any part of the carriageway available for through traffic at a road junction, a lay-by or a parking place is so indicated as aforesaid.

In this Regulation "central reservation" means any provision made in a road (not being the provision of a street refuge) for dividing the road for the safety or guidance of vehicular traffic.

Height of road markings and size of studs

26.—(1) Non-depressible studs incorporating reflectors and fitted as a part of a road marking shall either be in the shape of a circle having a diameter of not more than 20 millimetres in excess of the width of the road marking to which the studs are fitted or of a rectangle having a length of not more than 250 millimetres and a width of not more than 20 millimetres in excess of the width of the road marking to which the studs are fitted.

(2) Subject to paragraph (3), no road marking shall project above the surface of the carriageway in the immediate vicinity more than 6 millimetres at any point unless it is a road marking fitted with non-depressible studs when those studs shall not project above the said surface more than 18 millimetres at the highest point nor more than 6 millimetres at their edges, or unless it is the road marking shown in diagram 1003.4 when that marking shall not project above the said surface more than 125 millimetres at the highest point nor more than 6 millimetres at its edge.

(3) Depressible studs fitted in road markings and incorporating reflectors shall not project above the surface of the carriageway in the immediate vicinity more than 6 millimetres at their edges, nor at their highest points more than 25 millimetres, when not depressed or 20 millimetres when depressed by a force of 300 newtons and "newton" means the unit of force specified in paragraph 1.2.3 of Chapter A of the Annex to Council Directive 71/354 EEC(**a**) as amended by Council Directive 76/770/EEC(**b**).

In this Regulation, the expression "depressible studs", in relation to studs fitted in road markings, means studs so fitted that the height by which they project above the surface of the carriageway in the immediate vicinity is apt to be reduced when pressure is applied to those studs from above; and "non-depressible studs" and "depressed" shall be construed accordingly.

SECTION V

Miscellaneous Traffic Signs

Certain temporary signs

27.—(1) Notwithstanding the provisions of Regulation 9 and subject to the succeeding paragraphs of this Regulation, signs placed temporarily on or near a road—

(*a*) for conveying to traffic—

(i) information as respects deviations of, or alternative traffic routes,

(ii) information as respects the route which may conveniently be followed on the occasion of a sports meeting, exhibition or other public gathering, in each case attracting a considerable volume of traffic,

(iii) information as to the date from which works are to be executed on or near a road, or

(iv) a warning of a failure of street lighting;

(*b*) for conveying to vehicular traffic any prohibition, restriction or requirement of a description required for the purposes of a temporary statutory provision; or

(*c*) pending the erection of any permanent sign prescribed by these Regulations, for conveying to traffic the indication which such a permanent sign indicates,

may be of such size, colour and type as is specified in the following provisions of this Regulation.

(2) Every such sign placed as aforesaid (hereinafter referred to as a "temporary sign") shall be of a shape which—

(*a*) is rectangular;

(*b*) is rectangular, but with the corners rounded; or

(*c*) is rectangular, but with one end pointed.

(3) Every temporary sign shall be of such size as is necessary to accommodate the wording, numerals, arrows or chevrons and any symbol taken from any diagram shown in Schedule 1 appropriate to the purpose for which the sign is placed as aforesaid and to accommodate any arms, badge, device, words or letters incorporated in the sign in accordance with the provisions of paragraph (6).

(**a**) O.J. No. L243, 29.10 1971, p. 29. (**b**) O.J. No. L262, 27.9. 1976, p. 204.

(4) Every letter and numeral incorporated in a temporary sign other than any letter incorporated in the sign in accordance with the provisions of paragraph (6) shall be not less than 40 nor more than 250 millimetres in height, and every arrow so incorporated shall be not less than 250 nor more than 500 millimetres in length except that where an arrow is incorporated in the index part of a sign with a pointed end such arrow shall be not less than 100 nor more than 200 millimetres in length.

(5) Every letter, numeral, arrow, chevron or symbol incorporated in a temporary sign shall be—

(*a*) black on a background of white, or yellow; or

(*b*) white on a blue background.

(6) There may be incorporated in, or attached to, a temporary sign the arms, badge or other device of a highway authority, police authority or an organisation representative of road users, or words or letters indicating the highway authority, or that the sign is a police sign.

(7) No sign shall by virtue of this Regulation convey to traffic any information, warning, requirement, restriction or prohibition of a description which can be so conveyed either by a sign shown in a diagram in Part I, Part II or Part IV of Schedule 1 or by a sign so shown used in combination with or in conjunction with another sign shown in such a diagram.

Flashing beacons and flags

28.—(1) Beacons showing an intermittent amber light for conveying the warning that drivers of vehicles should take special care may be used in combination with any of the signs specified in the last preceding Regulation or with any of the signs shown in diagrams 562 to 569.1, 569.3 or 610 subject to the following conditions:—

(i) the light emitted by the lens or lenses of each such beacon shall be of peak intensity of not less than 100 candelas on the principal axis of the relevant lens;

(ii) the part of that beacon through which light is emitted shall be of such a shape and size that the perimeter of the area projected horizontally thereby on to any vertical plane shall be capable of lying wholly inside a square having sides of 200 millimetres in length and wholly outside a square having sides of 100 millimetres in length;

(iii) the height of the centre of the lenses from the surface of the carriageway in the immediate vicinity shall be not less than 800 nor more than 1500 millimetres; and

(iv) the rate of flashing shall be not less than 120 nor more than 150 flashes per minute and the period between flashes shall not exceed $\frac{1}{4}$ of a second.

(2) Beacons showing an intermittent blue light for conveying the warning that drivers of vehicles should take special care may be used by a constable, or a person acting under the instructions (whether general or specific) of the chief officer of police, in combination with any of the signs shown in diagrams 606, 609, 610 and 633 to 635 subject to the same conditions specified in paragraph (1) (iii) and (iv).

(3) Flags of an area of not less than 0·2 square metres and coloured red for conveying the warning that it would be dangerous for drivers to cause their vehicles to proceed may be used in an emergency at or in the vicinity of works being executed, or of an obstruction situated on or near a road.

Cones and cylinders

29.—(1) A device constructed of rubber or flexible plastic material and being of the conical shape shown in diagram 577 for conveying the warning that drivers of vehicles should follow a certain route around an obstruction or road works in a road may be placed temporarily on the carriageway thereof subject to the following conditions:—

(*a*) the height of the device shall be not more than one metre nor less than 450 millimetres;

(*b*) the device shall be coloured as follows:—

(i) the uppermost part of the device to a depth of not less than one quarter nor more than one third of the height thereof shall be coloured red;

(ii) the base indicated in the said diagram may be of any colour;

(iii) the lowermost part of the device (except the said base) to a height of 50 millimetres shall be coloured red; and

(iv) the remaining part of the device shall be coloured white; and

(*c*) that part of the device coloured white shall be illuminated with white reflecting material and that part of the device coloured red may be illuminated with red reflecting material.

(2) A device constructed of rubber or flexible plastic material and being of the cylindrical shape shown in diagram 578 for indicating to drivers of vehicles a temporary division of the carriageway made so as to separate traffic moving in one direction from traffic moving in the opposite direction or for so indicating a part of a dual-carriageway road where vehicles other than those used for fire brigade, ambulance or police purposes, are prohibited from proceeding from one carriageway to the other may be placed temporarily on the carriageway of the road subject to the following conditions:—

(*a*) the height of the device shall be not more than one metre nor less than 450 millimetres,

(*b*) it shall have a diameter of not more than 125 nor less than 75 millimetres; and

(*c*) the device shall be coloured in the same way as the device prescribed in paragraph (1) and the provisions of sub-paragraphs (*b*) and (*c*) thereof shall apply accordingly except that for the reference to diagram 577 in the said sub-paragraph (*b*)(ii) there shall be substituted a reference therein to diagram 578.

Refuge indicator lamps

30. A lamp in the form of an illuminated spherical globe for conveying the warning that drivers of vehicles are approaching a street refuge may be used subject to the following conditions:—

(*a*) the globe shall be white;

(*b*) the globe shall have a diameter of not less than 290 nor more than 310 millimetres; and

(*c*) the height of the centre of the globe from the surface of the carriageway in the immediate vicinity shall be not less than 3·8 nor more than 5 metres.

Light signals for control of vehicular traffic

31.—(1) Light signals may be used for the control of vehicular traffic and shall be of the size, colour and type prescribed by paragraph (2), by paragraph (3) or by paragraph (4).

(2) The size, colour and type of light signals prescribed by this paragraph shall be as follows:—

(*a*) three lights shall be used, one red, one amber and one green;

(*b*) the lamps showing the coloured lights aforesaid shall be arranged vertically, the lamp showing a red light being the uppermost and that showing a green light the lowermost;

(*c*) each lamp shall be separately illuminated and the effective diameter of the lens thereof shall be not less than 195 nor more than 220 millimetres unless the lens is a lens of the kind shown in diagram 3001 when instead the said diameter may be not less than 290 nor more than 310 millimetres;

(*d*) the height of the centre of the amber lens from the surface of the carriageway in the immediate vicinity shall be in the case of signals placed at the side of the carriageway or on a street refuge not less than 2·4 nor more than 4 metres and in the case of signals placed elsewhere and over the carriageway not less than 6·1 nor more than 9 metres;

(*e*) the centres of adjacent lenses shall be not less than 305 nor more than 360 millimetres apart;

(*f*) no lettering shall be used upon the lenses or in connection with a light signal;

(*g*) the sequence of the lights shown for the purpose of controlling vehicular traffic shall be as follows:—

(i) red,

(ii) amber and red together,

(iii) green,

(iv) amber.

(3) The size, colour and type of light signals prescribed by this paragraph shall be as follows:—

(*a*) Four lamps each showing an intermittent red light shall be used.

(*b*) The lamps shall be so fitted as to enclose a rectangular area bounded by the one pair of sides extending horizontally and terminating as to each side in the centres of each pair of lenses (in these Regulations called "the horizontal pairs") and by the other pair of sides extending vertically in relation to the ground and terminating as to each side in the centres of each pair of lenses (in these Regulations called "the vertical pairs").

(*c*) When the four lamps are erected beside the carriageway, the distance between the centres of the lenses for each of the horizontal pairs shall be not less than 945 nor more than 955 millimetres and for each of the vertical pairs shall be not less than 695 nor more than 705 millimetres in accordance with the arrangement shown in diagram 6032.

(*d*) When the four lamps are erected over the carriageway, the distance between the said centres for each of the horizontal pairs shall be not less than 1395 nor more than 1405 millimetres and for each of the vertical pairs not less than 545 nor more than 555 millimetres in accordance with the arrangement shown in diagram 6031.

(*e*) Subject to the provisions of the next following sub-paragraph, each lamp shall be separately illuminated and the effective diameter of the lens thereof shall be not less than 120 nor more than 130 millimetres.

(*f*) When the signal is operated, each lamp shall show its intermittent red light at a rate of flashing of not less than 60 nor more than 90 flashes per minute, and in such a manner that the lights of one of the vertical pairs are always shown when the lights of the other vertical pair are not shown.

(*g*) The height of the centres of the lenses comprising the lower of the horizontal pairs from the surface of the carriageway in the immediate vicinity shall be in the case of signals placed at the side of the carriageway not less than 1·8 nor more than 3·2 metres and in the case of signals placed over the carriageway not less than 5·8 nor more than 6·8 metres.

(*h*) No lettering of any kind shall be used upon any of the lenses.

(4) The size, colour and type of light signals prescribed by this paragraph shall be as follows:—

(*a*) two lamps each showing an intermittent red light and one lamp showing a steady amber light shall be used;

(*b*) the lamps showing an intermittent red light shall be arranged horizontally so that there is a distance of not less than 585 nor more than 665 millimetres between the centres of the lenses of the lamps;

(*c*) the lamp showing the amber light shall be placed below the red lenses in such a position that a vertical line passing through the centre of that lamp is horizontally equidistant from the vertical lines passing through the centre of each red lens and that the vertical distance between a horizontal line passing through the centres of the red lenses is not less than 235 nor more than 345 millimetres;

(*d*) each lamp shall be separately illuminated and the effective diameter of the lens thereof shall be not less than 195 nor more than 220 millimetres;

(*e*) when the lamps showing an intermittent red light are operated, each such lamp shall show a red light at a rate of flashing of not less than 60 nor more than 90 flashes per minute, and in such a manner that the light of one lamp is always shown at a time when the light of the other lamp is not shown;

(*f*) the height of the centre of the amber lens from the surface of the carriageway in the immediate vicinity shall be in the case of signals placed at the side of the carriageway or on a street refuge not less than 2·4 nor more than 4 metres and in the case of signals placed elsewhere and over the carriageway not less than 6·1 nor more than 9 metres;

(*g*) the lenses shall be provided with a rectangular backing board having an overall width of not less than 1·3 metres and extending not less than 300 millimetres above the centre of each of the red lenses and not less than 300 millimetres below the centre of the amber lens, which board shall be coloured black, save for a white border having a width of not less than 80 nor more than 100 millimetres on the side from which the lamps show;

(*h*) the sequence of the signal lights under this paragraph shown for the purpose of controlling vehicular traffic shall be amber followed by red;

(*i*) no lettering of any kind shall appear on any of the lenses.

(5) Light signals prescribed by paragraph (4) may be surmounted by a cross of the size, colour and type shown in diagrams 542 and 542.1.

32.—(1) Subject to the next following paragraph, a lens or lenses of the size and colour shown in diagram 3001 in Schedule 3, which, when illuminated, shows a green arrow—

(*a*) may be substituted for the lens showing the green light in the light signals referred to in Regulation 31(2) in any of the methods shown in diagrams 3003, 3005, 3006 and 3011 in the said Schedule;

(*b*) may be affixed to the light signals referred to in Regulation 31(2) or to those signals as altered in accordance with the preceding sub-paragraph in any of the methods shown in diagram 3002 and diagrams 3004 to 3011 in the said Schedule.

In this paragraph, the substitution authorised in sub-paragraph (*a*) thereof in the method shown in the said diagram 3011 shall be treated as having been effected by means of the upper arrow shown in that diagram, the lower arrow shown therein being treated as affixed in accordance with sub-paragraph (*b*) thereof.

(2) When a lens is, or lenses are, so affixed as provided in paragraph (1)(*b*) and any one lens so affixed is of the larger of the two sizes specified in diagram 3001 in the said Schedule, the distance between the centre of that lens and the centre of any other lens affixed next in position immediately above, below or to the side of that first mentioned lens shall be not less than 415 nor more than 440 millimetres.

(3) The direction in which the arrow shown in diagram 3003 in the said Schedule points may be varied so as to be—

(*a*) a direction which lies straight upright, or

(*b*) a direction which lies at any angle between 90 degrees either to the left or to the right of the said upright direction.

(4) The direction in which any arrow shown in any of the diagrams 3002, 3004 to 3006, 3009 and 3010 in the said Schedule points may be varied so as to be—

(*a*) a direction which lies straight upright, or

(*b*) a direction which lies between the direction shown in the diagram showing that arrow and the said upright direction.

(5) The direction in which the upper arrow shown in diagram 3007 of the said Schedule points may be varied so as to be a direction which lies at any angle from the upright position shown to an angle of 45 degrees to the left and the direction in which the upper arrow shown in diagram 3008 in that Schedule points may be so varied as aforesaid to an angle of 45 degrees to the right.

(6) The direction in which the lower arrow shown in each of the said diagrams 3007 and 3008 points may be varied so as to be a direction which lies at any angle from the position shown in each such diagram respectively to an angle of 45 degrees towards the upright position as shown for the upper arrow in each such diagram.

(7) When both arrows shown in diagram 3011 of the said Schedule are illuminated and extinguished simultaneously the direction in which the upper arrow shown in that diagram points may be varied so as to be a direction which lies at any angle from the position so shown for that arrow to an angle of 45 degrees to the right passing through an arc of 135 degrees and the direction in which the lower arrow so shown points may be varied so as to be a direction which lies at any angle from the position so shown for

that arrow to an angle of 45 degrees towards the upright position or alternatively so as to be a direction lying at any angle from a position in which that arrow faces in the opposite direction from that so shown to an angle 45 degrees towards the upright position.

(8) When both arrows shown in the said diagram 3011 are illuminated and extinguished independently of each other, the direction of each such arrow may be varied so as to be a direction which lies at any angle between 90 degrees either to the left or to the right of the upright position.

Portable light signals for control of vehicular traffic

33.—(1) Portable light signals may be used for the control of vehicular traffic in the circumstances specified at (*a*) to (*c*) of this paragraph—

(*a*) on a road where, owing to roadworks being in progress thereon or for some other reason, the width of the carriageway of that road is temporarily restricted so that it will carry only one line of traffic,

(*b*) at a level crossing where a road is crossed by a railway when work in relation to that crossing is being carried out, or

(*c*) during the progress of temporary schemes of traffic control, if the signals are being operated and maintained by, and under the regular supervision of, the police or have been erected at a site approved in writing by the highway authority.

(2) Such light signals shall comply with the provisions of sub-paragraphs (*a*), (*b*), (*c*), (*e*), (*f*) and (*g*) of paragraph (2) of Regulation 31 or of the said paragraph (2) as varied by Regulation 32.

Significance of light signals

34.—(1) The significance of the light signals prescribed by Regulation 31(2) or by Regulation 33 shall be as follows:—

(*a*) except as provided in the next following sub-paragraph, the red signal shall convey the prohibition that vehicular traffic shall not proceed beyond the stop line on the carriageway provided in conjunction with the signals or, if that line is not for the time being visible or there is no stop line, beyond the post or other structure on or in which the primary signals are mounted;

(*b*) on an occasion when a vehicle is being used for fire brigade, ambulance or police purposes and the observance of the prohibition conveyed by the red signal as provided by the last preceding sub-paragraph would be likely to hinder the use of that vehicle for the purpose for which it is being used on that occasion, then the said sub-paragraph shall not apply to that vehicle; but instead the prohibition conveyed to that vehicle by the red signal shall be that that vehicle shall not proceed beyond the stop line, or as the case may be as provided by the said sub-paragraph, beyond the said post or other structure in such a manner or at such a time—

(i) as is likely to cause danger to the driver of any other vehicle proceeding on or from another road or on or from another part of the same road in accordance with the indications of the light signals operating there in association with the said red signal or as to necessitate the driver of any other such vehicle to change its speed or course in order to avoid an accident, or

(ii) in the case of any traffic which is not vehicular, as is likely to cause danger to that traffic proceeding on or from another road or on or from another part of the same road;

(*c*) the amber-with-red signal shall be taken to denote an impending change in the indication given by the signals from red to green but shall not alter the prohibition conveyed by the red signal;

(*d*) the green signal shall indicate that vehicular traffic may pass the signals and proceed straight on or to the left or to the right;

(*e*) the amber signal shall, when shown alone, convey the prohibition that vehicular traffic shall not proceed beyond the stop line or, if that line is not for the time being visible or there is no stop line, beyond the said post or other structure, except in the case of any vehicle which when the signal first appears is so close to the said line, post or structure that it cannot safely be stopped before passing the line, post or structure.

(2) The significance of the light signals prescribed by Regulation 31(2) as varied in accordance with the provisions of Regulation 32, shall be as follows:—

(*a*) subject as provided in sub-paragraph (*d*) of this paragraph, the red signal shall convey the prohibition that vehicular traffic shall not proceed beyond the stop line on the carriageway provided in conjunction with the signals or if the stop line is not for the time being visible or there is no stop line, beyond the post or other structure on or in which the primary signals are mounted, except that when a vehicle is being used on such an occasion as is specified in paragraph (1)(*b*), the foregoing prohibition prescribed by this sub-paragraph shall not then apply to that vehicle but instead the prohibition conveyed to it on that occasion by the red signal shall be the same as that provided by paragraph (1)(*b*) in relation to the vehicle mentioned in that paragraph;

(*b*) subject as provided in sub-paragraph (*d*) of this paragraph, the amber-with-red signal shall denote an impending change in the indication given by the signals from red to green (where a green signal is provided) or from red to a green arrow or arrows but shall not alter the prohibition conveyed by the red signal;

(*c*) the green signal (where a green signal is provided) shall indicate that vehicular traffic may pass the signals and proceed straight on or to the left or to the right;

(*d*) any green arrow during such time as it is illuminated shall indicate that vehicular traffic may pass the signals and proceed in the direction indicated by the arrow notwithstanding any other indication given by the signals;

(*e*) the amber signal shall, when shown alone, convey the prohibition that vehicular traffic shall not proceed beyond the stop line, or if the stop line is not for the time being visible or there is no stop line, beyond the said post or other structure, except in the case of any vehicle which when the signal first appears is so close to the said line, post or structure that it cannot safely be stopped before passing the line, post or structure.

(3) Vehicular traffic passing any light signals in accordance with the foregoing provisions of this Regulation shall proceed with due regard to the safety of other users of the road and subject to the direction of any police constable in uniform or other duly authorised person who may be engaged in the regulation of traffic.

(4) The significance of the light signals prescribed by Regulation 31(3) shall be that the intermittent red lights when displayed at the side of the carriageway

convey the prohibition that vehicular traffic shall not proceed beyond those lights and when displayed over the carriageway so as to operate in relation to vehicular traffic proceeding in the traffic lane (as defined by Regulation 36(1)) situated immediately beneath them, the said lights convey the prohibition that such vehicular traffic as aforesaid shall not proceed beyond those lights:

Provided that this paragraph shall not apply to a vehicle when it is being used on such an occasion as is specified in Regulation 34(1)(*b*); and for that vehicle when it is being so used, the intermittent red lights whether so displayed at the side of or over the carriageway shall have no significance.

(5) The significance of the light signals prescribed by Regulation 31(4) shall be as follows:—

(*a*) the amber signal shall convey the prohibition that vehicular traffic shall not proceed beyond the stop line on the carriageway provided in conjunction with the signal or, if that line is not for the time being visible or there is no stop line, beyond the post or other structure on or in which the primary signals are mounted, except in the case of any vehicle which when the signal first appears is so close to the said post or structure, that it cannot safely be stopped before passing the line post or structure; and

(*b*) the intermittent red signals shall convey the prohibition that vehicular traffic shall not proceed beyond the stop line on the carriageway provided in conjunction with the signals or, if that line is not for the time being visible or there is no stop line, beyond the said post or structure.

(6) In this Regulation,

(*a*) the expression "Stop line" means the road marking shown in diagram 1001 placed on the carriageway in conjunction with light signals being either primary signals alone, or secondary signals alone or both primary and secondary signals;

(*b*) any reference to light signals, to the signals or to a signal of a particular colour, is, where secondary signals have been erected as well as primary signals, a reference to the light signals, signals or particular signal displayed by both the primary signals and the secondary signals or by either the primary signals operating without the secondary signals, or by the secondary signals operating without the primary signals;

(*c*) the expression "primary signals" means light signals erected on or near the carriageway of a road and sited in the vicinity of either one end or both ends of the stop line or, if there is no stop line, sited at either or both edges of the carriageway or part of that carriageway which is in use by the traffic approaching and controlled by the signals; and

(*d*) the expression "secondary signals" means light signals erected on or near the carriageway facing approaching traffic in the same direction as the primary signals but sited beyond those signals as viewed from the direction of travel of such traffic.

Light signals for pedestrians

35.—(1) Light signals for conveying to pedestrians the information mentioned in paragraph (4) may be used facing across the carriageway in conjunction with the light signals prescribed by Regulation 31(2) or those light signals as varied in accordance with the provisions of Regulation 32 and, if so used, shall be of the size, colour and type shown in diagram 4001 or 4002 in Schedule 4:

Provided that the light signals for conveying to pedestrians such information as aforesaid and which are associated as parts of the same electrical circuit shall be all of them of the same size, colour and type, that is to say, as shown either in the said diagram 4001 or alternatively in the said diagram 4002.

(2) The height of the lower edge of the container enclosing the light signals from the surface of the carriageway in the immediate vicinity shall be not less than 2·1 nor more than 2·6 metres.

(3) The said signals shall be so designed that—

(*a*) the red figure shown in the said Schedule (hereinafter referred to as "the red signal") can be internally illuminated by a steady light;

(*b*) the green figure shown in the said Schedule (hereinafter referred to as "the green signal") can be internally illuminated by a steady light; and

(*c*) when one signal is illuminated the other signal is not illuminated.

(4) (*a*) The period during which in the interests of safety pedestrians should not cross the carriageway shall be shown by the red signal during such time as it is illuminated; and

(*b*) the period during which in the interests of safety pedestrians should cross the carriageway shall be shown by the green signal during such time as it is illuminated by the steady light.

(5) A traffic sign of the size, colour and type shown in diagram 4003 may be erected for use in conjunction with either the sign shown in diagram 4001 or that shown in diagram 4002 for the purpose of conveying to pedestrians the indication specified above that diagram.

Light signals for lane control of vehicular traffic

36.—(1) In this Regulation the expression "traffic lane" means, in relation to a road, a part of the carriageway having as a boundary which separates it from another such part, a road marking of the type shown either in diagram 1004, 1005, 1007 or 1013.1.

(2) Light signals placed above the carriageway and facing the direction of the on-coming vehicular traffic may be used for the control of that traffic proceeding along the traffic lane over and in relation to which those signals have been so placed and, subject to the provisions of this Regulation, shall be of the size, colour and type shown in diagrams 5002 and 5004 if placed above the carriageway of a road which is a motorway or shown in diagrams 5001 and 5003 if placed above the carriageway of any other road.

(3) The height of the centre of each such signal from the surface of the carriageway in the immediate vicinity shall be not less than 5·5 metres nor more than 9 metres.

(4) The said signals shall be so designed that—

(*a*) the red cross shown in diagrams 5003 and 5004 (hereinafter referred to as "the red cross") can be internally illuminated in such manner as to show a steady red light,

(*b*) the white arrow shown in diagrams 5001 and 5002 (hereinafter referred to as "the white downward arrow") can be internally illuminated by a steady white light, and

(*c*) whenever the red cross is illuminated above a traffic lane, the white downward arrow above that traffic lane is not also then illuminated and whenever the white downward arrow is illuminated above that same lane, the red cross is not also then illuminated.

(5) The significance of the light signals prescribed by this Regulation shall be —

(*a*) the red cross conveys to vehicular traffic proceeding in the traffic lane above and in relation to which it is displayed the prohibition that such traffic shall not proceed beneath or beyond the red cross in the said traffic lane in the direction opposite to that in which the red cross faces until that prohibition is cancelled by a display over that traffic lane of the white downward arrow or by the display over that traffic lane or beside the carriageway of the traffic sign shown in diagram 6001 or of a traffic sign bearing the legend "End of lane control"; and

(*b*) the white downward arrow conveys to such traffic proceeding in the traffic lane above and in relation to which it is displayed the information that that traffic may proceed or continue so to do in the said lane beneath or beyond the said arrow and in the direction opposite to that in which that arrow faces.

School crossing patrol signs and warning lights

37.—(1) Except where the Secretary of State authorises the use of traffic signs of another description, every traffic sign which is exhibited by a school crossing patrol for the purpose of stopping any vehicle or vehicles in accordance with section 25 of the Act shall be of the size, colour and type shown in diagram 605.1.

(2) (*a*) A traffic sign for conveying the warning specified in the next following sub-paragraph to vehicular traffic which is approaching a place in a road where children on their way to or from school or on their way from one part of a school to another cross or seek to cross that road may be erected on or near a part of that road in advance, in relation to oncoming traffic, of the said place;

(*b*) the warning conveyed by the traffic sign mentioned in the preceding sub-paragraph shall be that such a place as aforesaid lies ahead and is either being patrolled by a school crossing patrol or is otherwise in use by children under the supervision of a teacher or other school officer, a traffic warden or a constable in uniform;

(*c*) the said sign shall be of the following size, colour and type, that is to say—

(i) 2 lamps mounted vertically one above the other, facing in the same direction and each showing an intermittent amber light shall be used;

(ii) each lamp shall be separately illuminated and the effective diameter of the lens thereof shall be not less than 135 nor more than 155 millimetres;

(iii) each lamp shall be so fitted that the centre of the light source which illuminates its lens is located on the axis of that lens; and

(iv) each lamp shall show an intermittent amber light at a rate of flashing of not less than 60 nor more than 90 flashes per minute and in such a manner that the light of one lamp is always shown at a time when the light of the other lamp is not shown.

Light signals for motorways

38. A traffic sign for conveying to the driver of a motor vehicle on a motorway the warning that, owing to the existence of a hazard thereon, he should drive at a speed which does not exceed 30 miles per hour shall consist of 2 beacons showing light signals of the following size, colour and type, that is to say—

(1) 2 lamps each showing an intermittent amber light shall be used;

(2) the lamps shall be arranged vertically so that there is a distance of not less than 825 millimetres nor more than 1 metre between the centres of the lenses of the lamps;

(3) each lamp shall be separately illuminated and the effective diameter of the lens thereof shall be not less than 115 nor more than 175 millimetres;

(4) each lamp shall show the said light at a rate of flashing of not less than 60 nor more than 90 flashes per minute, and in such a manner that the light of one lamp is always shown at a time when the light of the other lamp is not shown.

39.—(1) Subject to the provisions of these Regulations, a traffic sign for conveying to vehicular traffic on motorways a warning or information of the description specified in or under a diagram in Part I of Schedule 6 shall be of the size, colour and type shown in the diagram relating to that warning or that information.

In this paragraph, the reference to vehicular traffic, where the traffic sign is erected beside the carriageway, is a reference to all vehicular traffic facing that sign and proceeding along the carriageway beside which the sign is so erected, and where the traffic sign is erected over the carriageway so as to operate in relation to vehicular traffic facing that sign and proceeding in the traffic lane (as defined by Regulation 36(1)) situated immediately beneath it, is a reference only to such traffic so facing and proceeding in that lane.

(2) Each of the signs shown in any diagram in Part I of Schedule 6 shall, when displaying the pattern of circles indicated by the diagram relative to that sign, be illuminated by internal white or off-white lights so arranged as to form the said pattern and may be accompanied by four lamps each showing an intermittent amber light as provided in the next following paragraph.

(3) Where the said four lamps accompany any of the signs mentioned in the last preceding paragraph, those lamps shall be of the size, colour and type prescribed by this paragraph, that is to say—

(*a*) the lamps shall, in relation to the said pattern of circles, be so arranged as shown in diagram 6022 in Part II of Schedule 6 when erected beside the carriageway or as shown in diagram 6021 in the said Part II when erected over the carriageway;

(*b*) each lamp shall show an intermittent amber light and, subject to the provisions of sub-paragraph (*f*) of this paragraph, be separately illuminated; and the effective diameter of the lens thereof shall be not less than 120 nor more than 130 millimetres;

(*c*) the lamps shall be so fitted as to enclose a rectangular area bounded by the one pair of sides extending horizontally in relation to the ground and terminating as to each side in the centres of each pair of lenses (in these Regulations called "the horizontal pairs") and by the other pair of sides extending vertically in relation to the ground and terminating as to each side in the centres of each pair of lenses (in these Regulations called "the vertical pairs");

(*d*) when the four lamps are erected beside the carriageway, the distance between the centres of the lenses for each of the horizontal pairs shall be not less than 695 nor more than 705 millimetres and for each of the vertical pairs shall be not less than 945 nor more than 955 millimetres;

(*e*) when the four lamps are erected over the carriageway, the distance between the said centres for each of the horizontal pairs shall be not less than 1045 nor more than 1055 millimetres and for each of the vertical pairs not less than 545 nor more than 555 millimetres;

(*f*) when the sign is operated, each lamp shall show the said light at a rate of flashing of not less than 60 nor more than 90 flashes per minute, and in such a manner that the lights of one of the horizontal pairs are always shown when the lights of the other horizontal pair are not shown;

(*g*) the height of the centres of the lenses comprising the lower of the horizontal pairs from the surface of the carriageway in the immediate vicinity shall be in the case of signs placed beside the carriageway not less than 1·8 nor more than 3·2 metres and in the case of signs placed over the carriageway not less than 5·8 nor more than 6·8 metres;

(*h*) no lettering of any kind shall be used upon any of the lenses.

(4) The light signals prescribed by paragraph (3) shall convey to traffic the warning that the display of a traffic sign shown in a diagram in Part I of Schedule 6 is due to the existence of temporary hazardous conditions on or near the motorway.

(5) Where the circumstances so require, the indications given by the signs shown in Part I of Schedule 6 may be varied as in this paragraph provided, that is to say—

(*a*) any indication given by such a sign may be varied in the respect (if any) in which it is shown below the diagram relating to that sign that the indication may be varied;

(*b*) in the sign shown in diagram 6001, the numerals may be varied to accord with the circumstances.

Road danger lamps

40.—(1) Subject to the provisions of these Regulations, a lamp showing either a steady or an intermittent light may be used to indicate to traffic the limits of a temporary obstruction of a road and shall be of the size, colour and type prescribed by paragraph 2.

(2) (*a*) The colour of the light shown by the said lamp whether steady or intermittent shall be amber.

(*b*) Each lens of the lamp shall be—

(i) if the light so shown is emitted from the lamp in only one, two or three horizontal directions, of such a shape and size that the perimeter of its horizontally projected area on to any vertical plane shall be capable of lying wholly inside a circle having a diameter of 150 millimetres and wholly outside a circle having a diameter of 100 millimetres, and

(ii) if the light so shown is emitted from the lamp in every horizontal direction, of such a shape and size that the perimeter of its horizontally projected area on to any vertical plane shall be capable of lying wholly within a square having sides of 125 millimetres in length and wholly outside a square having sides of 40 millimetres in length.

(*c*) Each such lamp shall be illuminated separately and by a single source of light.

(*d*) The height of the centre of any such lens from the surface of the road in the immediate vicinity shall not exceed 1·2 metres.

(*e*) There shall be displayed in association with that lens a device having an area of not less than 50 square centimetres and fitted with amber reflectors or amber reflecting material.

(*f*) Where a lamp is used which shows a steady light, then the luminous intensity of that light shall not be less than 0·5 candela measured within 5 degrees above and below and 10 degrees left and right of the principal axis if the light so shown is emitted from the lamp in only one, two or three directions, and measured within 5 degrees above and below the horizontal plane around the vertical axis of symmetry if the said light is so emitted in every direction.

(*g*) Where a lamp which shows an intermittent light is used, then that lamp shall be of such a size and type that the rate of flashing shall be not less than 900 flashes per minute and the peak luminous intensity measured in accordance with the last preceding sub-paragraph not less than 1 candela; except that where such a lamp is erected within 50 metres of a street lamp lit by electricity on a road subject to a speed limit of 40 miles per hour or less, that lamp may, as an alternative to the size and type last mentioned, be of such a size and type that the said rate shall be not less than 120 nor more than 150 flashes per minute and the said intensity so measured shall be not less than 1·5 candela.

SCHEDULE 1 (See Regulations 9 — 19)

Dimensions in any diagram shown in this Schedule are expressed in millimetres unless otherwise specified.

PART I—Warning signs

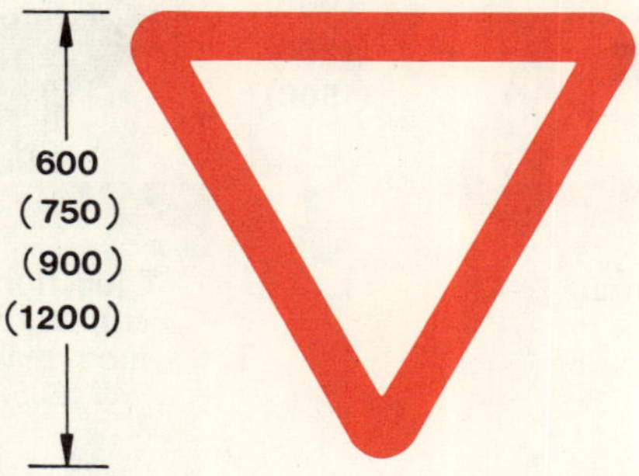

Junction ahead controlled by sign in diagram 601.1 or 602
(See Direction 11)
501

Plate for use with sign in diagram 501
(See Directions 11 and 12)
502

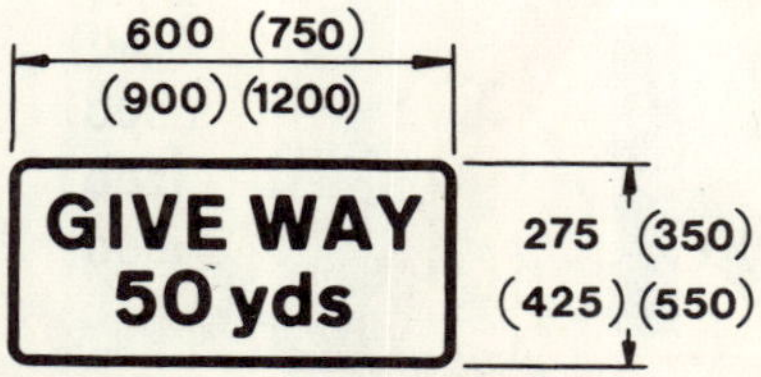

Plate for use with sign in diagram 501
(See Directions 11 and 12)
503

Cross roads ahead
504.1

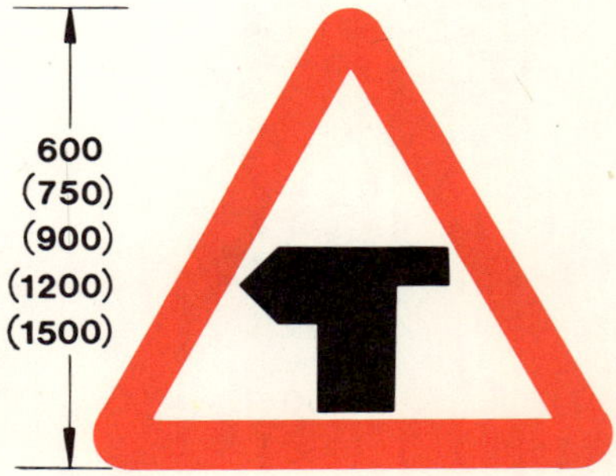

T junction ahead
Permitted variant:
The symbol may be reversed
505.1

Side road ahead
Permitted variants:
The symbol may be reversed and the thickness of the symbol may be varied to indicate the direction of the major road
506.1

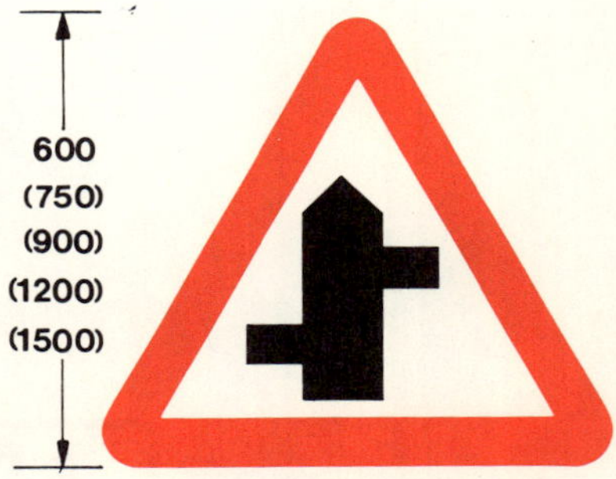

Staggered junction ahead
Permitted variants:
The symbol may be reversed and the thickness of the symbol may be varied to indicate the direction of the major road
507.1

Traffic merges ahead
Permitted variant:
The symbol may be reversed
508

Same as 508
Permitted variant:
The symbol may be reversed
509

Roundabout ahead
510

Plate for use with signs in diagrams 504.1 to 507.1, 510, 512, 513, 516, 517 and 520
Permitted variant:
When used in combination with any of the signs in diagrams 504.1 to 507.1 may be varied to read "Heavy plant crossing"
(See Direction 12)
511

Bend to the right ahead
Permitted variant:
The symbol may be reversed to indicate a bend to the left ahead
512

Double bend ahead, first to the left
Permitted variant:
The symbol may be reversed to indicate a double bend ahead, first to the right
513

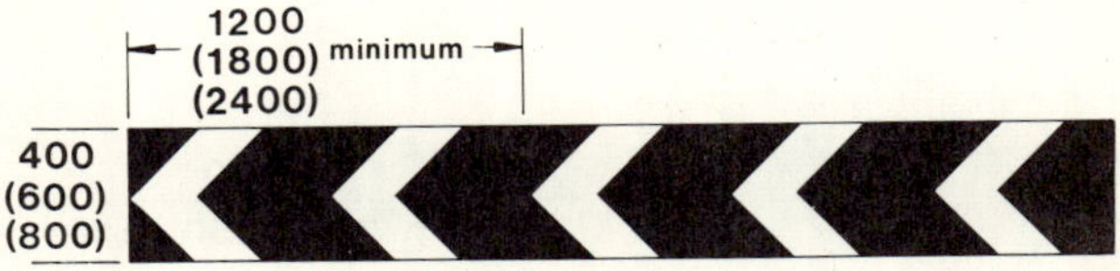

Sharp deviation of route to the left
515

Road narrows on both sides ahead
516

Road narrows on right ahead
Permitted variant:
The symbol may be reversed to indicate that road narrows on left ahead
517

Convergence of traffic to single file in each direction
Plate for use with signs in diagrams 516 and 517
(See Direction 12)
518

Road only wide enough for one line of vehicles
Plate for use with signs in diagrams 516 and 517
(See Direction 12)
519

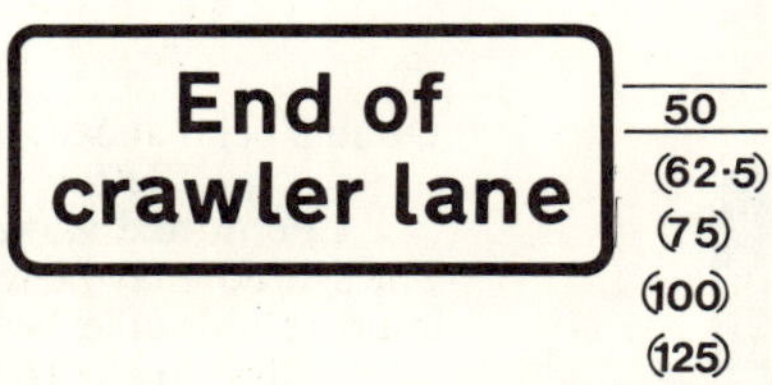

Plate for use with sign in diagram 517
(See Direction 12)
519.1

Dual carriageway ends ahead
520

Two-way traffic
521

Two-way traffic ahead across a one-way carriageway
522

Steep hill downwards ahead
523.1

Steep hill upwards ahead
524.1

Plate for use with signs in diagrams 523.1 and 524.1 (See Direction 12)
525

Plate for use with signs in diagrams 512, 513, 523.1 and 524.1 (See Direction 12)
526

Plate for use with signs in diagrams 523.1 and 524.1 (See Direction 12)
527

Hump bridge ahead
528

Opening or swing bridge ahead
529

Tunnel ahead
529.1

Headroom at hazard
Permitted variant: Metric units may be substituted for imperial units within the warning triangle
(See Direction 11)
530

Limits within which headroom indicated is available at hazard
Permitted variant: Same as for 530
(See Direction 11)
532.1

Electrified overhead cable ahead
(See Direction 11)
533

Plate for use with sign in diagram 533
(See Direction 12)
534.1

Plate for use with sign in diagram 533
(See Direction 12)
534.2

Plate for use with sign in diagram 533
(See Direction 12)
535.1

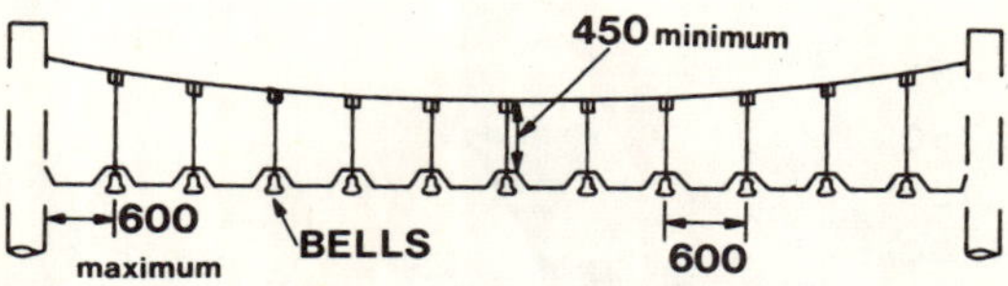

Load gauge to afford audible warning of the maximum safe height of vehicles about to pass under electrified overhead cable
(See Direction 22)
536

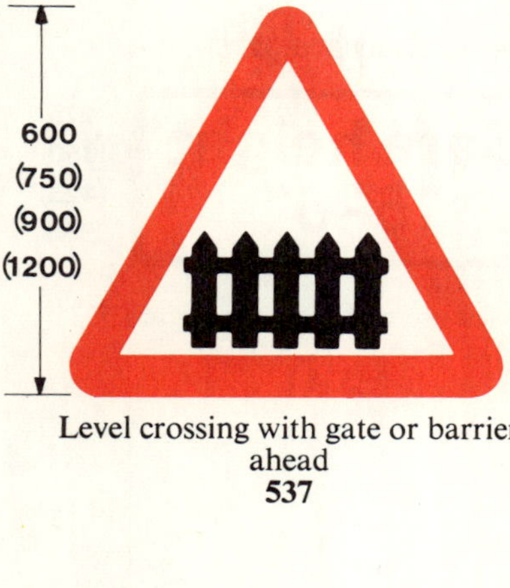

Level crossing with gate or barrier ahead
537

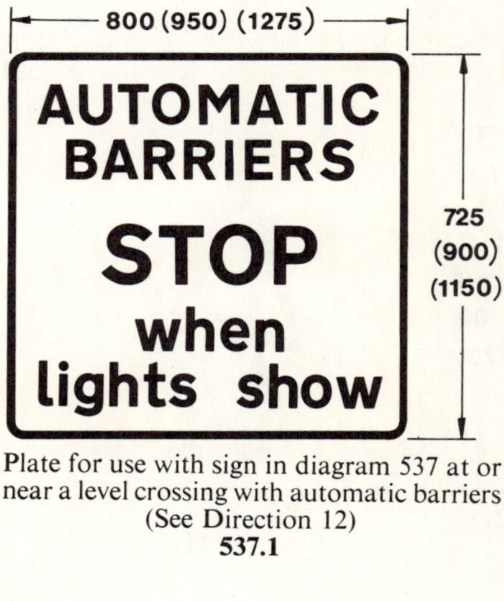

Plate for use with sign in diagram 537 at or near a level crossing with automatic barriers
(See Direction 12)
537.1

Plate for use with signs in diagrams 529, 529.1, 537 (except when erected at or near a level crossing with automatic barriers) and 558
(See Direction 12)
537.2

Plate for use with diagram 562 to give warning of the presence of signals ahead of the type prescribed by Regulation 31 (4) installed at or near a fire station
Permitted variant:
"Ambulance" may be substituted for "Fire" when appropriate
(See Direction 12)
537.3

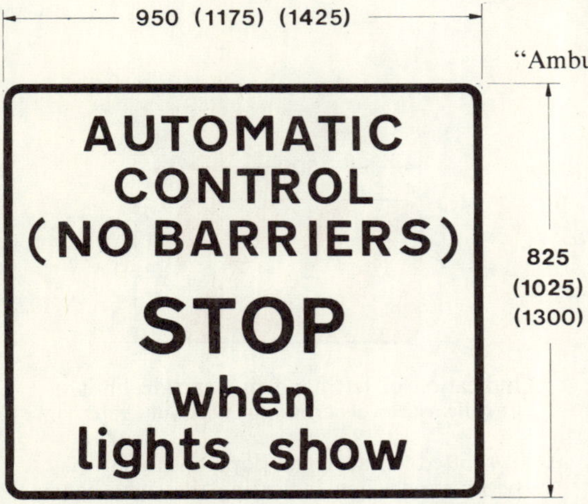

Plate for use with sign in diagram 538 at or near a level crossing where signals prescribed by Regulation 31 (4) are installed
(See Direction 12)
537.4

Level crossing without gate or barrier ahead
538

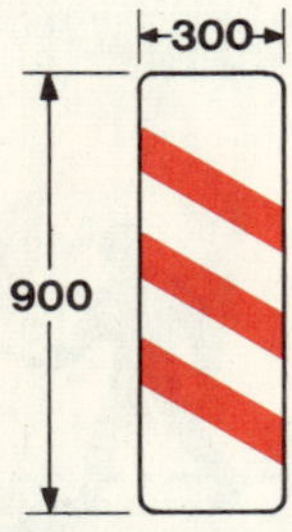

Concealed level crossing ahead
539

Same as 539
540

Same as 539
541

Permitted variant: In the signs in diagrams 539, 540 and 541 the slope of the bars may be reversed when erected on the right hand side of a carriageway

Location of single track railway level crossing without gate or barrier
542

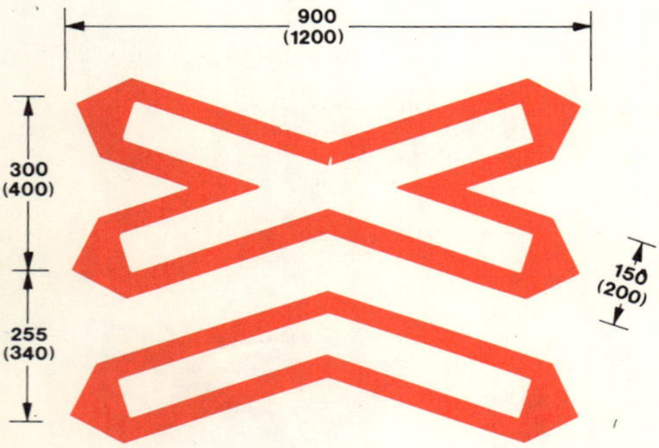

Location of level crossing without gate or barrier over more than one line of railway
542.1

Indication of left hand or nearside limit of a railway level crossing without gate or barrier
Permitted variant: The slope of the bar may be reversed when indicating the right hand or offside limit of a railway level crossing without gate or barrier
542.2

Traffic signals ahead
543

Pedestrian crossing ahead
544

Pedestrians in road ahead
544.1

Elderly or handicapped pedestrians
(See Direction 11)
544.2

Children going to or from school
or playground
(See Directions 11 and 15)
545

Plate for use with sign in diagram 545
(See Direction 12)
546

Plate for use with sign in diagram 545
(See Directions 12 and 15)
547.1

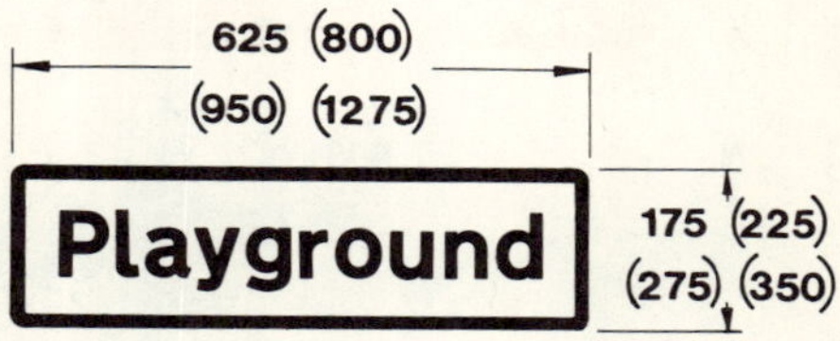

Plate for use with sign in diagram 545
(See Direction 12)
547.2

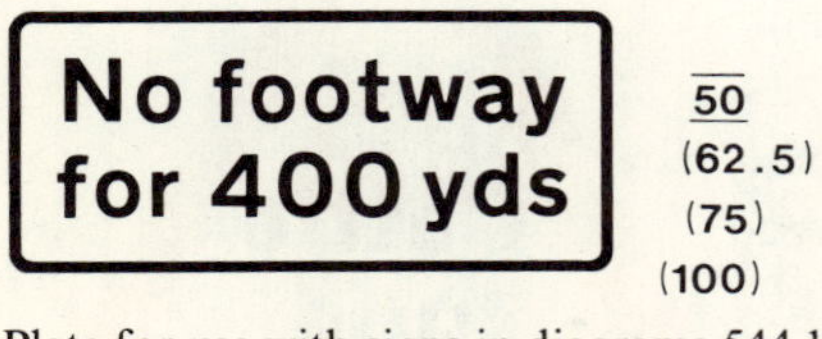

Plate for use with signs in diagrams 544.1
and 545
(See Direction 12)
547.3

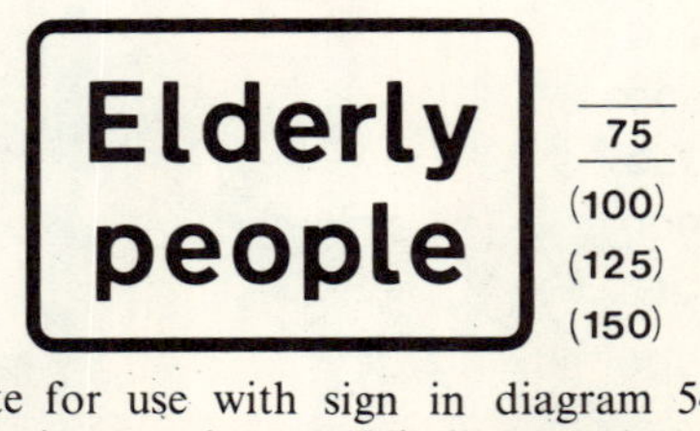

Plate for use with sign in diagram 544.2
Permitted variants: "Blind" or "Disabled"
may be substituted for "Elderly"
(See Direction 12)
547.4

Cattle
548

Sheep
549

Wild horses or ponies
550

Accompanied horses or ponies crossing the road ahead
550.1

Wild animals
551

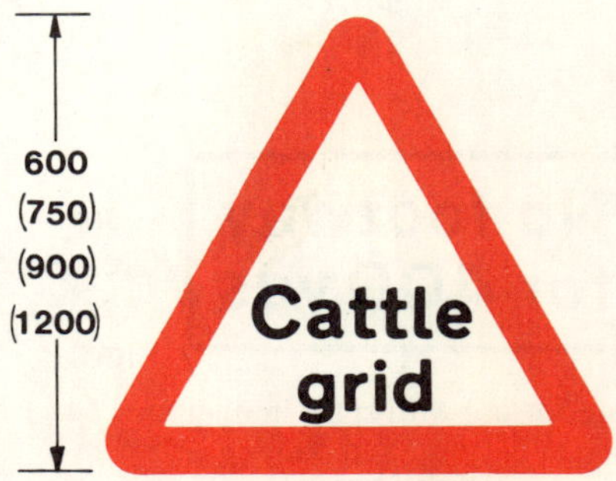

Cattle grid ahead
552

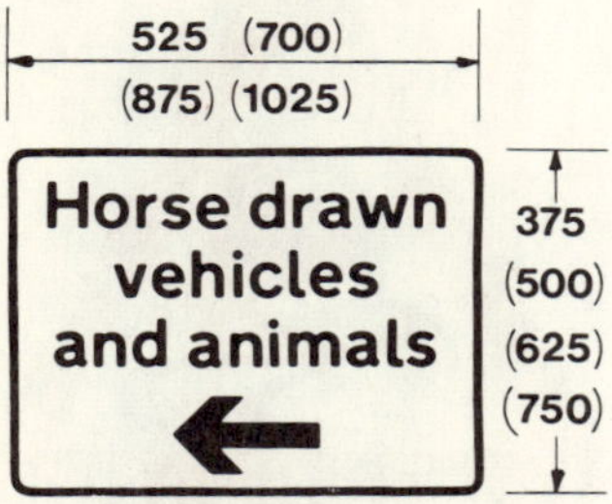

By-pass of cattle grid
Plate for use with sign
in diagram 552
(See Direction 12)
553

Worded warning sign
Permitted variants:
"Flood", "Fog", "Gate", "Gates", "Ice" or "Snow drifts" may be substituted for "Ford"
554

Indication to drivers after crossing a ford or before descending a down gradient
554.1

Quayside or river bank ahead
Permitted variant:
The symbol may be reversed
555

Uneven road
556

Plate for use with sign in diagram 556 at or near a railway level crossing or with sign in diagram 528 at or near a hump bridge
(See Direction 12)
556.3

Plate for use with sign in diagram 556 near a railway level crossing or with sign in diagram 528 near a hump bridge
(See Direction 12)
556.4

Slippery road
557

Low flying aircraft or sudden aircraft noise
558

Risk of falling or fallen rocks
Permitted variant:
The symbol may be reversed
559

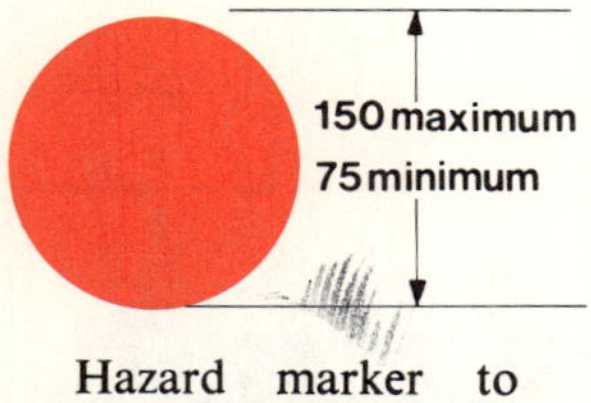

Hazard marker to indicate edge of carriageway or obstruction near that edge
Permitted variant:
The portion of the sign coloured red to be coloured white or amber as prescribed
(See Direction 23)
560

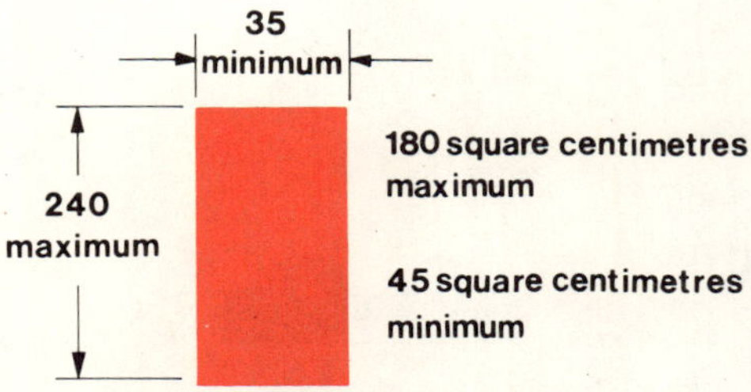

Same as 560
(See Direction 23)
561

Other danger ahead
(See Direction 11)
562

Plate indicating nature of other danger, for use with sign in diagram 562
Permitted variants: "Blasting", "Dust cloud", "Fallen tree", "Frost damage", "Overhead cable repairs", "Road liable to flooding", "Smoke", "Surveying" or "Census" may be substituted for "Accident"
(See Directions 11 and 12)
563

Road works or temporary obstruction of the carriageway ahead
(See Direction 17)
564

Plate indicating nature of road works for use with sign in diagram 564
Permitted variants: "Blasting", "Grass cutting", "Gritting", "Gully emptying", "Hedge cutting", "Road sweeping", "Salting", "Sign cleaning", "Snow ploughing", "Surveying", "Tree cutting" or "Overhead works" may be substituted for "Line painting"
(See Directions 12 and 17)
564.1

Diversion to the other carriageway of a dual carriageway road ahead
Permitted variant:
The symbol may be reversed
(See Direction 17)
564.5

Loose chippings
(See Direction 17)
565.1

Permitted variants: "Ramp ahead", "Road ahead closed", "Road closed", "Temporary road surface", "Works traffic only", "No works traffic", "Traffic control ahead", "Traffic signal maintenance" (Dimension 450 may be substituted for 750), "Give way markings erased" or "Stop markings erased" may be substituted for "Slow wet tar"
(See Direction 17)
565.2

To indicate to vehicular traffic the place beyond which traffic shall not proceed when a temporary red light signal conforming to Regulation 33 (2) is displayed and no stop line is placed on the carriageway
Permitted variant: "Stop sign" may be substituted for "Red Light"
(See Direction 17)
565.3

To indicate a temporary absence of road markings
Permitted variant: "At level crossing" may be substituted for "For 2 miles"
(See Direction 17)
565.4

(See Direction 17)
566

Permitted variants: "Right" or "Both ways" may be substituted for "Left"
(See Direction 17)
567

Direction of temporary pedestrian route
(See Direction 17)
567.1

To indicate direction for emergency vehicles to a temporary incident control point
Permitted variant: "Incident control"
(See Direction 17)
567.2

Sharp deviation of route to the left at or near road works or other temporary obstruction
(See Direction 17)
569

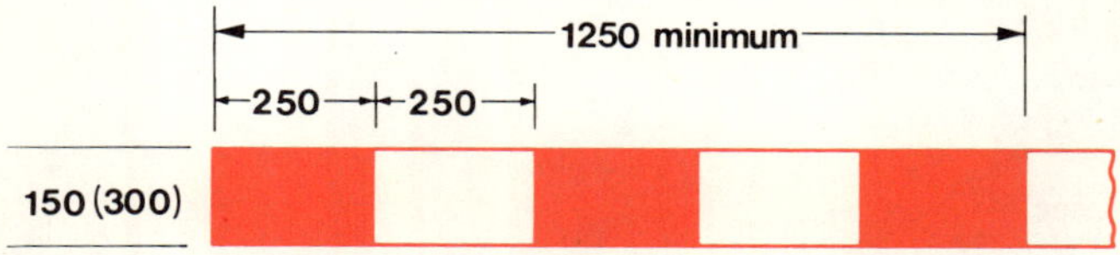

Traffic lane or carriageway closed to traffic
(See Direction 17)
569.1

Permitted variants: "New road layout", "New traffic signals", "Changed priorities", "New one-way system", "Gap closed" or "New traffic islands" may be substituted for the first two lines and a distance expressed to the nearest 50 yards may be inserted before the word "Ahead"
(See Direction 19)
569.2

New level crossing control ahead
(See Direction 19)
569.3

To indicate failure of light signals ahead
569.4

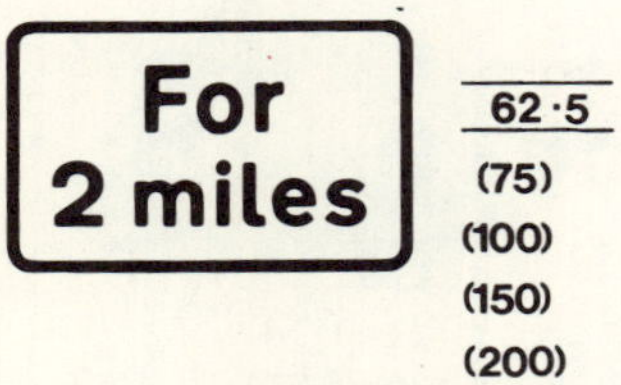

Distance over which hazard or prohibition extends
Plate for use with signs in diagrams 513, 518, 519, 521, 523.1, 524.1, 548 to 551, 554 (when varied to "Flood"), 556, 557 to 559, 564, 565.1, 614, 615, 632, 642, 811, 858, 858.1 and 858.2
(See Direction 12)
570

Distance to hazard
Plate for use with signs in diagrams 518, 519, 523.1, 524.1, 529, 530, 554 and 564
(See Direction 12)
571

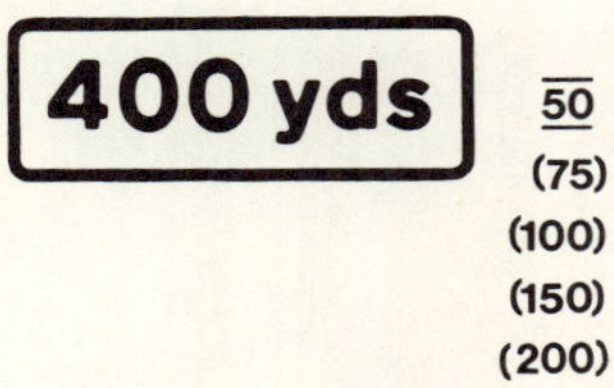

Distance to hazard
Plate for use with signs in diagrams 504.1 to 509, 516 to 520, 523.1, 524.1, 529, 529.1, 530, 533, 537, 538, 543 to 545, 554, 555, 562, 564, 564.5, 858, 858.1 and 858.2
(See Direction 12)
572

Distance and direction to hazard
Plate for use with signs in diagrams 516, 517, 529, 529.1, 530, 533, 537, 538, 543 to 545, 554, 555, 562, 564, 858, 858.1 and 858.2
Permitted variant: The distance may be omitted
(See Direction 12)
573

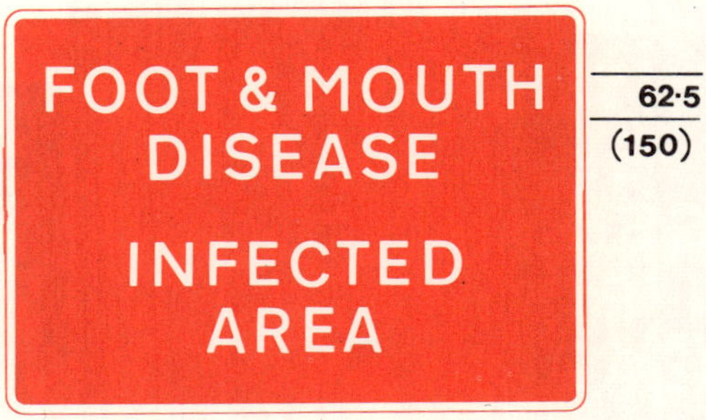

Permitted variants: "Rabies" may be substituted for "Foot and Mouth Disease". "Ahead" may be inserted after "Area" or "End of" may be inserted before "Infected"

(See Direction 16)

574

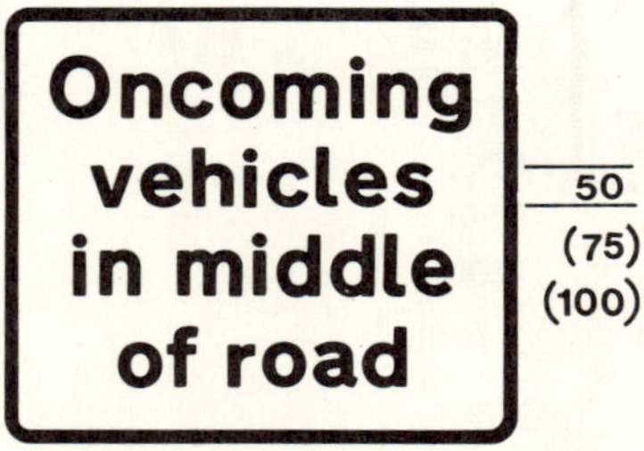

Plate for use with signs in diagrams 516, 517, 528, 529.1 and 530

(See Direction 12)

575

Temporary sign for pedestrians to indicate that a Zebra or Pelican pedestrian crossing is not in use as such a crossing

576

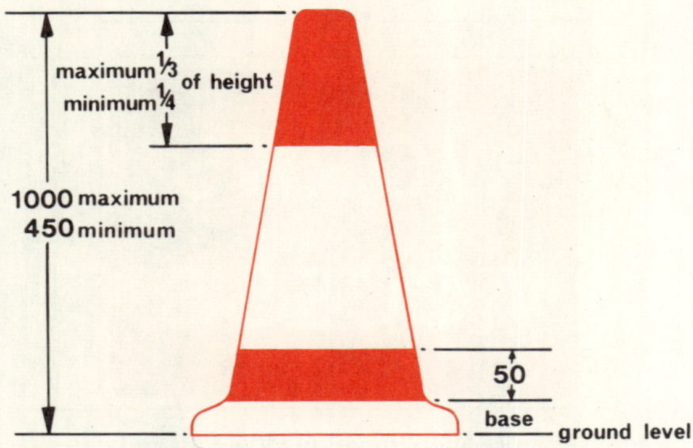

Traffic cone to delineate the edge of a route for vehicular traffic through or past a temporary obstruction

577

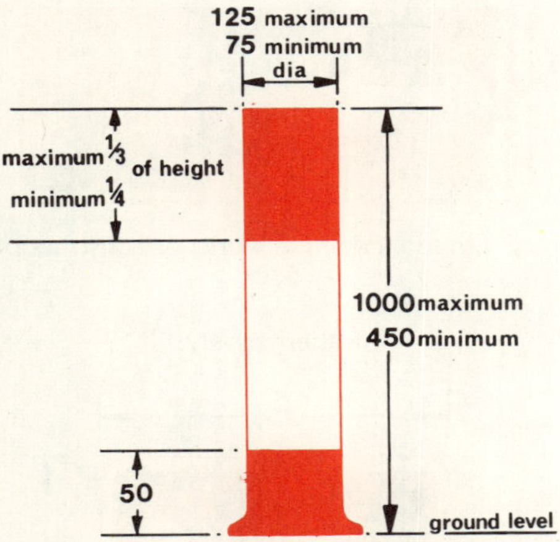

Traffic cylinder to indicate the temporary division of traffic flows into opposing directions on one carriageway, or to mark a boundary between two carriageways of a dual carriageway which may not be crossed except for fire brigade, ambulance or police purposes

578

Plate for use with diagram 506.1 to indicate a temporary access to a construction or road works site
(See Direction 12)
579

Temporary sign to guide road works or construction traffic
580

or alternatively

SCHEDULE 1 (See Regulations 9—19)

PART II—Regulatory signs

To indicate to vehicular traffic the requirements prescribed in Regulation 11 (1) (*b*)
(See Directions 5, 10, 11 and 25)
601.1

To indicate to vehicular traffic the requirements prescribed in Regulation 11(1)(*c*)(i)
(See Directions 10 and 11)
602

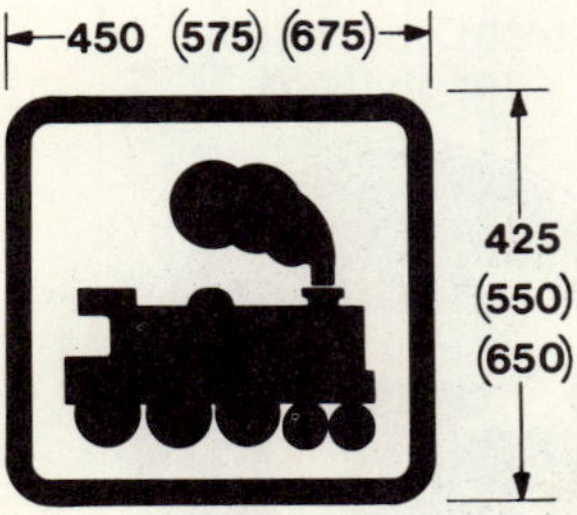

Plate for use with sign in diagram 602 at an open level-crossing without light signals to indicate the requirements prescribed by Regulation 11 (1) (*c*) (ii)
(See Direction 12)
602.1

Manually operated temporary sign to indicate to vehicular traffic that they shall not proceed into the length of road where one-way working is necessary
(See Direction 18)
603

Manually operated temporary sign to indicate to vehicular traffic that they may proceed into the length of road where one-way working is necessary
(See Direction 18)
604

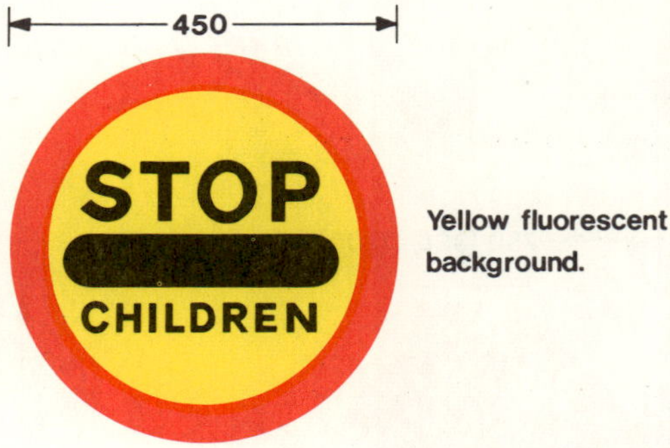

Sign exhibited by a school crossing patrol for the purpose of stopping any vehicle or vehicles in accordance with section 25 of the Road Traffic Regulation Act 1967
605.1

Vehicular traffic must proceed in the direction indicated by the arrow
(See Direction 6)
606

Plate for use with signs in diagrams 606 and 609
(See Directions 6 and 12)
607

Vehicular traffic must turn left ahead
Permitted variant:
The direction of the arrow may be reversed to indicate vehicular traffic must turn right ahead
(See Direction 6)
609

Plate for use with signs in diagrams 501, 601.1, 602, 606, 609 and 610
(See Direction 12)
608

To indicate to vehicular traffic the requirements prescribed in Regulation 9A(2) or (3)
Permitted variant: The arrow may be pointed downwards to the right
610

Vehicles entering the junction give priority to vehicles from the right at the transverse road marking shown in diagram 1003.3 associated with the sign or, if the line is not for the time being visible, at the road junction and proceed past the marking shown in diagram 1003.4 in the direction indicated by the arrows (See Directions 10 and 25)
611.1

To indicate to vehicular traffic that by passing either side of the sign the same destination is reached
611

No right turn for vehicular traffic (See Direction 6)
612

No left turn for vehicular traffic (See Direction 6)
613

No U Turns
for vehicular traffic
(See Direction 6)
614

Priority to vehicles
from the opposite direction
(See Direction 18)
615

No entry for vehicular traffic
(See Direction 6)
616

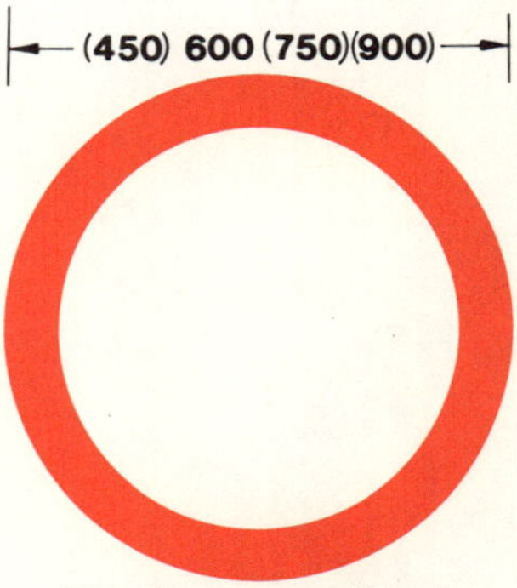

All vehicles prohibited
(See Directions 6 and 11)
617

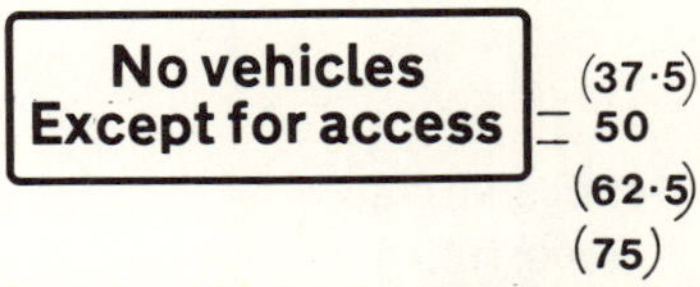

Plate for use with sign in diagram 617 to indicate exemption for access to premises and land adjacent to the prohibited road or roads.
Permitted variants: "Except for access" may be omitted or "for access" may be varied to read "for loading" to indicate an exemption for loading or unloading in the prohibited road or roads and for access to off-street garageing from those roads, or "disabled badge holders" (in which case the black on orange symbol shown in diagram 661 shall be added), or "permit holders", or "buses and for access", or "buses coaches and for access", or "buses and for loading", or "buses coaches and for loading" or "for loading and disabled badge holders (in which case the black on orange symbol shown in diagram 661 shall be added) or "for loading and permit holders"
(See Directions 6 and 12)
618.1

Plate for use
with sign in diagram 617
(See Directions 6 and 12)
618

All motor vehicles prohibited
(See Direction 6)
619

All motor vehicles except motor bicycles without side-car prohibited
(See Direction 6)
619.1

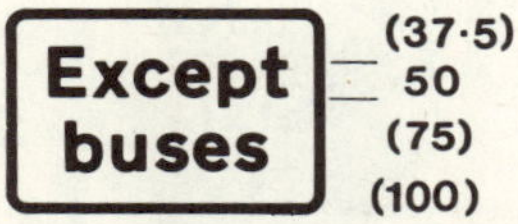

Plate for use with signs in diagrams 606, 609, 612, 613, 616, 619, 619.1, 626.1, 628.1, 629 and 629.2 and indicating exemption for stage carriages, scheduled express carriages, school buses and works buses

Permitted variants: There may be added, when used in conjunction with the sign in diagram 626.1, a weight in tonnes not to be exceeded by the vehicles or vehicles and load qualifying for exemption and, when used in conjunction with the sign in diagram 628.1, an axle weight in tonnes not to be so exceeded as aforesaid

(See Directions 6 and 12)
619.3

Plate for use with signs in diagrams 606, 609, 612, 613, 616, 619, 619.1, 626.1, 628.1, 629, and 629.2 and indicating exemption for vehicles constructed to carry 12 or more passengers

Permitted variants: Same as 619.3

(See Directions 6 and 12)
619.4

Plate for use with signs in diagrams 619, 619.1, 621, 622.1A, 622.5, 626.1, 628.1, 629, 629.1 and 629.2 to indicate exemption for access to premises and land adjacent to the prohibited road or roads

Permitted variants: Same as for 618.1

(See Directions 6 and 12)
620

Plate for use with the sign in diagram 619 to indicate an exemption for goods vehicles to enter the street for loading and unloading of goods

(See Directions 6 and 12)
620.1

All vehicles constructed or adapted to carry more than 12 passengers prohibited except stage carriages, scheduled express carriages, school buses and works buses
(See Direction 6)
621

Goods vehicles exceeding the maximum gross weight indicated on the goods vehicle symbol prohibited
Permitted variant: The weight may be varied to "16.5T" (16.5 tonnes)
(See Direction 6)
622.1A

End of prohibition of goods vehicles exceeding the maximum gross weight previously indicated to traffic
(See Direction 6)
622.2

Plate to give reason for the imposition of a temporary restriction on classes of vehicles for use with signs in diagrams 621, 622.1A, 622.4, 626.1, 628.1, 629, 629.1 and 632
Permitted variant: "Ice" may be substituted for "Snow drifts"
(See Direction 12)
622.3

Track laying vehicles prohibited
Permitted variant:
"No articulated vehicles"
(See Direction 6)
622.4

Horsedrawn vehicles prohibited
(See Direction 6)
622.5

Pedal cycling prohibited
(See Direction 6)
624

Route shall not be used except by non-mechanically propelled pedal cycles
(See Direction 6)
625

Pedestrians prohibited
(See Direction 6)
625.1

Plate for use with signs shown in diagrams 625 and 815 to indicate that mopeds may use the cycle track
(See Direction 12)
625.2

Vehicles or vehicles and load exceeding the weight indicated in tonnes prohibited
(See Direction 6)
626.1

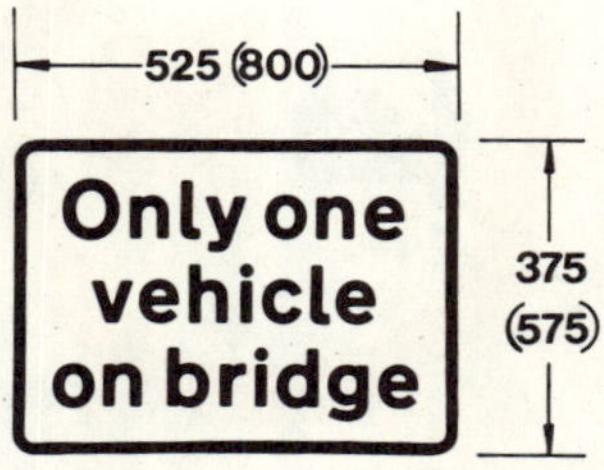

Plate for use with signs in diagrams 626.1 and 628.1
(See Directions 6 and 12)
627

Vehicles or vehicles and load exceeding the weight indicated in tonnes on any one axle prohibited
(See Direction 6)
628.1

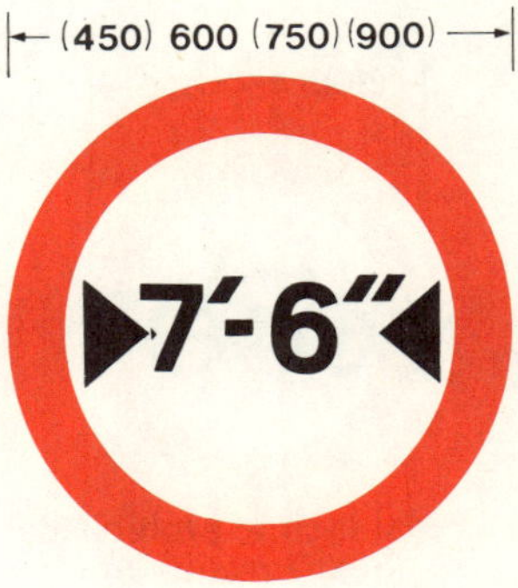

Vehicles exceeding width indicated prohibited
Permitted variant:
Metric units may be substituted for imperial units within the prohibitory circle
(See Directions 6 and 11)
629

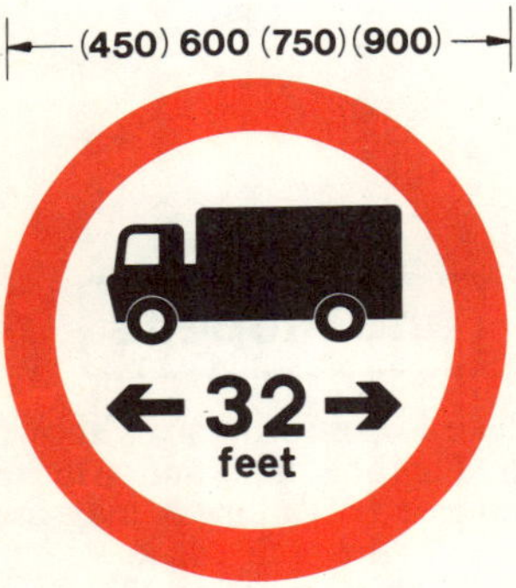

Vehicles or combinations of vehicles exceeding length indicated prohibited
Permitted variant: Same as 629
(See Directions 6 and 11)
629.1

Vehicles exceeding height indicated prohibited
Permitted variant: Same as 629
(See Directions 6 and 11)
629.2

No overtaking
(See Directions 6 and 11)
632

Manually operated temporary sign to indicate to vehicular traffic the requirement not to proceed beyond the sign where displayed by a police constable in uniform or traffic warden
633

Temporary sign to indicate potential danger ahead and the need to proceed with caution
(See Direction 18(3))
634

Temporary sign to indicate an accident ahead and the need to proceed with caution
(See Direction 18(3))
635

Temporary sign to indicate prohibition of waiting except for loading and unloading at the time it is displayed
(See Direction 6)
636

Legend for use with sign in diagram 636
(See Directions 6 and 12)
636.1

Plate showing continuous prohibition on waiting except for loading and unloading
(See Directions 6 and 13)
637

Plate showing continuous prohibition on loading and unloading
Permitted variant:
"at bus stop" may be inserted after "No loading"
(See Directions 6 and 14)
638

Plate showing hours during and direction in which waiting is prohibited except for loading and unloading
(See Directions 6 and 13)
639

Plate showing hours during which waiting by goods vehicles over 5 or 7·5 tonnes maximum gross weight is prohibited except for loading and unloading
Permitted variant: "7·5" may be substituted for "5" on the goods vehicle symbol
(See Direction 6)
639.2

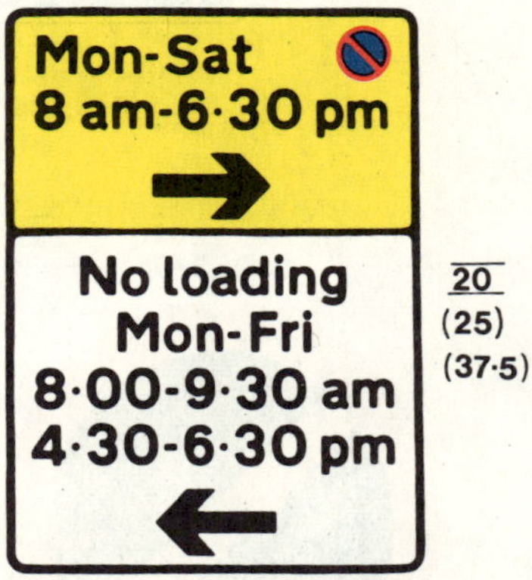

Plate showing (upper portion) times and direction in which waiting is prohibited except for loading and unloading and (lower portion) times during and direction in which loading and unloading are prohibited
Permitted variant: (lower portion) "at bus stop" may be inserted after "No loading"
(See Directions 6, 13 and 14)
640

Sign to appear on parking meter cover showing prohibition on waiting, loading and unloading at a parking place where parking is temporarily suspended
Permitted variants:
"During meter control" may be added
"No loading" may be omitted
640.1

Plate showing hours during and direction in which waiting by goods vehicles over 5 or 7·5 tonnes maximum gross weight is prohibited except for loading and unloading
Permitted variant: "7·5" may be substituted for "5" on the goods vehicle symbol
(See Direction 6)
640.2A

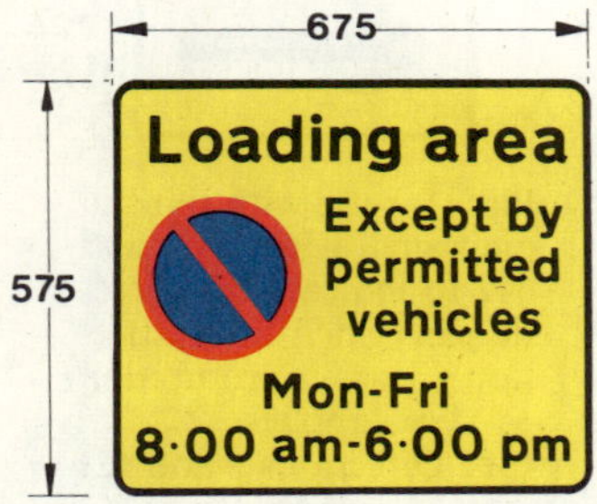

Entrance to a designated loading area in which waiting except by permitted vehicles is prohibited during the hours shown
(See Direction 6)
640.3

Sign showing hours during which waiting except by permitted vehicles is prohibited in a designated loading area
(See Direction 6)
640.4

End of loading area in which waiting except by permitted vehicles is prohibited
(See Direction 6)
640.5

Plate showing hours
during which waiting is limited
(See Directions 6, 13 and 28)
641

No stopping
on main carriageway
(See Direction 6)
642

Plate for use with diagram 642
(See Directions 6 and 12)
642.1

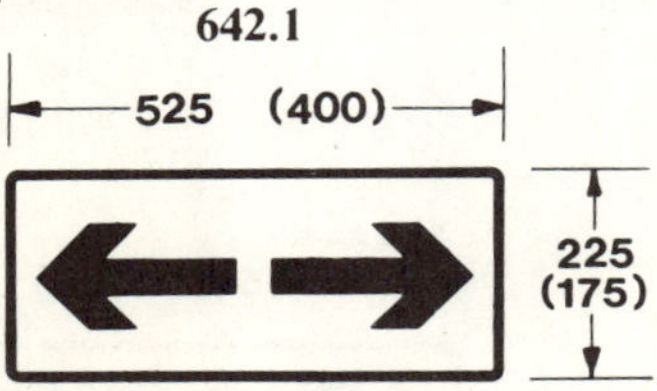

Plate for use with signs in diagrams 636, 641 and 642 to indicate that the restriction or prohibition applies in both directions
(See Directions 6 and 12)
643

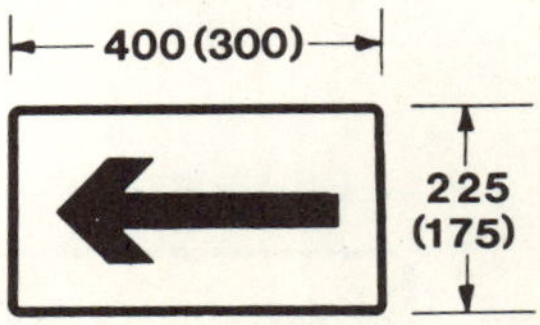

Plate for use with signs in diagrams 636, 641 and 642 to indicate the direction in which the restriction or prohibition applies
(See Directions 6 and 12)
644

Plate for use with and showing end of an indication given by signs in diagrams 564, 614, 615, 632, 642 and 811
(See Direction 12)
645

No stopping during periods indicated except for as long as may be necessary for the purpose of setting down or picking up passengers
(See Directions 6 and 13)
646

(See Direction 6)
647

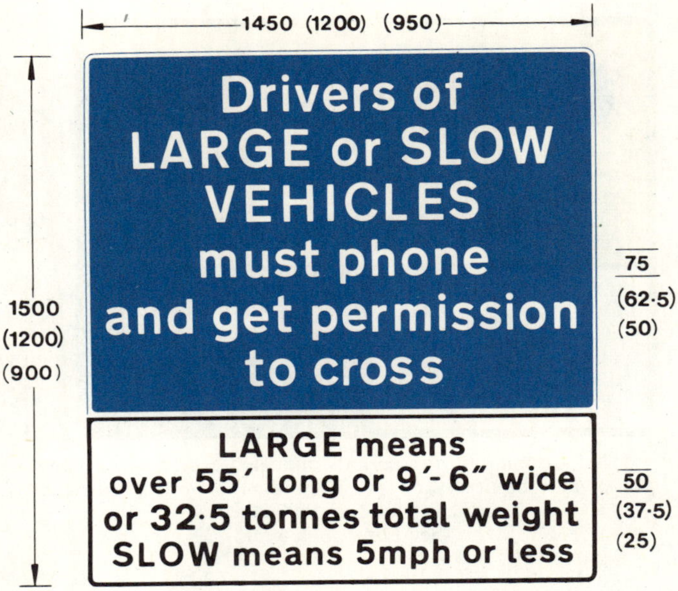

To indicate to vehicular traffic the requirements prescribed by Regulation 11 (2)

649.1

Prohibition on stopping by vehicles other than stage and scheduled express carriages between 7 am and 7 pm

Permitted variant: "except for stage buses" may be substituted for "except buses" where the prohibition on stopping applies to scheduled express carriages

(See Directions, 6, 10 and 30)

650

Prohibitions imposed on use of verges maintained in a mown or ornamental condition
Permitted variants: The pedestrian symbol and the word "Pedestrians" may be omitted or the word "Animals" may be omitted or the symbol and both those words may be omitted
(See Direction 6)
651

One way traffic
(See Direction 6)
652

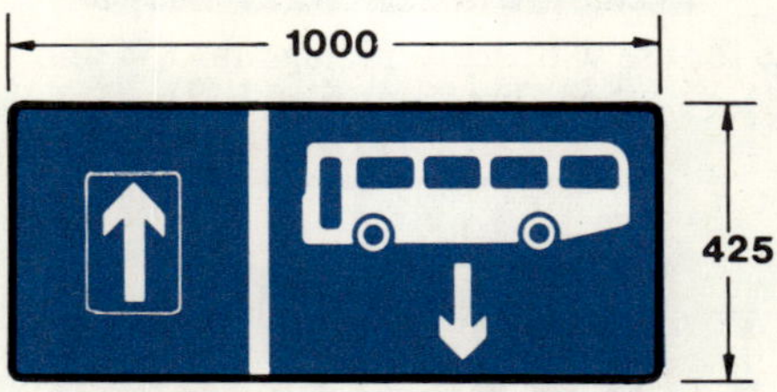

One way traffic on either side of the white line representing the marking shown in diagram 1049, the side of the carriageway to the right of that line being reserved for the use of stage carriages, scheduled express carriages, school buses and works buses except that any vehicle travelling along the left hand side of the carriageway may cross the line to stop to load or unload where this is not prohibited
(See Directions 6, 10 and 30)
653

Lane marked on the carriageway by the marking in diagram 1048 and bounded by the marking in diagram 1049 reserved for stage carriages, scheduled express carriages, school buses, works buses and pedal cycles except that any vehicle may cross the line to stop, to load, or unload where this is not prohibited

Permitted variants: The word "taxi" may be added beside the bicycle symbol where hackney carriages are permitted to use the lane. The legend "& coaches" may be placed in black letters on the bus symbol where all vehicles constructed or adapted to carry 12 or more passengers are permitted to use the lane

(See Directions 6, 10 and 30)

654

(See Direction 6)

655

Plate for use with signs in diagrams 654 and 812.1

(See Directions 6 and 12)

656

Plate for use with signs in diagrams 654 and 812.1

Permitted variants: "7.30 am" or "8 am" may be substituted for "7 am"; "9 am" or "9.30 am" may be substituted for "10 am"; "4.30 pm" or "5.00 pm" may be substituted for "4 pm" and "6 pm" or "6.30 pm" may be substituted for "7 pm". Either the morning or afternoon period may be omitted

(See Directions 6 and 12)

656.1

Parking place reserved for permit holders

Permitted variants: "Card holders", "Doctor permit holders", "Large or slow vehicles", "Business permit holders", or "Resident permit holders" may be substituted for "Permit holders" and up to three code letters coloured black and corresponding with details in the permit may be added to the sign to identify parking places

(See Direction 6)

660

Plate for use with signs in diagrams 660 and 661

Permitted variant: "At any time" may be substituted for "8 am–6 pm" without prejudice to Regulation 12(1)*(g)*

(See Directions 6 and 12)

660.2

Parking place reserved
for disabled badge holders
(See Direction 6)
661

Plate for use with sign in diagram 801 at parking places in disc zones showing hours during which waiting is limited and that display of disc is required
(See Directions 6 and 12)
662

SCHEDULE 1 (See Regulations 9—19)

PART III—Directional informatory signs

(75)
100
(150)
(200)
(250)

Route number of, and next place of traffic importance on, roads extending from a junction ahead. A route shown in brackets is not at the junction but may be reached by proceeding in the direction indicated
(See Direction 7)
701

(150)
(200)
250

Route number of, and next place of traffic importance on, a road at a junction $\frac{1}{2}$ mile ahead
(See Direction 7)
702

(150)
(200)
250

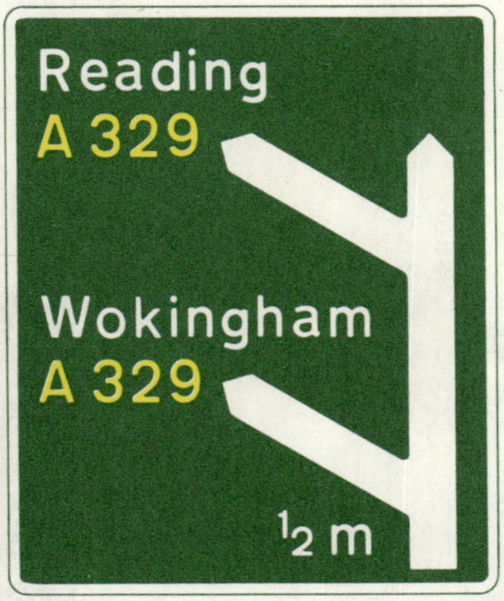

Same as 702 with variation to indicate two route numbers and next places of traffic importance at road junctions ahead
(See Direction 7)
702.1

100
(75)
(150)
(200)
(250)

Route number of, and next place of traffic importance on, roads extending from a junction immediately ahead
(See Direction 7)
703

(75)
100
(150)
(200)
(250)

Same as 703 with variations to indicate appropriate traffic lanes for traffic to the places shown
(See Direction 7)
703.1

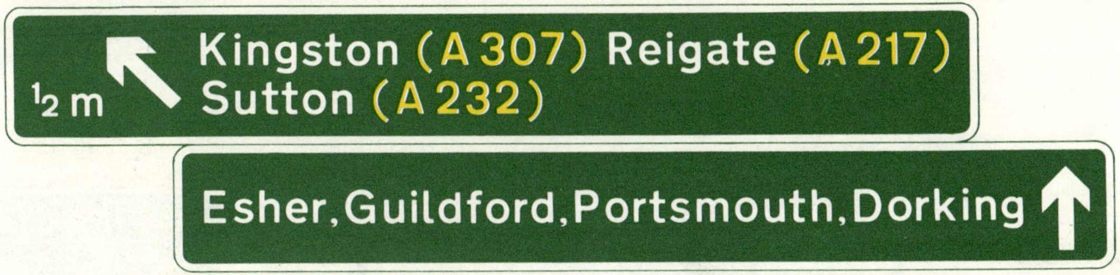

100
(150)
(200)
(250)

Route numbers of roads extending from a junction ahead and places to which they lead when the sign is placed over the carriageway

Permitted variants: "$\frac{1}{2}$ m" may be omitted or replaced by "$\frac{1}{3}$ m" or by "$\frac{2}{3}$ m"

(See Direction 7)

703.2

(100)
150
(200)
(250)

Same as 703 with variations to indicate appropriate traffic lanes for traffic to the places shown when the sign is placed over the carriageway

(See Direction 7)

703.3

Route number of, and next place of traffic importance on, roads extending from a junction ahead
(See Direction 7)
704

Same as 704
(See Direction 7)
705

Same as 704 with variations for approach to a junction with a ring road or by-pass. Routes shown in brackets are not at the junction but may be reached by proceeding in the direction indicated
(See Direction 7)
706

100
(75)
(150)
(200)
(250)

Same as 704 except that the relative importance of each road is shown by differing widths of the route symbol and the route shown in brackets is not at the junction but may be reached by proceeding in the direction indicated
(See Direction 7)
707

100
(75)
(150)
(200)
(250)

Same as 707
(See Direction 7)
708

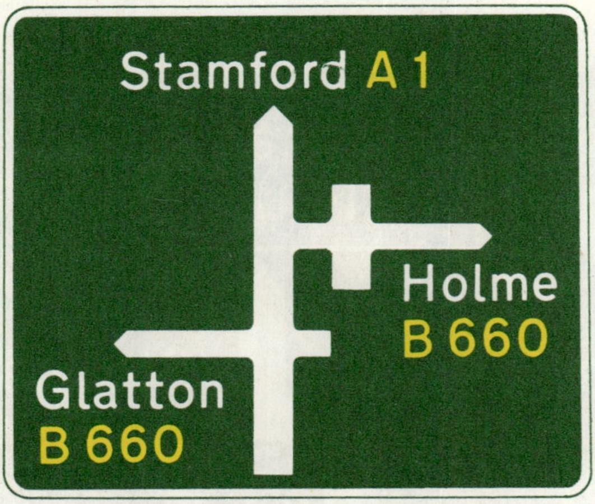

100
(75)
(150)
(200)
(250)

Route number of, and next place of traffic importance on, roads extending from a junction on a dual carriageway
(See Direction 7)
709

(250)
(200)
(150)
(75)
100

Same as 704 with variations for roundabout junction
(See Direction 7)
710

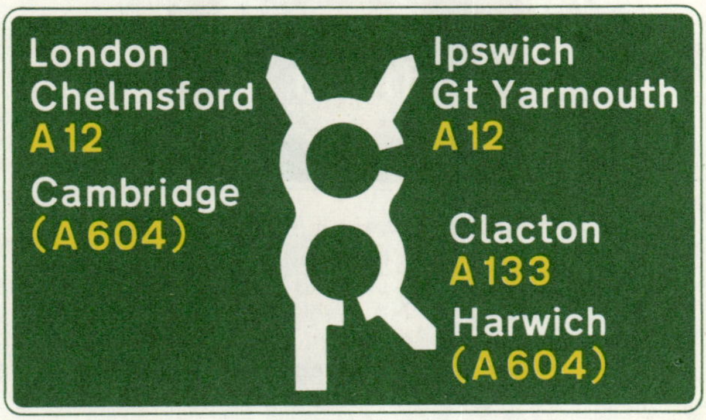

(75)
100
(150)
(200)
(250)

Route number of, and next place of traffic importance on, roads extending from a double roundabout junction ahead
(See Direction 7)
710.1

Same as 704 with variations for roundabout junction with a motorway. The motorway route shown in brackets is not at the junction but may be reached by proceeding in the direction indicated
(See Direction 7)
711.1

Same as 704 with variation for a road where entry is prohibited
Permitted variants: The No entry symbol may be replaced by a No right turn, No left turn symbol or a red bar as indicated in diagrams 816 and 817 where appropriate
(See Directions 6 and 7)
712

Same as 704 with variation for a road on which a hazard or a limited prohibition exists

Permitted variants: The Safe height at hazard ahead symbol may be replaced by a symbol shown in diagrams 513, 516, 523.1, 524.1, 528, 529, 533 (with 534.1 or 534.2), 537, 538, 554 "Ford", 556 (with 556.3), 619, 619.1, 621, 622.1A, 622.4, 622.5, 626.1, 628.1, 629, 629.1 or 629.2

(See Directions 6 and 7)

712.1

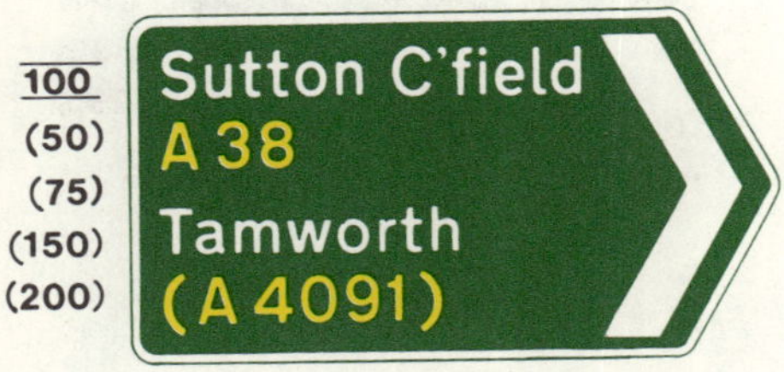

Direction of route and places. The route shown in brackets may be reached by proceeding in the direction indicated

(See Direction 7)

713

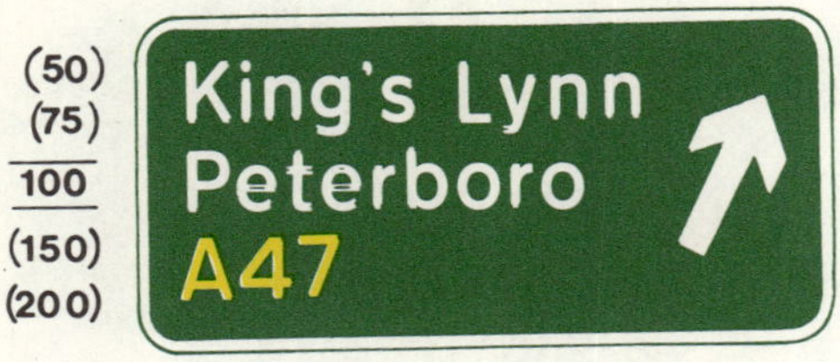

Direction of route and places

(See Direction 7)

714

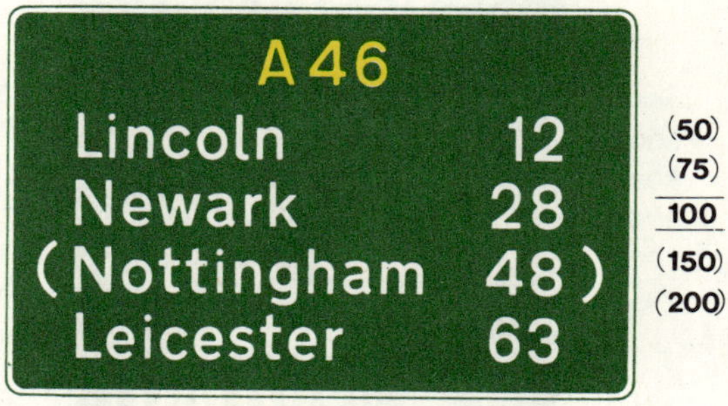

Route number of primary route with names of, and distances in miles to, places of traffic importance to which it leads. The bracketed name and figures indicate a place which can be reached by a road which branches off the primary route and the distance in miles to that place
Permitted variant: "Ring road" in white lettering may be substituted for the route number
(See Direction 7)
715

Route to which road is leading
(See Direction 7)
716

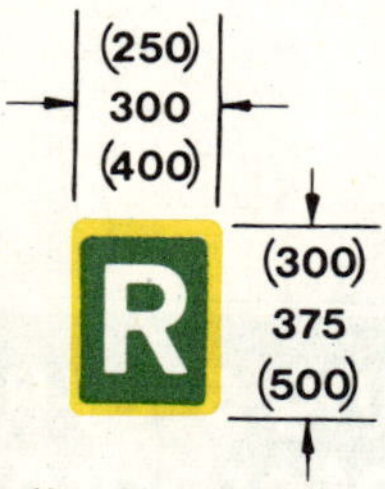

Indication that a primary route forms part of a ring road
(See Direction 7)
717

(200)
(150)
(75)
(50)
100

Same as 704
The relative importance of each road
is shown by differing widths of the route symbol
(See Direction 7)
718

(200)
(150)
100
(75)
(50)

Route number, next place of traffic importance and appropriate traffic lanes to the places shown from a junction ahead
(See Direction 7)
718.1

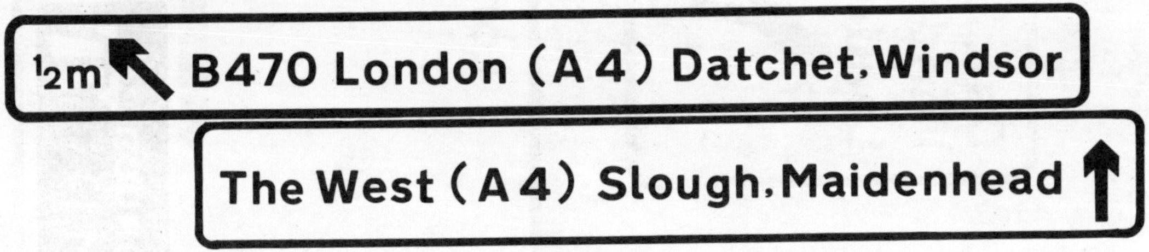

100
(150)
(200)
(250)

Route number of, and next place of traffic importance on, roads extending from a junction ahead when the sign is placed over the carriageway
Permitted variants: The route number may be omitted and the border coloured blue when used to indicate local directions. "½ m" may be omitted or replaced by "⅓ m" or by "⅔ m"
(See Direction 7)
718.2

Route number of, next place of traffic importance on and appropriate traffic lanes for traffic to the places shown from a junction ahead when the sign is placed over the carriageway

Permitted variants: The route number may be omitted and the border coloured blue when used to indicate local directions

(See Direction 7)

718.3

Same as 701

(See Direction 7)

719

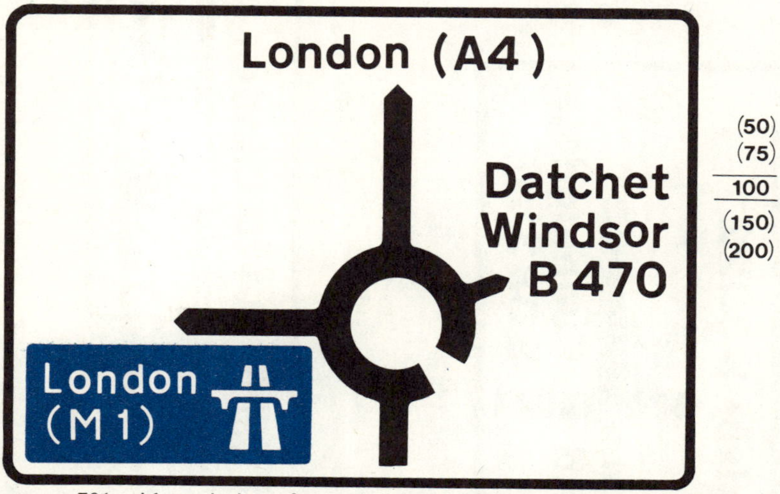

Same as 701 with variations for roundabout junction with a motorway. The motorway route shown in brackets is not at the junction but may be reached by proceeding in the direction indicated. The relative importance of each road is shown by differing widths of the route symbol

(See Direction 7)

719.1

Same as 712 with variation for a road where entry is prohibited
Permitted variants: Same as 712
(See Directions 6 and 7)
719.2

Same as 704 with variation for a road on which a hazard or a limited prohibition exists
Permitted variant: The goods vehicle prohibited symbol may be replaced by a symbol shown in diagrams 513, 516, 523.1, 524.1, 528, 529, 530, 533 (with 534.1 or 534.2), 537, 538, 554 ("Ford"), 556 (with 556.3), 619, 619.1, 621, 622.4, 622.5, 626.1, 628.1, 629, 629.1 or 629.2
(See Directions 6 and 7)
719.3A

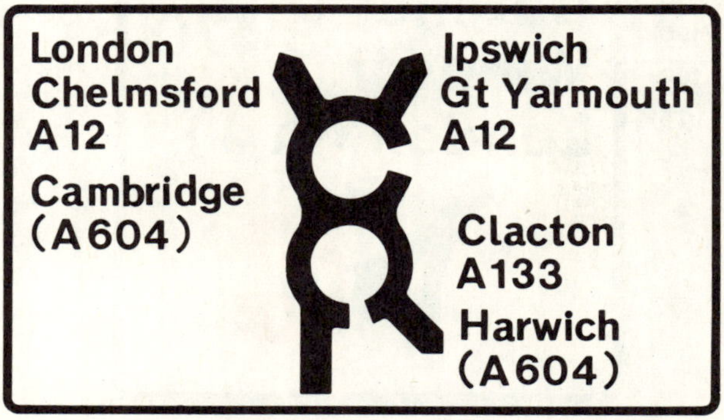

(50)
(75)
100
(150)
(200)

Route number of, and next place of traffic importance on, roads extending from a double roundabout junction ahead
(See Direction 7)
719.4

100
(50)
(75)
(150)
(200)

Same as 704
(See Direction 7)
720

(50)
(75)
100
(150)
(200)

Route number of, and next place of traffic importance on, roads extending from a junction of a non-primary route with a motorway ahead
(See Direction 7)
721.1

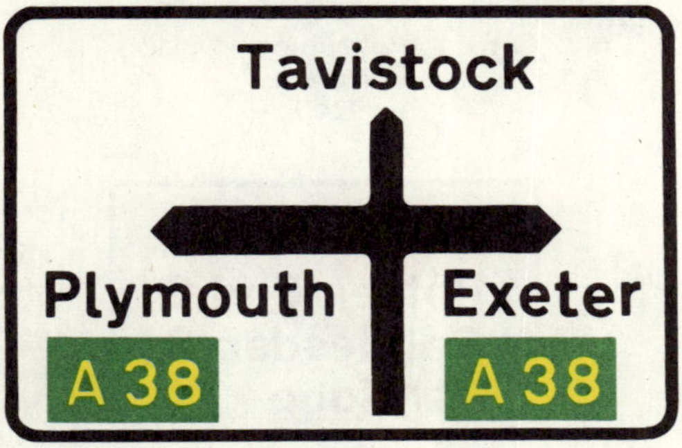

100
(50)
(75)
(150)
(200)

Same as 721.1 with variation for a junction of a non-primary route with a primary route ahead
(See Direction 7)
722

100
(50)
(75)
(150)
(200)

Same as 722
(See Direction 7)
723

(50)
(75)
100
(150)

Direction of non-primary route and mileage to place named
Permitted variant: Mileage may be omitted
(See Direction 7)
724

100
(50)
(75)
(150)

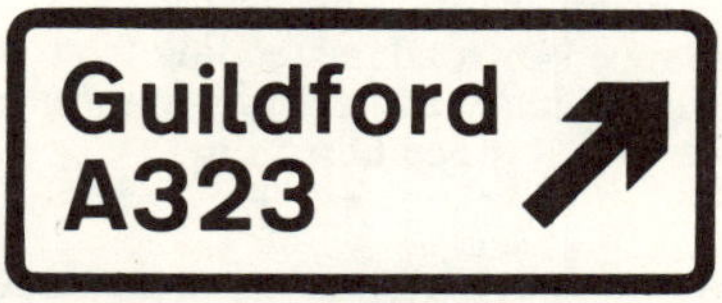

Direction of route and places
(See Direction 7)
724.1

(50)
(75)
100
(150)

Route number of non-primary route with names of and distances in miles to places to which it leads. The bracketed name and figure indicate a place which can be reached by a road which branches off the non-primary route and the distance to that place
Permitted variant: "Ring road" may be substituted for the route number
(See Direction 7)
724.2

(50)
75
(100)
(150)
(200)

Route number of road
(See Direction 7)
725

SCHEDULE 1 *PART III*—Directional informatory signs (contd.)

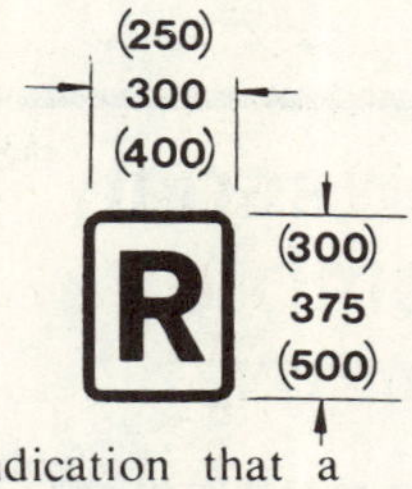

Indication that a non-primary route forms part of a ring road (See Direction 7)

726

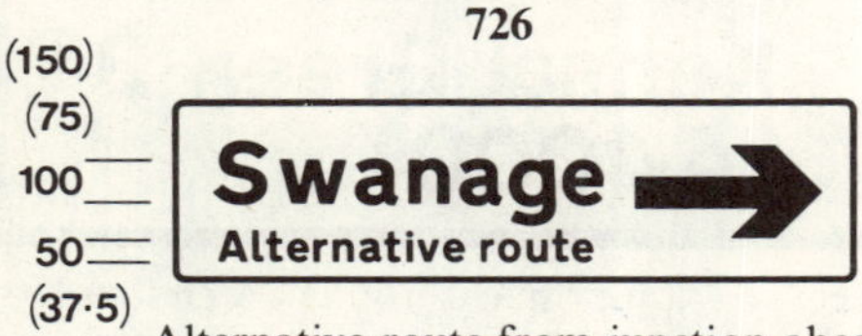

Alternative route from junction ahead to place named

Permitted variants: "Alternative route for light cars", "Alternative tourist route", "Scenic route", "Avoiding ford", "Avoiding low bridge", "Avoiding town centre", "Coastal route" or "Avoiding steep hill" may be substituted for "Alternative route"

727

Route suitable for goods vehicles to the routes or places named from a junction ahead

Permitted variant: Place name or "Docks" may be substituted for route numbers shown in brackets

727.2

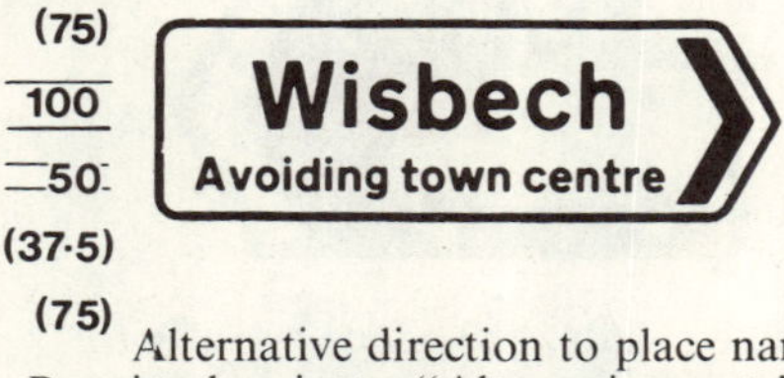

Alternative direction to place named

Permitted variants: "Alternative route", "Alternative route for light cars", "Alternative tourist route", "Scenic route", "Avoiding ford", "Avoiding low bridge", "Coastal route" or "Avoiding steep hill" may be substituted for "Avoiding town centre"

728

Route number of non-primary route extending from a junction ahead and direction to local and other places with mileage. The route shown in brackets is not at the junction but may be reached by proceeding in the direction indicated

728.1

Direction of non-primary route and direction to local and other places with mileage

728.2

Route suitable for goods vehicles to the routes or places named from a junction

Permitted variant: Place name or "Docks" may be substituted for route numbers shown in brackets

728.3

75

(50)
(100)
(150)
(200)

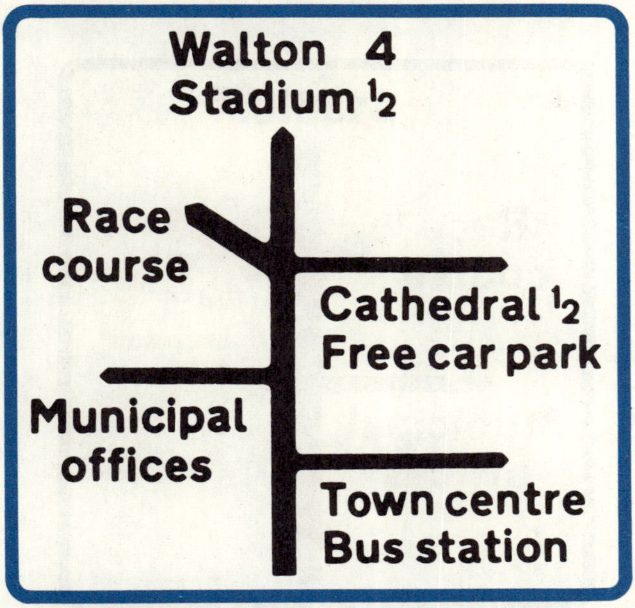

Direction from junction ahead to local places with mileage. The relative importance of each road is shown by differing widths of the route symbol

729

75

(50)
(100)
(150)
(200)

Same as 729 with variation for a road on which a prohibition exists

Permitted variants: The No entry symbol may be replaced by a No right turn or No left turn symbol or a red bar as indicated by diagrams 816 and 817 where appropriate (See Direction 6)

729.1

Same as 729 with variation for a road on which a hazard exists
Permitted variants: The Safe height at hazard ahead symbol may be replaced by a symbol shown in diagrams 513, 516, 523.1, 524.1, 528, 529, 533 (with 534.1), 537, 538, 554 ("Ford"), 556 (with 556.3) 619, 619.1, 621, 622.1A, 622.4, 622.5, 626.1, 628.1, 629, 629.1, 629.2 or red bar from diagrams 816 or 817 as appropriate
(See Direction 6)
729.2

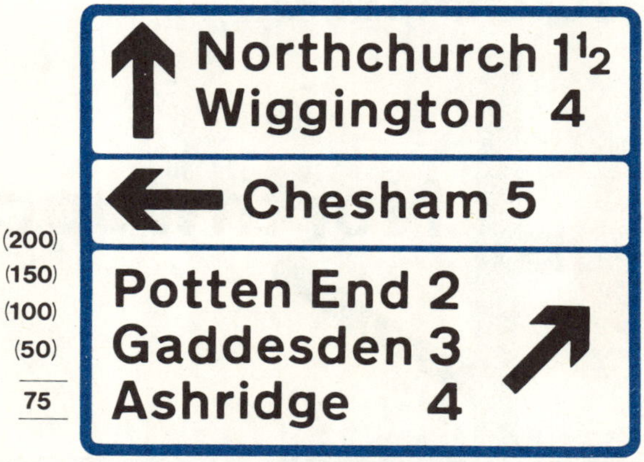

Direction from junction ahead to local places with mileage
730

SCHEDULE 1 *PART III*—Directional informatory signs (contd.)

(37·5)
(50)
75
(100)
(150)

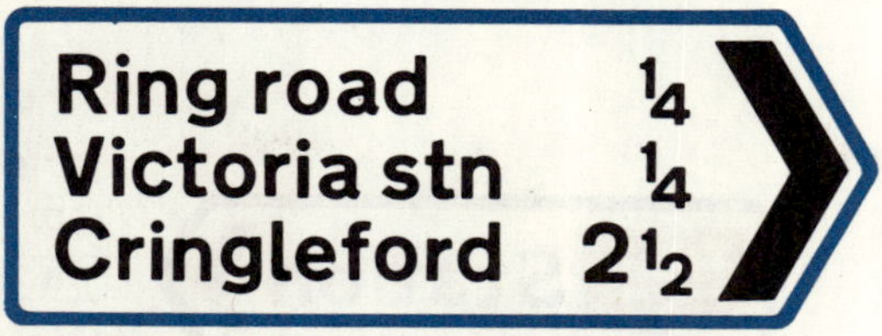

Direction to local places with mileage
Permitted variants: The symbol shown in diagram 736.1 may be added and the mileage may be omitted

732

(37·5)
(50)
75
(100)
(150)

Same as 730

732.1

(50)
75
(100)
(150)

Names of, and distances in miles to, local places to which a road leads. The bracketed name indicates a place which can be reached by a road which branches off the route and the distance in miles to that place

732.2

50

Direction of route recommended for pedal cyclists and mileage to place named
Permitted variant: mileage may be omitted

732.4

(37·5)
(50)
(75)
100
(150)

Direction to airport with mileage. The direction of the aircraft symbol shall accord with that of the destination
Permitted variant:
The word "Airport" may be added

733

(37·5)
(50)
(75)
100
(150)

Direction to airport. The direction of the aircraft symbol shall accord with that of the destination
Permitted variant:
The word "Airport" may be added

733.1

Direction to a railway station
Permitted variants: The name of the station may be included. The London Transport symbol shown in diagram 734.3 may replace the British Rail symbol
734.1

Same as 734.1
Permitted variant: Same as 734.1
734.2

Direction to stations
734.3

Same as 734.3
734.4

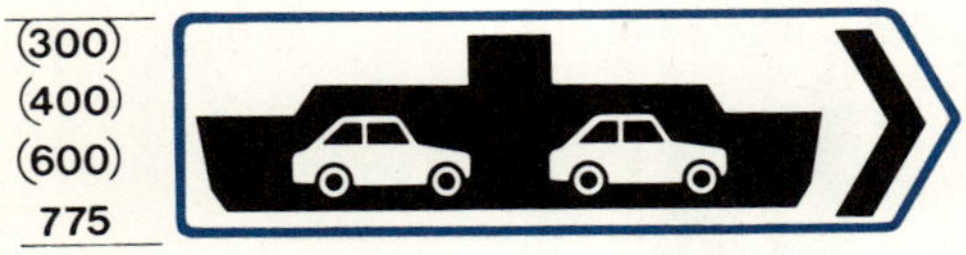

Direction to car ferry
Permitted variants: The words "Pedestrian ferry" may replace the symbol to indicate direction to a ferry available only for pedestrians. The goods vehicle symbol shown in diagram 728.3 may be substituted for the left hand car symbol where appropriate. The name of the quay may be added below the symbol
734.5

Direction to Public Telephone
Permitted variant: The words "Public telephone" may be added
734.6

(75) 100 (150)

Direction to a service area at which fuel, parking, cafeteria and restaurant facilities are available 24 hours a day (See Direction 5)

734.7

(37·5) (50) (75) 100 (150)

Direction and distance to parking place
Permitted variants: Either the word "Free" or the distance or both may be omitted and any one or a combination of two of the following symbols may be added namely the bus in diagram 803.1, the goods vehicle in diagram 804.1, the motor car in diagram 804.2 or the caravan drawn by a motor vehicle in diagram 804.3

734.8

(50) (75) 100 (150) (200)

Direction to parking place
Permitted variant: The word "Free" may be omitted and any one or a combination of two of the following symbols may be added, namely the bus in diagram 803.1, the goods vehicle in diagram 804.1, the motor car in diagram 804.2 or the caravan drawn by a motor vehicle in diagram 804.3

734.9

(300) (400) (600) 775

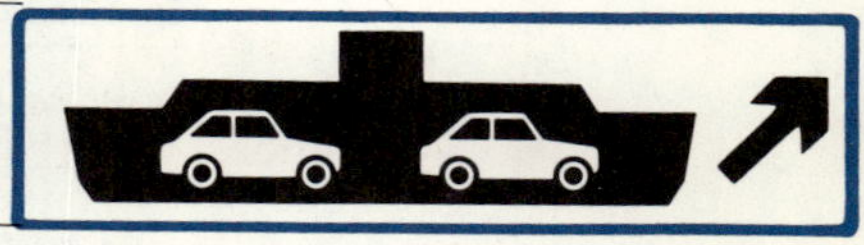

Direction to car ferry on a road extending from a junction ahead
Permitted variants: Same as 734.5

734.10

(37·5) (50) (75) 100 (150)

Direction to toilets
Permitted variants: "Ladies toilet" or "Mens toilet" may be substituted for "Toilets"

736

(37·5) (50) (75) 100 (150)

Direction to toilets including facilities for the disabled
Permitted variants: Same as 736

736.1

(37·5) 50 (75) (100)

Direction to a place which can be reached by a by-way open to all traffic

737.1

SCHEDULE 1 *PART III*—Directional informatory signs (contd.)

37.5
(50)

Direction of route for pedestrians to local places where this differs from the route for vehicular traffic
Permitted variant: The disabled persons symbol shown in diagram 736.1 may be added in white between worded legend and pedestrian symbol
739

225
(300)

Direction of route for pedestrians to railway stations where this differs from the route for vehicular traffic
Permitted variants: The British Rail or London Transport symbol may be omitted as appropriate
739.1

37·5
(50)

Direction of route for pedestrians to bus stop where this differs from the route for vehicular traffic
Permitted variants: "Coach" may be substituted for "Bus" "Station" may be substituted for "Stop" and one or more bus destinations may be added in white
739.2

37·5
(50)

Direction of route for pedestrians to a Tourist information point provided and maintained in position by the authorities listed at diagram 758 for the period specified at diagram 758 where this differs from the route for vehicular traffic
739.3

Direction to Ministry
of Defence establishment
741

Direction to a Ministry of Defence establishment on a road extending from a junction ahead.
741.1

Direction to an Ancient Monument
Permitted variants: The approved Ancient Monument symbol may be added in green. Colouring may be varied to blue lettering, symbol and border on a white ground for use in Scotland
742.1

Direction to an Ancient Monument on a road extending from a junction ahead
Permitted variants: Same as 742.1
742.2

Direction to a National Trust property
742.3

Direction to a National Trust property on a road extending from a junction ahead
742.4

Position of a county boundary, or in Scotland a regional boundary
Permitted variants: The name of a country may be added to or substituted for that of a county or region. The crest may be omitted. The lettering may be in any colour except red providing a contrast is maintained with the background. The background may be any colour except red, yellow or dark green
743.1

Name of town or village commencing immediately ahead
Permitted variants: The name of a river, inland waterway or a road junction may be substituted for the name of a town or village. The name of the district council may be omitted. In London the name of a London Borough may be substituted for the district council name. The crest of a town, village or in London the Borough may be added. The lettering may be in any colour except red providing a contrast is maintained with the background. The background may be any colour except red, yellow or dark green. The names of one or two towns or villages outside the United Kingdom with which the town or village indicated by the sign is associated may be added beneath that indication either preceded by the words "TWINNED WITH" or "TWIN TOWN" or "TWIN TOWNS" as is appropriate or in the case of a town's indication followed by whichever of the latter two expressions is appropriate
744.1

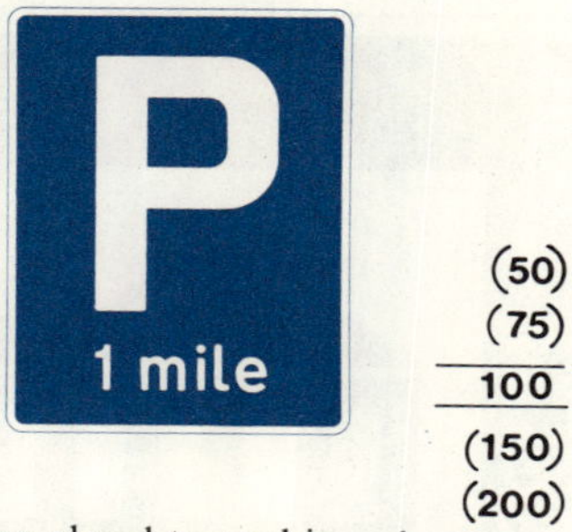

Distance ahead to parking place
Permitted variants: Any one or more of the following words may be added to or substituted for "P", namely "Information", "Viewpoint", "Toilets"

746.2

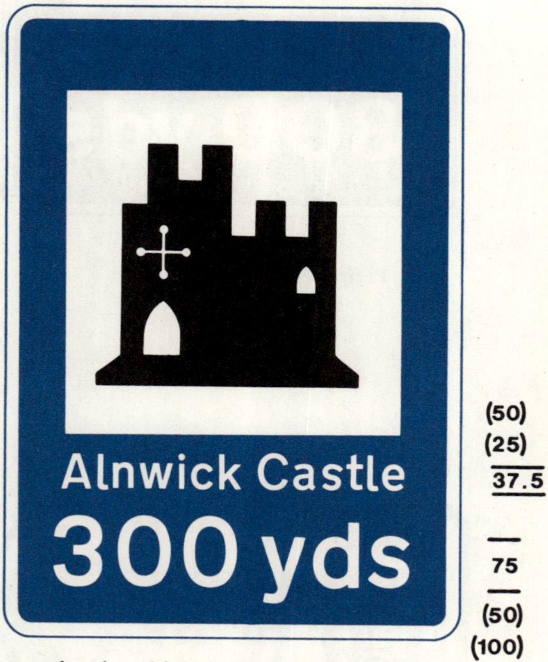

Distance ahead to historic property regularly open to the public at least 50 days in any year and listed as a building of special architectural or historic interest under the provisions of the Town and Country Planning Act 1971 or the Town and Country Planning (Scotland) Act 1972, or as an ancient monument under the Historic Buildings and Ancient Monuments Act 1953

Permitted variant: The distance may be replaced by a horizontal arrow when entrance to historic property is immediately ahead

747

Same as 747
Permitted variant: Same as 747
748

Direction and distance to historic property regularly open to the public at least 50 days in any year and listed as a building of special architectural or historic interest under the provisions of the Town and Country Planning Act 1971 or the Town and Country Planning (Scotland) Act 1972, or as an ancient monument under the Historic Buildings and Ancient Monuments Act 1953
Permitted variant: The symbol shown in diagram 747 may be substituted as appropriate
749

(50)
75
(100)

Distance ahead to camping and caravan site licensed under the Caravan Sites and Control of Development Act 1960 and/or the Public Health Act 1936 and having a minimum of 20 pitches for casual overnight use

Permitted variants: The tent or caravan symbol may be omitted as appropriate and the distance replaced by a horizontal arrow when entrance to camp or caravan site is immediately ahead

750

(37·5)
50
(75)
(100)
(150)

Direction and distance to camping and caravan site licensed under the Caravan Sites and Control of Development Act 1960 and/or the Public Health Act 1936 and having a minimum of 20 pitches for casual overnight use

Permitted variant: The tent or caravan symbol may be omitted as appropriate

751

Distance ahead to hostel managed by the Youth Hostels Association or the Scottish Youth Hostels Association
Permitted variant: Same as 747
752

Distance ahead to picnic area
Permitted variant: Same as 747
752.1

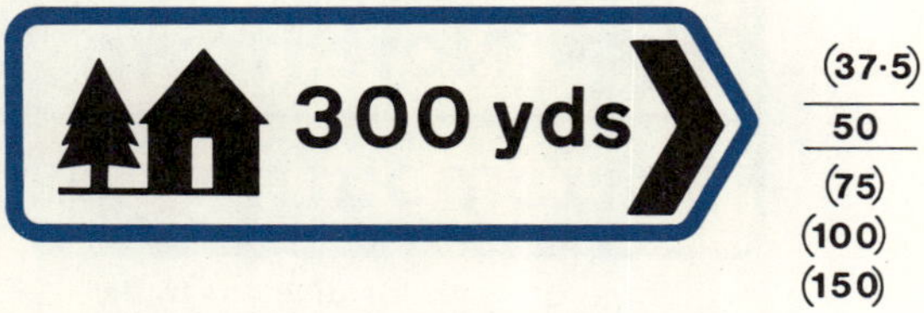

Direction and distance to hostel managed by the Youth Hostels Association or the Scottish Youth Hostels Association
753

Direction and distance to picnic area
753.1

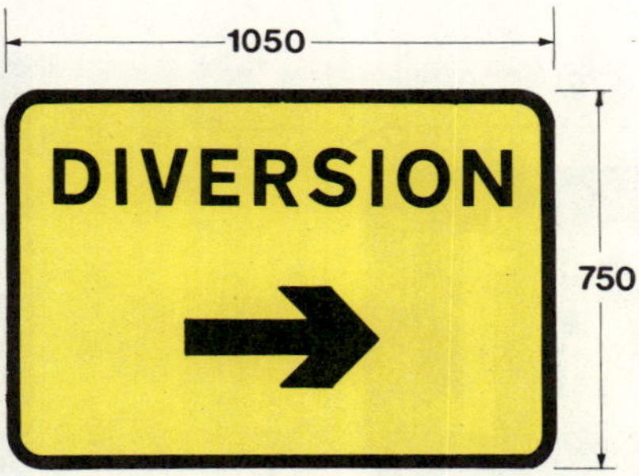

Temporary indication of alternative route avoiding road closure
Permitted variant: The arrow may be replaced by distances up to 400 yards to the nearest 50 yards or the word "end"
(See Direction 17)
754

Temporary sign for diverted traffic from a junction ahead
(See Direction 17)
755

Temporary sign showing direction of route for diverted traffic
(See Direction 17)
755.1

Temporary sign for diverted traffic
to places named from a junction ahead
(See Direction 17)
756

Temporary sign showing direction of route for diverted traffic to places indicated
(See Direction 17)
756.1

European route number of road
and its direction
757

Indication of Tourist information point provided by or recognised by any tourist board or local authority, the Countryside Commission, Countryside Commission for Scotland, Forestry Commission, National Trust, National Trust for Scotland or British Waterways Board, for the purpose of offering travellers information about Great Britain and maintained in position for at least 4 months in any one year

Permitted variant: An arrow to left or right or a distance up to 800 yards to the nearest 50 yards may be added beneath the word "information"
758

(37·5) 50 (75) (100) (150)

Same as 758 but showing direction and distance
759

(50) 75 (100) (150) (200)

Direction of route extending from a junction ahead to destination shown avoiding a prohibited movement where the route begins before the junction affected by the prohibition
Permitted variants: The No right turn symbol may be replaced by a No left turn symbol, No motor vehicles symbol or a No goods vehicles symbol
(See Direction 6)
760

(50) 75 (100) (150) (200)

Direction of route extending from a junction ahead to destination shown avoiding a prohibited movement where the route begins at or beyond the junction affected by the prohibition
Permitted variants: Same as 760
(See Direction 6)
761

Parking place
801

To indicate parking permitted on verge or footway or part of verge or footway
(See Direction 6)
801.3

To indicate end of parking permitted on verge or footway
(See Direction 6)
801.4

To indicate parking permitted on verge or footway or part of verge or footway where waiting restrictions are in force at certain times
(See Direction 6)
801.5

Plate for use with sign in diagram 801 indicating a picnic area
(See Direction 12)
802.1

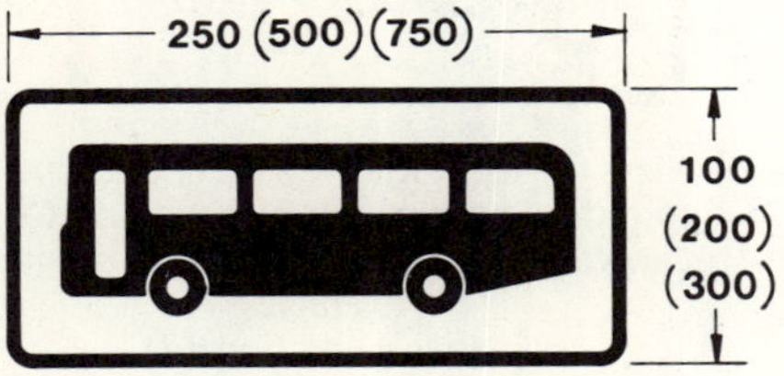

Plate for use with sign in diagram 801 to indicate a parking place for vehicles constructed or adapted to carry 12 or more passengers
(See Direction 12)
803.1

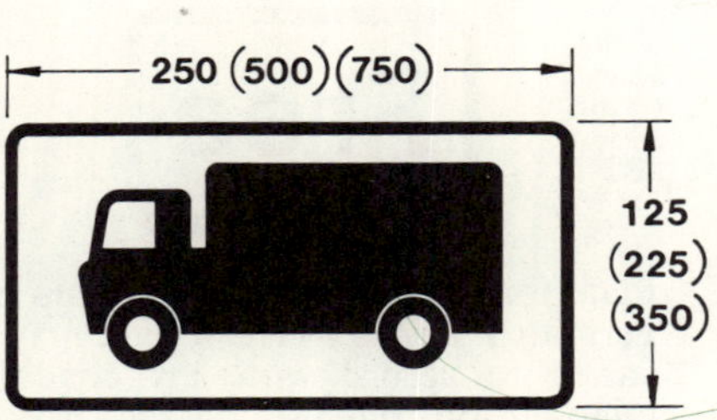

Plate for use with sign in diagram 801 to indicate a parking place for goods vehicles
(See Direction 12)
804.1

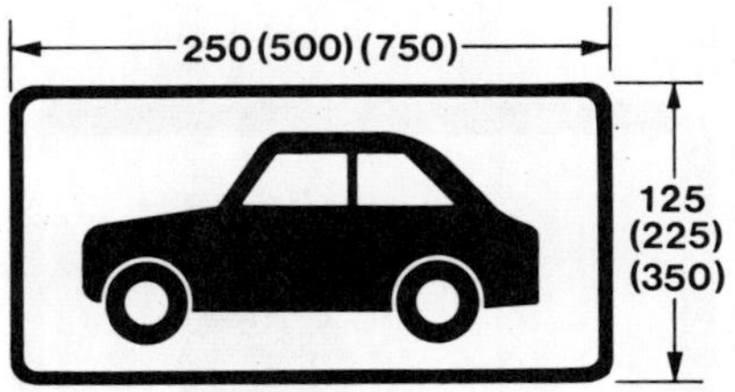

Plate for use with the sign in diagram 801 to indicate a parking place for motor cars
(See Direction 12)
804.2

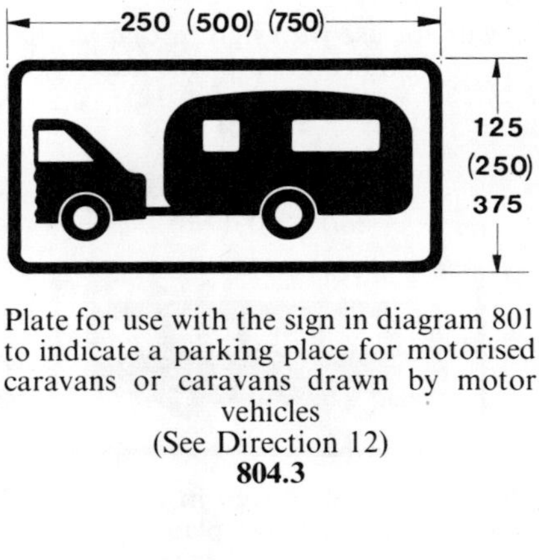

Plate for use with the sign in diagram 801 to indicate a parking place for motorised caravans or caravans drawn by motor vehicles
(See Direction 12)
804.3

Plate for use with sign in diagram 801 Permitted variants: The legend may be varied to accord with any condition imposed on the use of the parking place without prejudice to Regulation 12(1)(*g*), or to "Viewpoint" or "Information".
(See Direction 12)
805

Entrance to controlled parking zone
Permitted variants: "Controlled", "Disc" or "Ticket" may be substituted for "Meter". "Disc and" or "Ticket and" may be inserted before "Meter"
(See Directions 6, 28 and 37)
806

Same as 806 and 807 combined
Permitted variants: Same as 806
(See Directions 6, 28 and 37)
806.1

Entrance to a controlled parking zone applying to goods vehicles over 5 or 7.5 tonnes maximum gross weight
Permitted variant: "7·5" may be substituted for "5" on the goods vehicle symbol
(See Direction 6)
806.3

Plate for use with sign in diagram 806
(See Directions 6, 12 and 37)
807

Exit from controlled parking zone
(See Directions 6 and 37)
808.1

Exit from a controlled parking zone applying to goods vehicles over 5 or 7·5 tonnes maximum gross weight
Permitted variant: "7·5" may be substituted for "5" on the goods vehicle symbol
(See Direction 6)
808.3

To inform pedestrians of one way traffic
(See Direction 6)
810

To inform pedestrians of a lane or lanes reserved for stage carriages, scheduled express carriages, school buses and works buses
Permitted variant: Symbol may be reversed with door replaced by fifth window and "right" varied to read "left"
(See Direction 6)
810.1

Priority over vehicles
from the opposite direction
(See Direction 18)
811

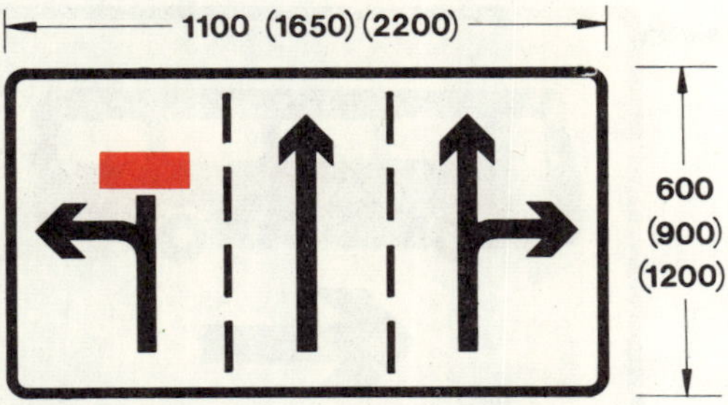

Left hand lane for traffic turning left only
Permitted variants: The centre lane may be omitted and the symbols otherwise varied to accord with the circumstances. The words "Except buses" may be added above the red bar

812

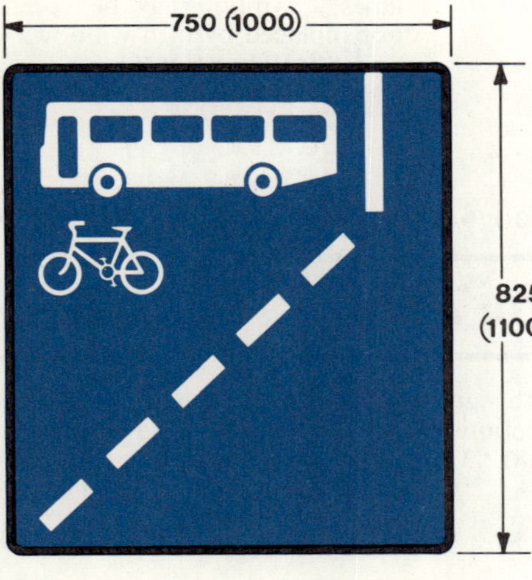

Lane reserved for stage carriages, scheduled express carriages, school buses, works buses and pedal cycles ahead
Permitted variants: The word "taxi" may be added between the bus and cycle symbols where hackney carriages are permitted to use the lane. The legend "& coaches" may be placed in black letters on the bus symbol where all vehicles constructed or adapted to carry 12 or more passengers are permitted to use the lane
(See Direction 6)

812.1

Lane reserved for stage carriages, scheduled express carriages, school buses and works buses on road at junction ahead
Permitted variants: Arrow may be reversed and the position of the symbol and arrow altered to accord with the circumstances. The arrow may be omitted. Where this occurs the words "Bus lane "shall read "Bus lanes". Symbol may be reversed with door replaced by fifth window
(See Direction 6)
812.2

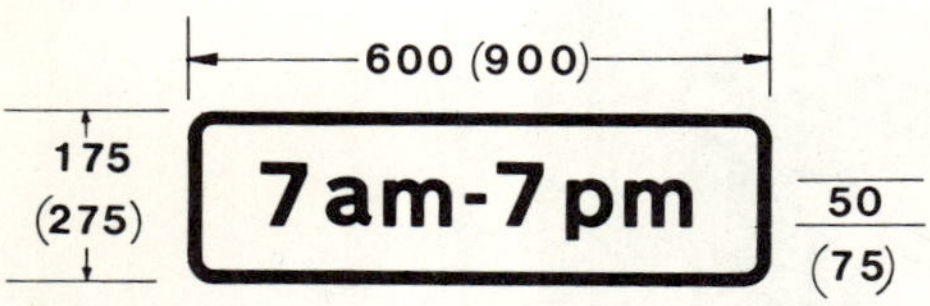

Plate for use with sign in diagram 812.2
(See Directions 6 and 12)
812.3

Plate for use with sign in diagram 812.2
Permitted variants: Same as 656.1
(See Directions 6 and 12)
812.4

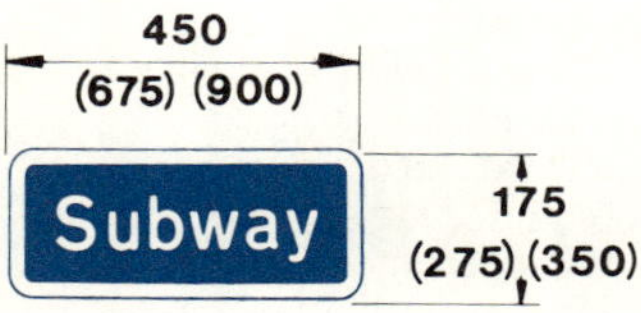

Entrance to pedestrian subway
814

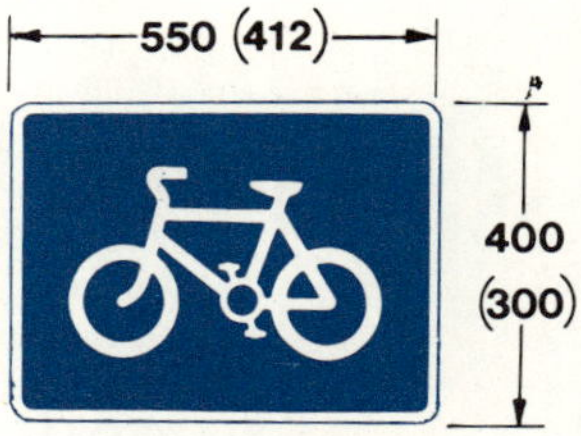

Route recommended for pedal cyclists
815

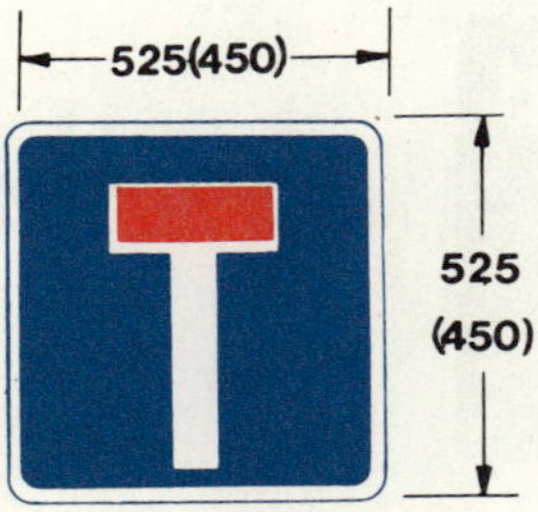

No through road
for vehicular traffic
816

Same as 816
for use with a
street nameplate
816.1

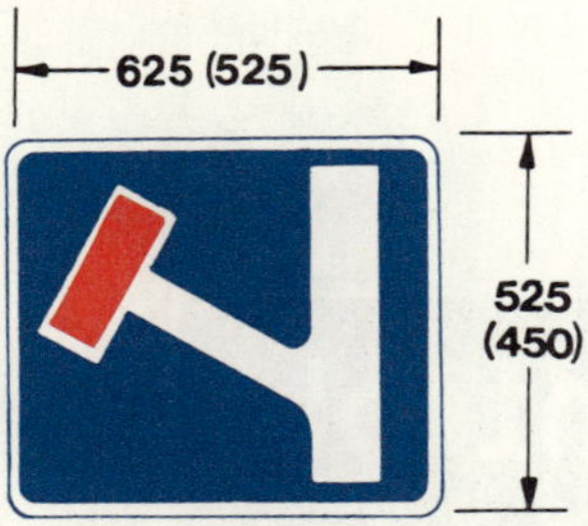

No through road for vehicular traffic in direction indicated from junction ahead
Permitted variants: The symbol may be reversed or otherwise varied to accord with the circumstances
817

Plate for use with signs in diagrams 816, 816.1 and 817
(See Direction 12)
817.1

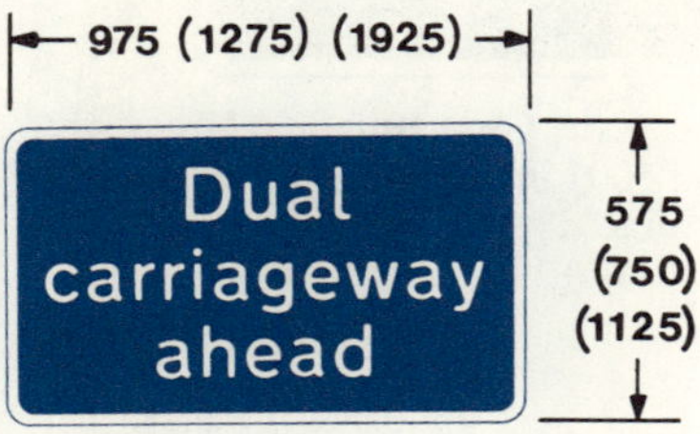

To indicate the presence of a dual carriageway on route directly ahead
818

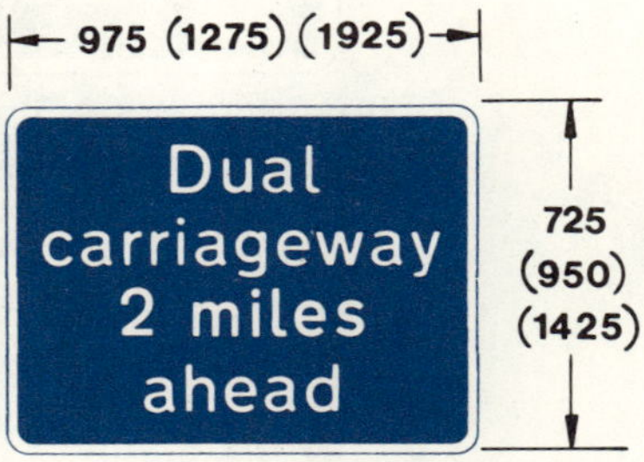

Same as 818 with distance not greater than 2 miles
818.1

To indicate a prohibition, restriction or requirement ahead
Permitted variant: The legend may be varied to accord with the prohibition, restriction or requirement imposed provided that no vulgar fraction shall be used to indicate weight
(See Direction 6)
818.2

Indication of the presence ahead of lane control signals conforming to diagrams 5001 and 5003 in Schedule 5 to these Regulations
(See Direction 6)
819.1

Indication of the presence of lane control signals conforming to diagrams 5001 and 5003 in Schedule 5 to these Regulations on the road across the junction immediately ahead
(See Direction 6)
819.2

Indication of the point beyond which lane control ceases to operate
(See Direction 6)
819.3

Permitted variants: "caravans", "coaches", "heavy goods vehicles", "long vehicles" or "wide vehicles" may be substituted for "motors"
820

Permitted variant: "Use passing places to permit overtaking" may be substituted for "with passing places"
821

Passing place
on a single track road
822

823 **824** **825**

Diagrams 823, 824 and 825: To indicate distance in hundreds of yards to the next point at which a driver may leave a motorway or other route or a roundabout
Permitted variants: The slope of the bars may be reversed when erected on the right hand side of a carriageway. On primary routes the background shall be green. On non-primary routes the symbol and border shall be black and the background white
(See Direction 8)

Gauge
indicating
depth of
water at a ford
826

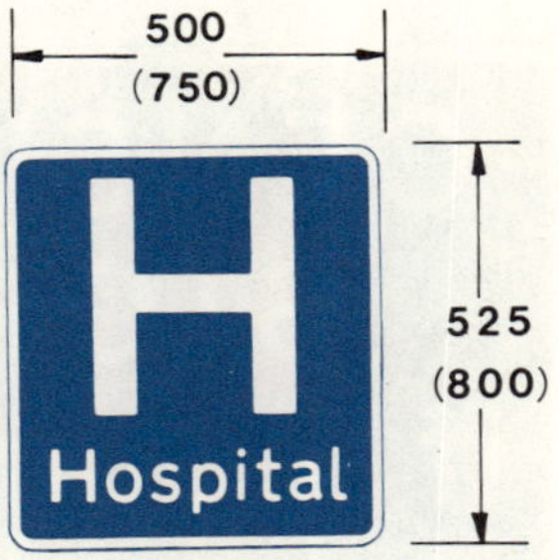

Hospital ahead
827

An electrically operated sign which, when illuminated so that the black letters of the legend appear against a red flashing background, indicates to road users the likely passage of another train over the level crossing
828.1

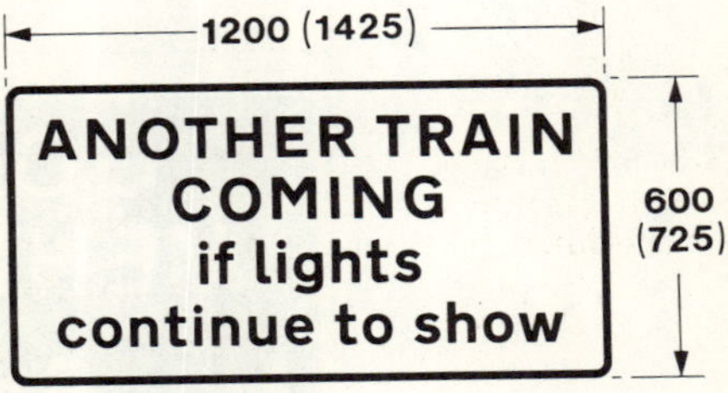

Indication to users of an automatic railway level crossing within the meaning of Regulation 25(1) where there is more than one line of railway
828.2

Permitted variant:
"weight check" may be substituted for "census" where the sign is to be used in connection with a vehicle examination under s.160 Road Traffic Act 1972 (see Direction 20 and where used for a traffic survey s.22A of that Act)
830

Permitted variant: Same as 830
(See Direction 20)
830.1

A goods vehicle may be required to stop ahead by a police constable in uniform for the purposes of section 53, 56 or 160 of the Road Traffic Act 1972
830.2

Permitted variant: Same as 830
(See Direction 20)
831

Permitted variant: Same as 830
(See Direction 20)
832

Permitted variant: "GOODS VEHICLE" may be substituted for "Department of Transport"
832.1

To indicate a vehicle condition inspection by the Department of Transport
832.2

To regulate the use of a private access to a public road
(See Direction 21)
833

Same as 833
(See Direction 21)
834

Same as 833
(See Direction 21)
835

Same as 833
(See Direction 21)
836

Distance to named service area at which fuel, parking, cafeteria and restaurant facilities are available
Permitted variants: The name of the area may be varied having regard to the place where the sign is erected, the numeral "$\frac{1}{2}$" may be varied to read "$\frac{1}{3}$" or "1" and the name may be omitted
(See Directions 5 and 8)
837.1

Direction to named service area at which fuel, parking, cafeteria and restaurant facilities are available
Permitted variants: The name of the area may be varied having regard to the place where the sign is erected and that name may be omitted
(See Directions 5 and 8)
838.1

Distance to next two service areas
Permitted variants: Second mileage may be omitted and the words "and information" may be substituted
(See Directions 5 and 8)
838.2

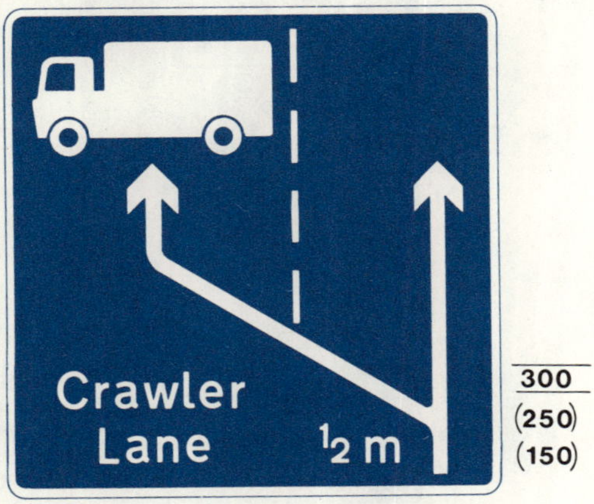

To indicate on a motorway or a dual carriageway the presence and distance ahead of an additional lane for the use of slow moving vehicles
838.3

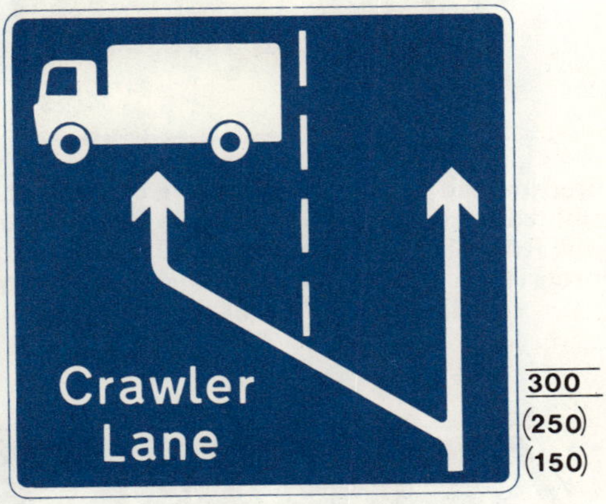

To indicate on a motorway or a dual carriageway the presence of an additional lane for the use of slow moving vehicles
838.4

Distance to motoring organisation telephone
Permitted variants: The badge of the Royal Scottish Automobile Club or the Automobile Association may be substituted as appropriate. The legend and border of the sign shall be black and the background yellow to indicate an Automobile Association telephone
841

Direction and distance to motoring organisation telephone
Permitted variants: The badge of the Royal Automobile Club or the Royal Scottish Automobile Club may be substituted as appropriate and in such cases the legend and border of the sign shall be white and the background blue
841.1

Direction and distance to motoring organisation service centre
Permitted variant: The badge of the Royal Scottish Automobile Club may be substituted as appropriate
842.1

Direction and/or distance
to Automobile Association service
842.2

Direction or direction and distance to Automobile Association service
Permitted variant: The distance may be omitted
842.3

Distance ahead to motoring organisation service centre
Permitted variant: The badge of the Royal Scottish Automobile Club may be substituted as appropriate
842.4

Fire rendezvous point
843

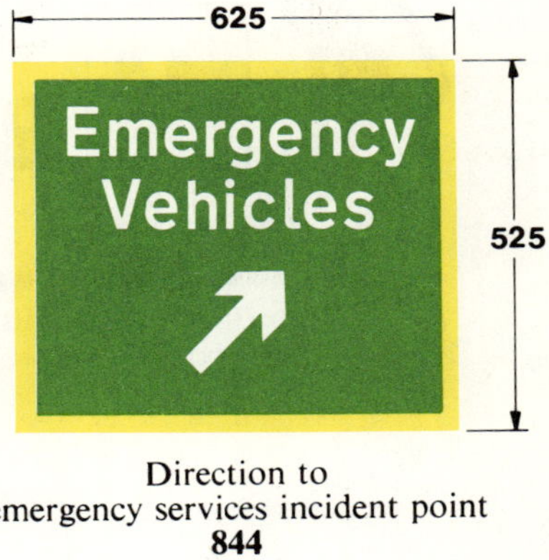

Direction to emergency services incident point
844

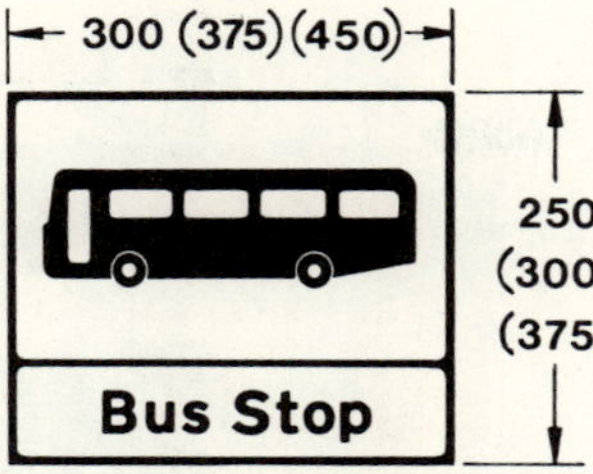

Stopping place for stage and scheduled express carriages
Permitted variants: "Coach" or "Bus and coach" may be substituted for "Bus". External borders may be omitted. The black transverse line above the legend may be thickened to a maximum of 10 millimetres
845

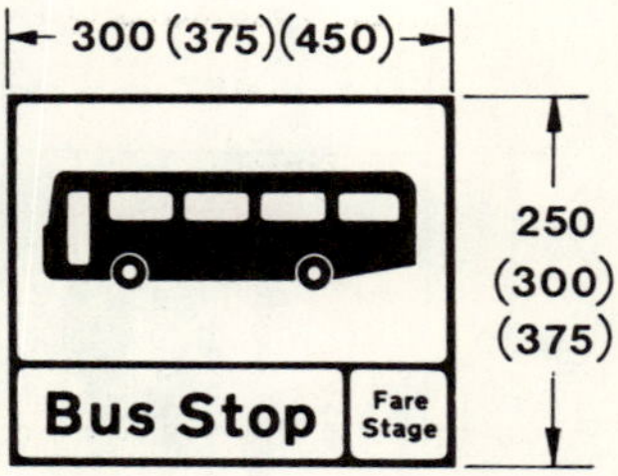

Same as 845
846

Same as 845
847

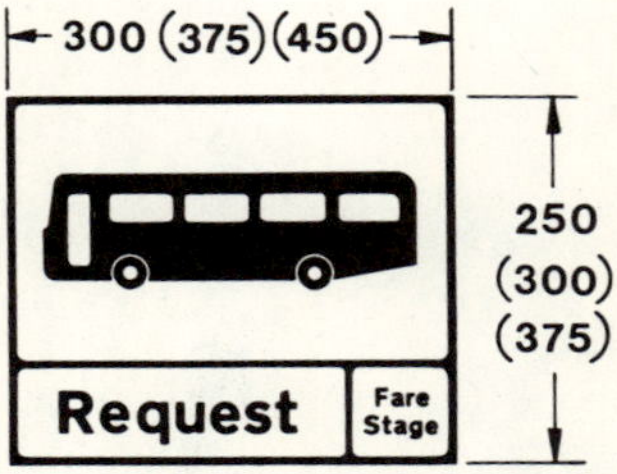

Same as 845
848

845–852 Note: Supplementary plates may be added to give additional information

Stopping place for London Transport stage carriages or scheduled express carriages only or in combination with other companies
Permitted variants:
"coach" may be substituted for "bus" and the portions shown red may be shown coloured green
849

Place where London Transport stage carriages or scheduled express carriages only or in combination with other companies may stop
Permitted variants:
"coach "may be substituted for "bus" and the portions shown red may be shown coloured green
850

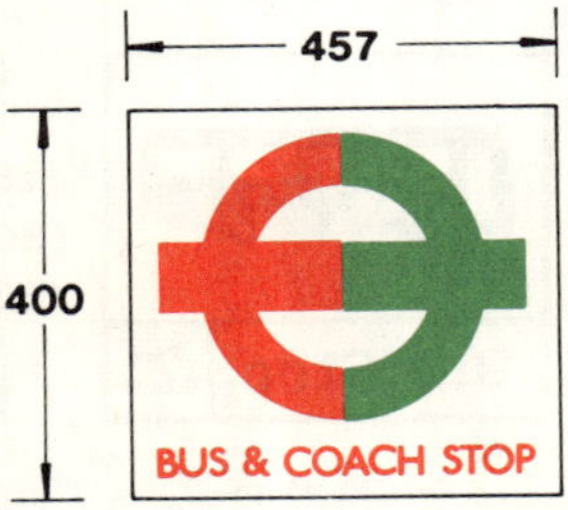

Stopping place for London Transport stage carriages and scheduled express carriages only or in combination with other companies
851

Place where London Transport stage carriages and scheduled express carriages only or in combination with other companies may stop
852

Emergency telephone or a telephone at or near a level crossing
854

Direction to an emergency telephone or to a telephone at or near a level crossing
855

To indicate where large or slow vehicles should wait near an automatic railway level crossing within the meaning of Regulation 11(2) before the driver complies with Regulation 11(2)(*b*)
856

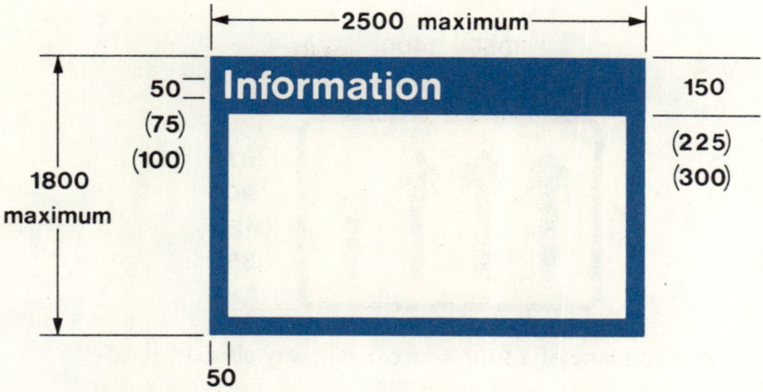

Information board to indicate to pedestrians useful information about facilities in a nearby place. White area to be filled with map and/or any legend not exceeding 25 mm in letter height in any colours
Permitted variants: "Tourist information" may be substituted for "Information" and any one or a combination of two of the following symbols may be added within the blue top border namely the tourist information symbol in diagram 758, the English Tourist Board symbol, the Wales Tourist Board symbol or the Scottish Tourist Board symbol

857

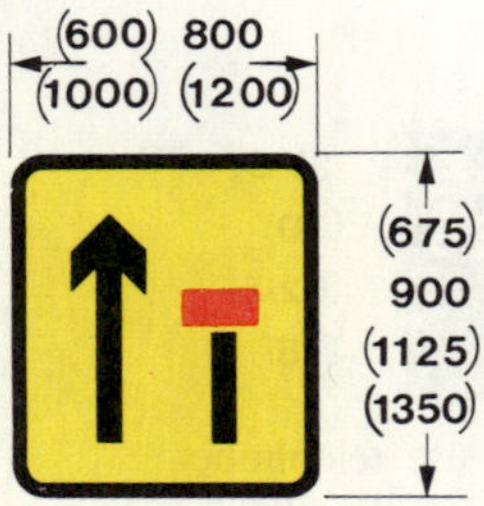

Right hand lane of a two lane carriageway of a dual carriageway road closed to traffic ahead
Permitted variants: The symbols may be reversed to indicate left hand lane is closed to traffic ahead. The following colour combination may be substituted for the colours shown; a blue background with a white border and white symbols except for the horizontal bar line which shall remain red
(See Direction 17)

858

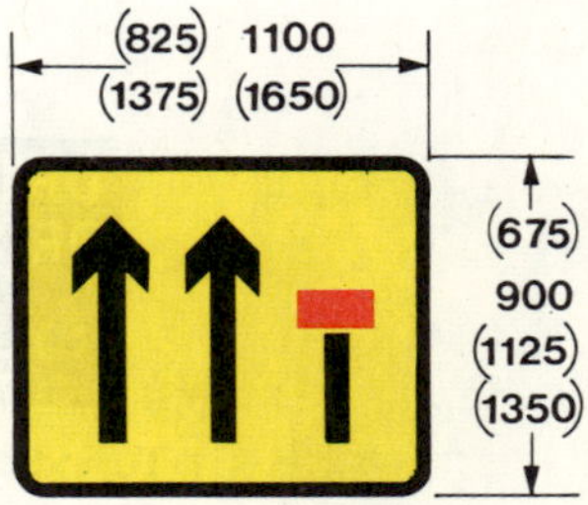

Right hand lane of a three lane carriageway closed to traffic ahead
Permitted variants: The symbols may be varied to indicate which lane is or lanes are closed to traffic, provided that the centre lane is not shown as closed and the other lanes are shown as open unless the right hand arrow is reversed to indicate two-way traffic. The following colour combination may be substituted for the colours shown; a blue background with a white border and white symbols except for the horizontal bar line which shall remain red
(See Direction 17)

858.1

Right hand lane of a four lane carriageway closed to traffic ahead
Permitted variants: The symbols may be varied to indicate which lane is or lanes are closed to traffic, provided that if either one of the two centre lanes is shown as closed then the outside lane adjacent to it shall also be shown as closed and if both centre lanes are so shown, then either one of the two outside lanes shall also be so shown unless one of the arrows representing a lane not so shown is reversed to indicate two-way traffic. The following colour combination may be substituted for the colours shown; a blue background with a white border and white symbols except for the horizontal bar line which shall remain red
(See Direction 17)
858.2

To indicate a requirement to use telephone apparatus at a railway level crossing ahead
Permitted variant: "LONG LOW" may be substituted for "LARGE OR SLOW"
861

Permitted variants: The appropriate telephone number (and exchange name where necessary) shall be substituted for "01–234–56789" and "RLY" may be substituted for "BR" in the legend
862

To indicate to vehicular traffic not to stop in such a manner that a vehicle or any part of a vehicle is at rest within the area of a railway level crossing
863

SCHEDULE 1 (See Regulations 9—19)

PART V—Directional and other informatory signs on motorways

Motorways Traffic Regulations for the time being in force under s.13 of the Act start to apply to the road at this point
(See Direction 9)
901.1

Route number and direction to place indicated
(See Direction 9)
903.1

Same as 903.1 but where more than one destination is shown
(See Direction 9)
904.1

Route number of road extending from a junction 1 mile ahead and number of that junction
(See Direction 9)
905

PART V—Directional and other informatory signs on motorways (contd.)

(250)
300

Route number of, and next place of traffic importance on, a road extending from a junction ½ mile ahead and number of that junction
(See Direction 9)
906

(250)
300

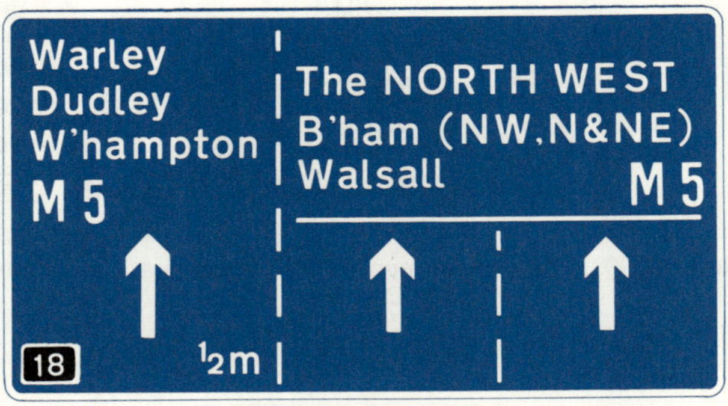

Route number of and next places of traffic importance and an indication of appropriate traffic lanes for traffic to the places shown from a junction ahead and number of that junction
Permitted variant: The arrow on the left may be angled to point 22½° to the left
(See Direction 9)
906.1

SCHEDULE 1

PART V—Directional and other informatory signs on motorways (contd.)

(250)
300

Route numbers and next places of traffic importance from an exit road ½ mile ahead and a further exit road in close proximity to the first exit road
(See Direction 9)
906.2

(250)
300

Route number of, and next place of traffic importance on, a road at a junction with a motorway, places to which the motorway leads and number of that junction
(See Direction 9)
907

PART V—Directional and other informatory signs on motorways (contd.)

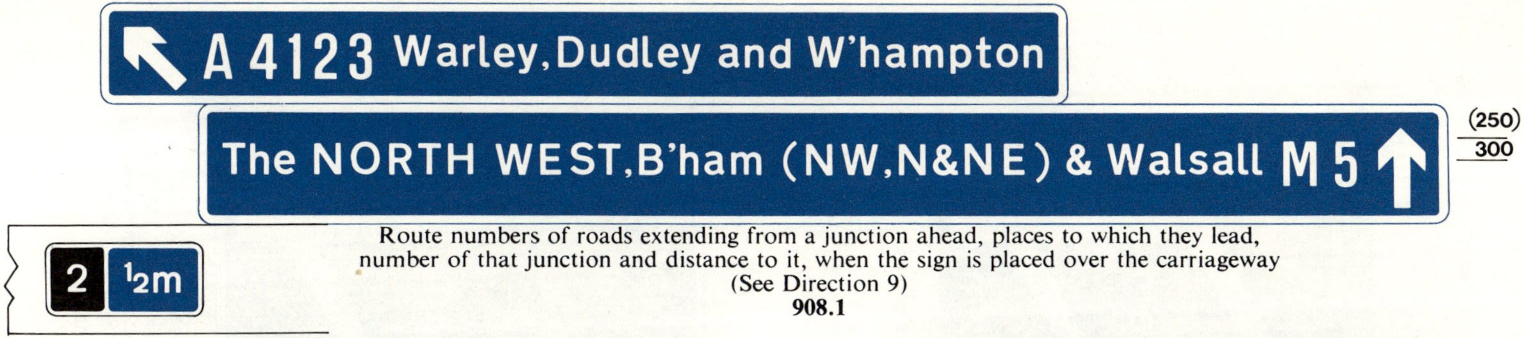

Route numbers of roads extending from a junction ahead, places to which they lead, number of that junction and distance to it, when the sign is placed over the carriageway
(See Direction 9)
908.1

Route numbers of roads extending from a junction ahead, places to which they lead, number of that junction and appropriate traffic lanes for traffic to those places when the sign is placed over the carriageway
Permitted variants:
The distance to the junction may be added. When motorway signals are present the alternative arrow design shown in Part IV of Schedule 7 may be provided
(See Direction 9)
908.2

PART V—Directional and other informatory signs on motorways (contd.)

Route number of road and place to which it leads from a junction with a motorway
(See Direction 9)
909.1

Direction of route
(See Direction 9)
910

Same as 910
(See Direction 9)
910.1

Route number of motorway with names of and distances in miles to places of traffic importance to which it leads
(See Direction 9)
911

PART V—Directional and other informatory signs on motorways (contd.)

Direction to nearest emergency telephone box on same side of road
(See Direction 9)
912

Side of emergency telephone box
Permitted variant: the letters and numerals of the telephone location may be varied
(See Direction 9)
913.2

Back of emergency telephone box
Permitted variant: Same as 913.2
(See Direction 9)
913.3

SCHEDULE 1

PART V—Directional and other informatory signs on motorways (contd.)

Distance to next
service area
(See Direction 9)
915

Distance to next
two service areas
(See Direction 9)
916

Direction to service area
(See Direction 9)
916.1

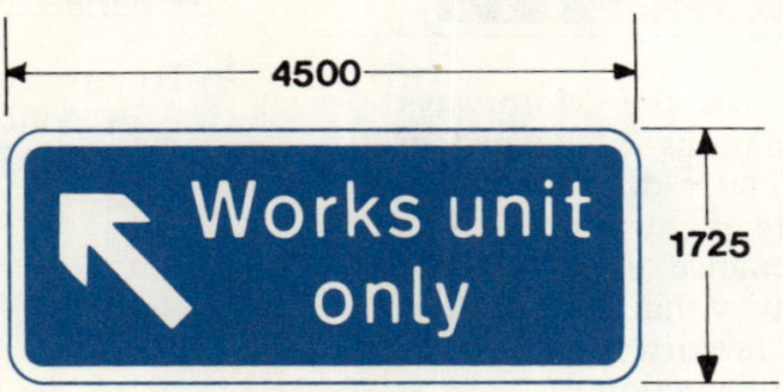

(See Direction 9)
917

PART V—Directional and other informatory signs on motorways (contd.)

To indicate that the Motorways Traffic Regulations (as defined in the caption under diagram 901.1) cease to apply 1 mile ahead
Permitted variant:
"½" may be substituted for "1"
(See Direction 9)
918.1

To indicate that the Motorways Traffic Regulations (as defined in the caption under diagram 901.1) cease to apply at a junction
(See Direction 9)
919.1

To indicate that the Motorways Traffic Regulations (as defined in the caption under diagram 901.1) cease to apply at entry to a service area, maintenance compound or similar facility within the length of a motorway
(See Direction 9)
920

To indicate a waiting place for police vehicles only
(See Direction 9)
925

SCHEDULE 2 (See Regulations 20—26 and Direction 31)

Markings on the road

Dimensions in any diagram shown in this Schedule are expressed in millimetres unless otherwise specified

Transverse line (stop line) to indicate the position beyond which vehicular traffic must not proceed when required to stop by light signals or the police
(See Directions 24 and 34)
1001

Transverse line to indicate the position beyond which vehicular traffic must not proceed when required to stop by the sign shown in diagram 601.1
(See Direction 25)
1002.1

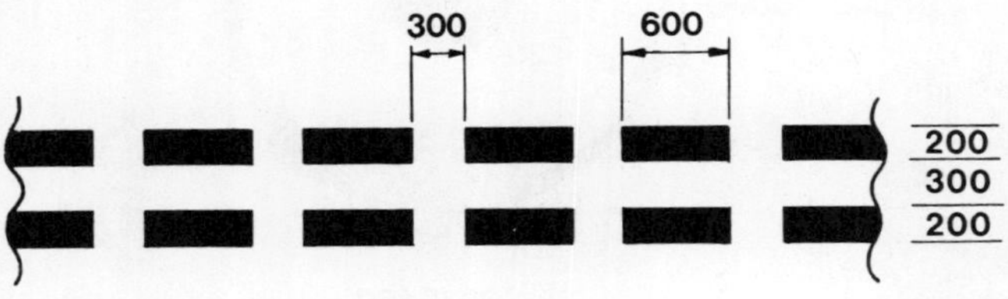

Transverse marking to indicate to vehicular traffic the requirement prescribed by Regulation 22(2)
1003

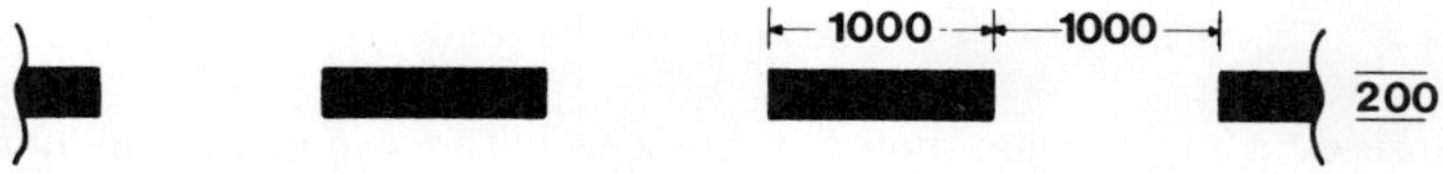

Transverse marking to indicate to vehicular traffic approaching a roundabout the position at or immediately beyond which the said vehicles should give way to vehicular traffic circulating on the carriageway of the roundabout

1003.1

Transverse marking to indicate position where pedestrians should wait at a level crossing when the barriers are closed or when the light signals as prescribed by Regulation 31(4) are showing or if there are neither barriers nor light signals where they should wait until it is safe to proceed

1003.2

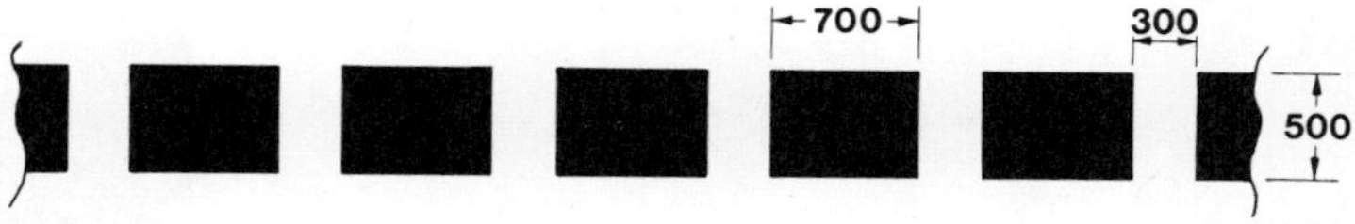

Transverse marking to indicate to vehicular traffic approaching a roundabout with a small central island or approaching a junction marked by signs conforming to that shown in diagram 611.1 the position at or immediately beyond which the said vehicles should give way to vehicular traffic circulating on the carriageway of the roundabout

1003.3

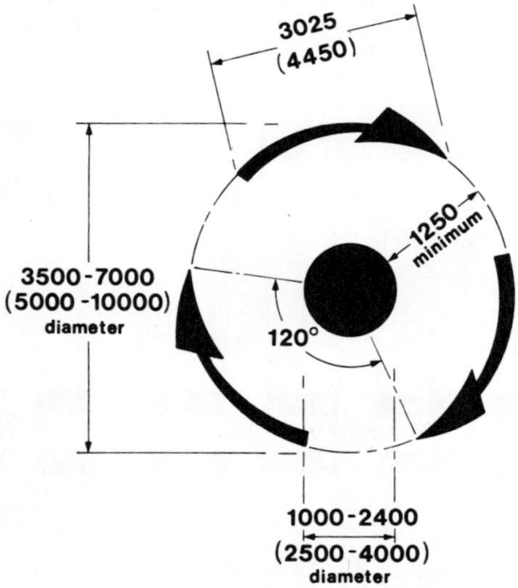

To indicate to vehicular traffic the direction of traffic flow at a junction marked by signs conforming to that shown in diagram 611.1

(See Direction 25)

1003.4

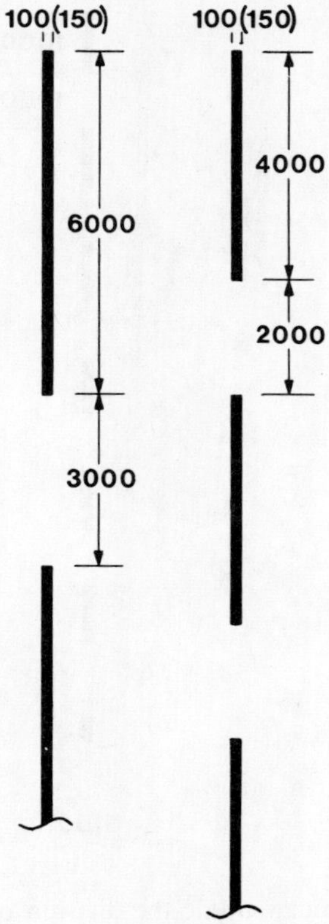

1004

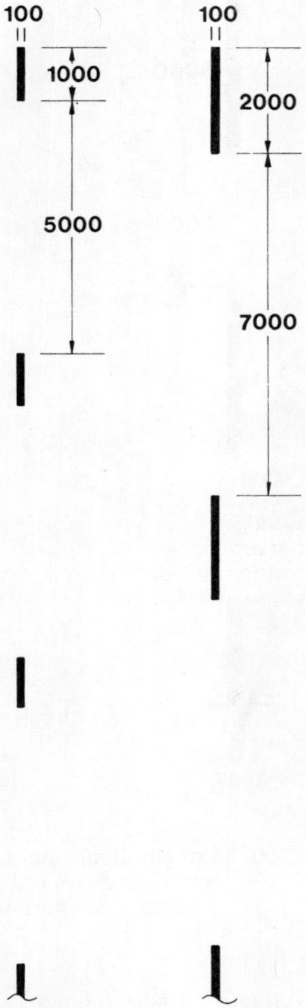

1005

Diagram 1004: Alternative methods of marking a longitudinal line to warn vehicular traffic when approaching or negotiating a hazard not to cross or straddle the line unless it is seen by the driver to be safe to do so

Diagram 1005: Alternative methods of marking a longitudinal line to indicate to vehicular traffic the division of the carriageway into traffic lanes

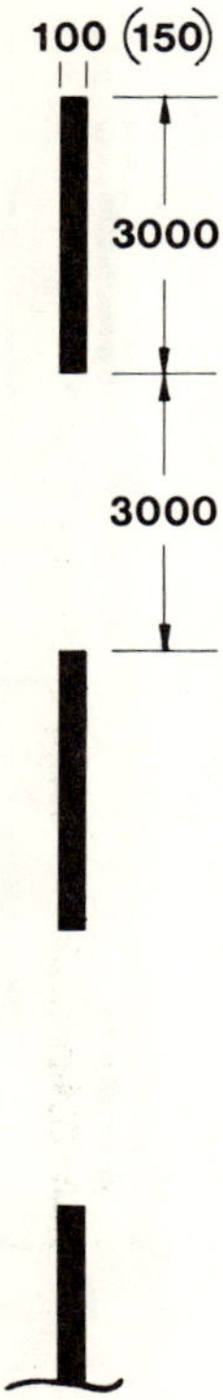

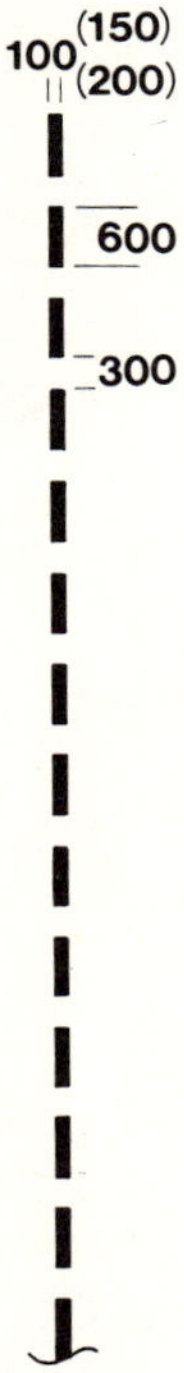

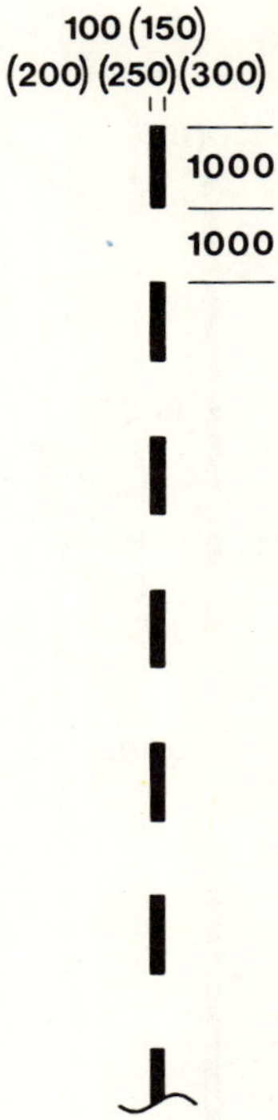

1007 **1009** **1010**

Diagram 1007: Longitudinal line to indicate to vehicular traffic the division between opposing flows on a carriageway having four or more lanes or being 10 metres or more wide

Diagram 1009: Longitudinal line to indicate to vehicular traffic the edge of the carriageway at a road junction

Diagram 1010: Longitudinal line to indicate to vehicular traffic the edge of the carriageway at a road junction or a layby

1011

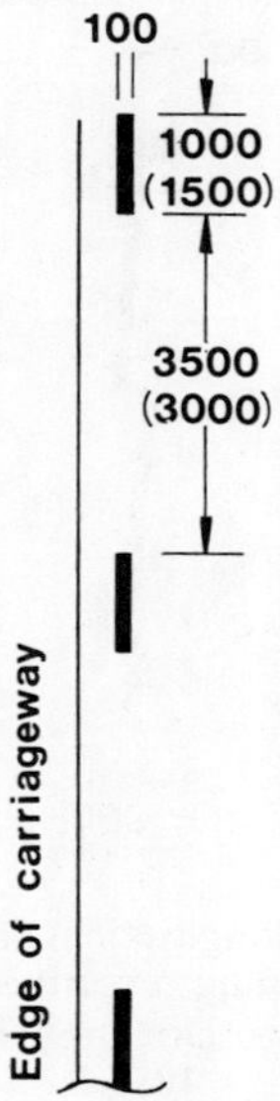

1012

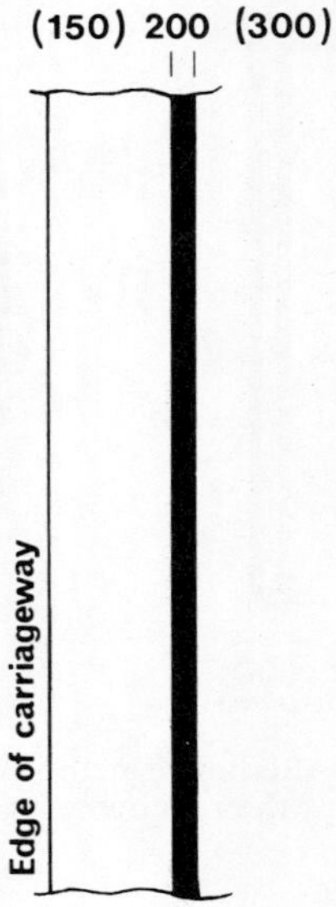

1012.1

Diagram 1011: Longitudinal line to indicate to vehicular traffic the edge of the carriageway at a bend or similar hazard

Diagram 1012: Longitudinal line to indicate to vehicular traffic the edge of the carriageway elsewhere than at a bend or similar hazard, a road junction or a lay-by

Diagram 1012.1: Longitudinal line to indicate to vehicular traffic on a motorway or other dual carriageway road or on a single carriageway all purpose road the edge of that part of the carriageway available for through traffic where a hard shoulder or a hard strip is provided

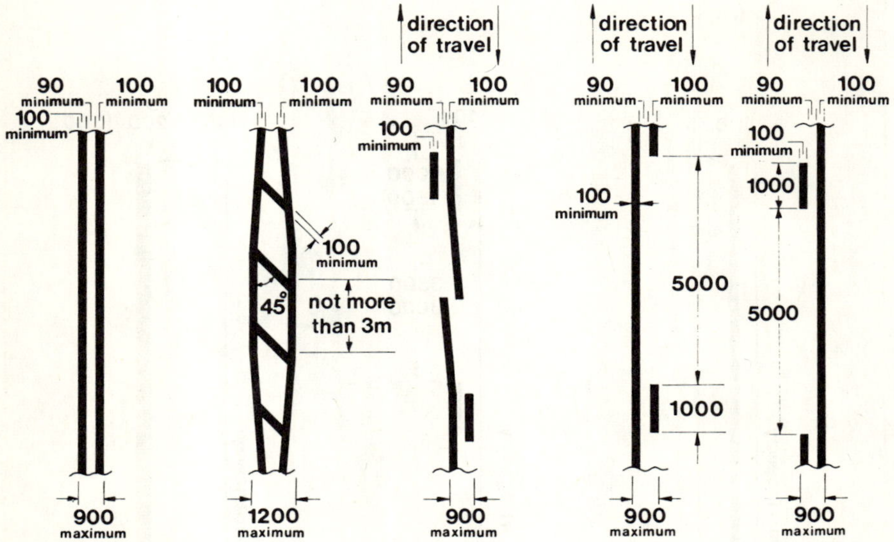

Alternative methods of marking longitudinal lines to indicate to vehicular traffic the requirements and the warning prescribed by Regulation 23(2) and (5)
(See Direction 42)
1013.1

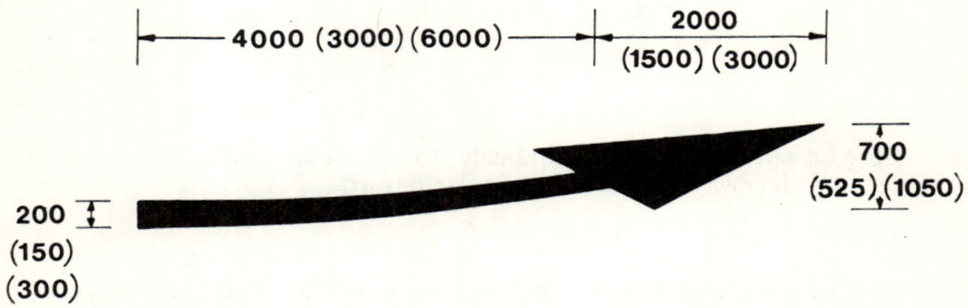

To warn vehicular traffic of the presence ahead of a road marking of the type shown in diagrams 1013.1, 1040, 1040.1 or 1049 and to indicate which side of the carriageway traffic should travel past that marking, or to warn vehicular traffic approaching a length of road on which there is the need to pass a temporary obstruction on the carriageway
Permitted variant: The arrow may be reversed when used in connection with a temporary obstruction or in advance of the road marking shown in diagram 1049
(See Direction 42)
1014

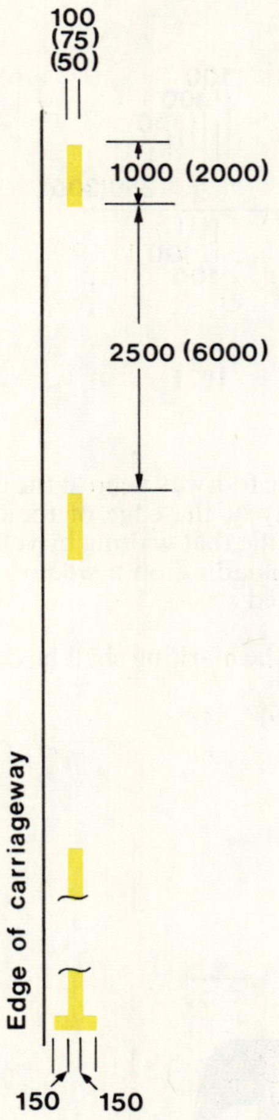

1016.1

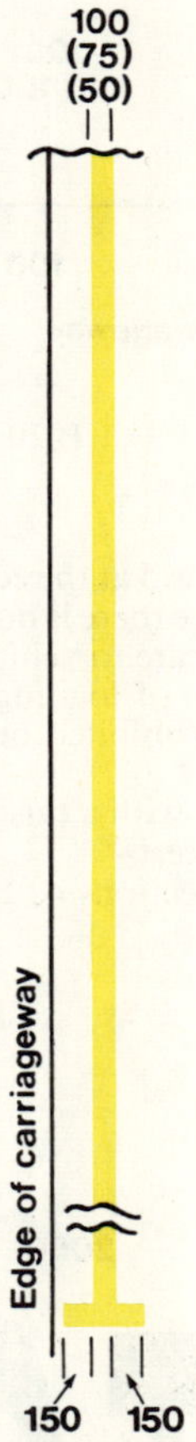

1017

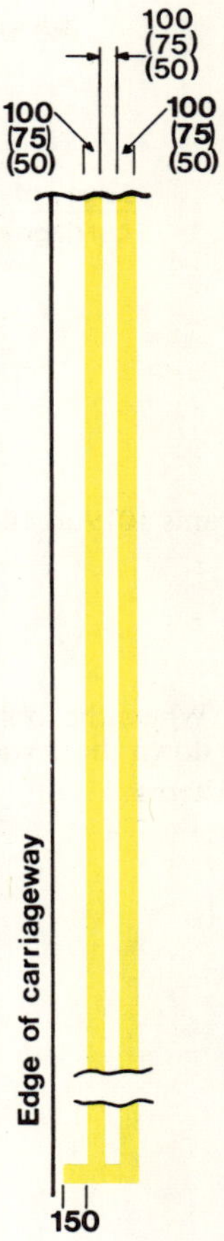

1018

Edge of carriageway **Edge of carriageway** **Edge of carrlageway**

Diagrams 1016.1 to 1018: Longitudinal lines to be laid near the edge of the carriageway to indicate to vehicular traffic that waiting by vehicles on a side of a length of road is prohibited or restricted

Note: When one of these types of longitudinal lines is used alone, the short transverse line shall be provided at each end. When two or more of these types of lines are used in continuous sequence, the short transverse line shall be provided at each end of the sequence and also at any point where the pattern of the longitudinal lines changes

(See Directions 6, 26 and 28)

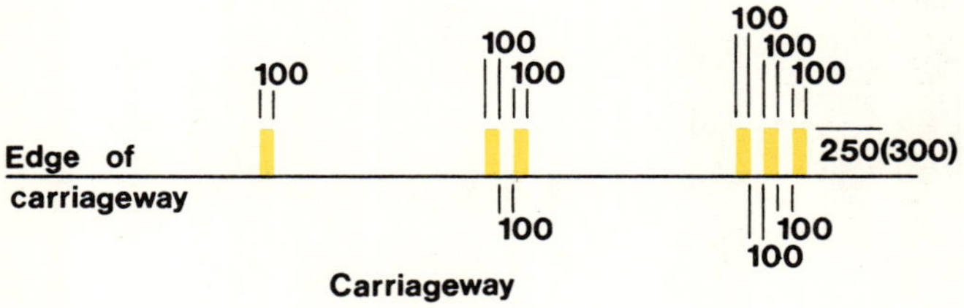

1019 **1020** **1021**

Diagrams 1019 to 1021: Lines to be laid at the edge of the footway nearest the carriageway, or where there is no footway at the edge of the carriageway, to indicate to vehicular traffic that waiting by vehicles for the purposes of loading and unloading on a side of a length of road is prohibited or restricted

Note: Where the footway is provided with a raised kerb the marking shall be continued down the vertical face of the kerb

(See Directions 6, 27 and 29)

To indicate to vehicular traffic the approach to a road junction at or near which is placed the sign shown in diagram 601.1 and the road marking 1002.1

(See Direction 25)

1022

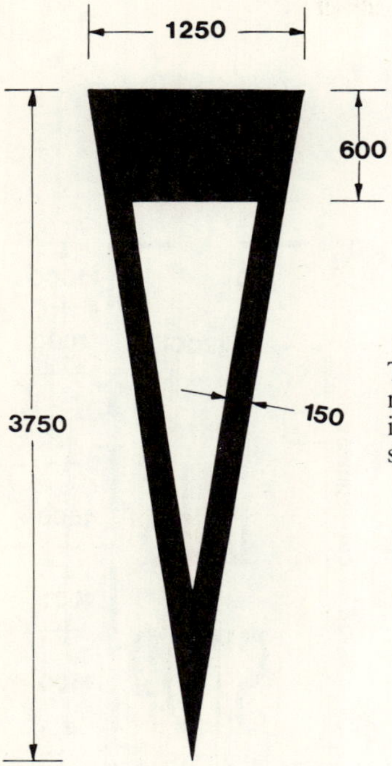

To indicate to vehicular traffic the approach to a road junction at or near which is placed the marking shown in diagram 1003 or both the marking shown in diagram 1003 and the sign shown in diagram 602
(See Direction 30)
1023

To indicate to vehicular traffic potential danger ahead and the need to proceed with caution
1024

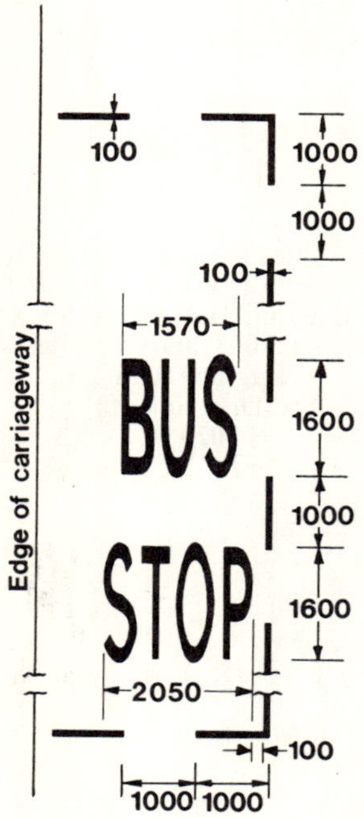

1025

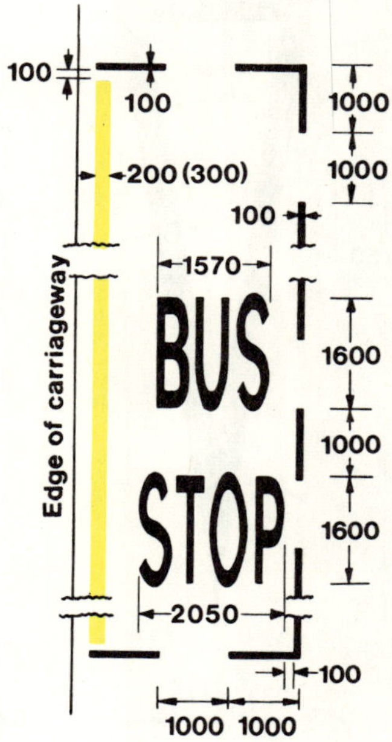

1025.1

Diagram 1025: To indicate to vehicular traffic limits of a bus stop on that part of the carriageway also used by through traffic

Diagram 1025.1: To indicate to vehicular traffic limits of a bus stop on that part of the carriageway also used by through traffic subject to restrictions on stopping by vehicles other than stage and scheduled express carriages between 7 am and 7 pm
Permitted variant: The word "Stage" may be added above "Bus Stop" where the restrictions on stopping apply to scheduled express carriages
(See Directions 6 and 30)

Note: Where the bus stop is one where there are frequent or multiple services or vehicles with different entrance positions, the length of the bay may be increased as necessary in stages of 2 metres from a minimum of 19 metres. The words "bus stop" must be repeated once for each complete 12 metres length in excess of the minimum length

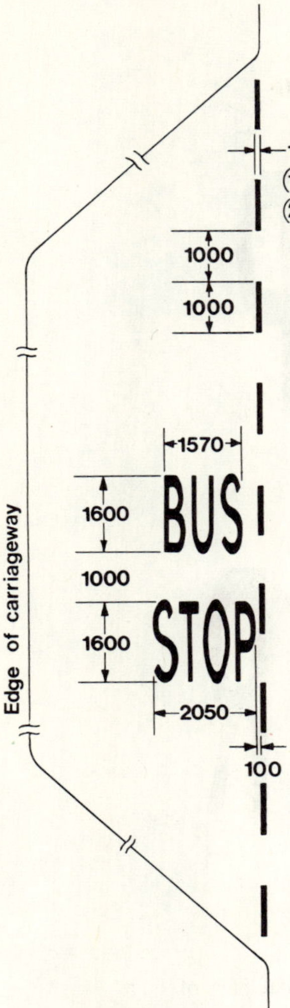

1025.2

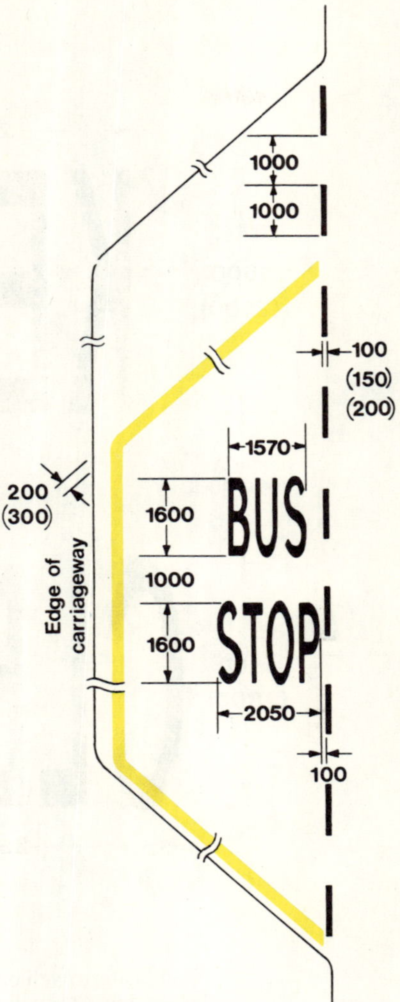

1025.3

Diagram 1025.2: To indicate to vehicular traffic limits of a bus stop in a lay-by
Permitted variant: The shape of the marking may be varied having regard to the place where the marking is situated

Diagram 1025.3: To indicate to vehicular traffic limits of a bus stop in a lay-by subject to restrictions on stopping by vehicles other than stage and scheduled express carriages between 7 am and 7 pm
Permitted variants: The word "Stage" may be added above "Bus Stop" where the restrictions on stopping apply to scheduled express carriages. The shape of the marking may be varied having regard to the place where the marking is situated

(See Directions 6 and 30)

Note: The expression "Stage Bus" in the permitted variants for diagrams 1025.1 and 1025.3 means for the purpose of the indication "Stage carriage"

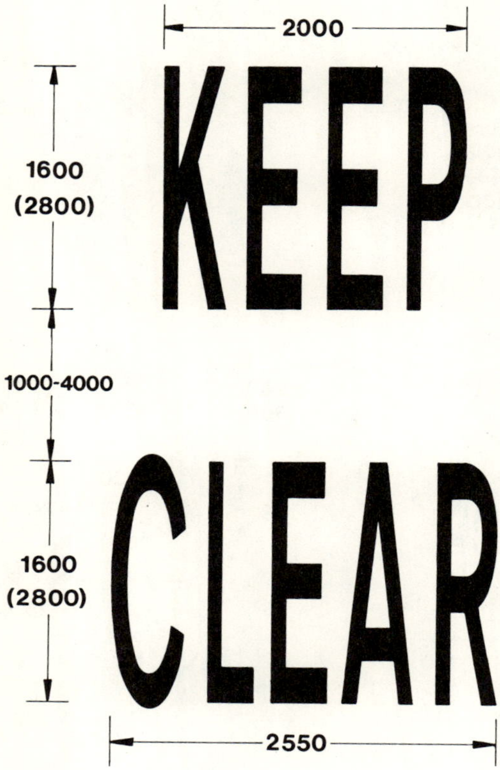

To indicate to vehicular traffic that part of the carriageway which should be left clear of stationary vehicles
1026

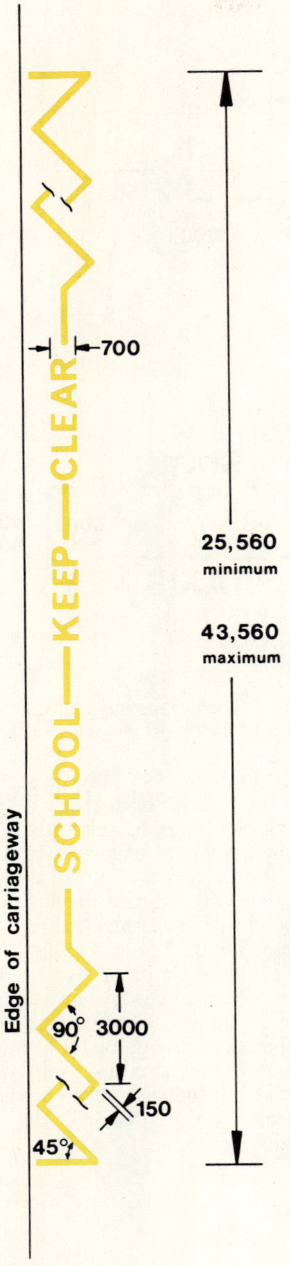

To indicate to vehicular traffic that part of the carriageway outside a school entrance which should be kept clear of stationary vehicles

Permitted variant: The legend "school" may be omitted and the minimum length reduced when the marking is used to indicate that part of the carriageway outside a hospital, ambulance station or fire station which should be kept clear of stationary vehicles

1027.1

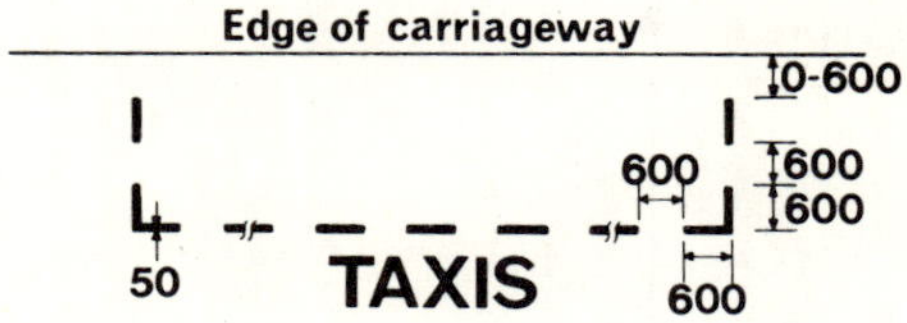

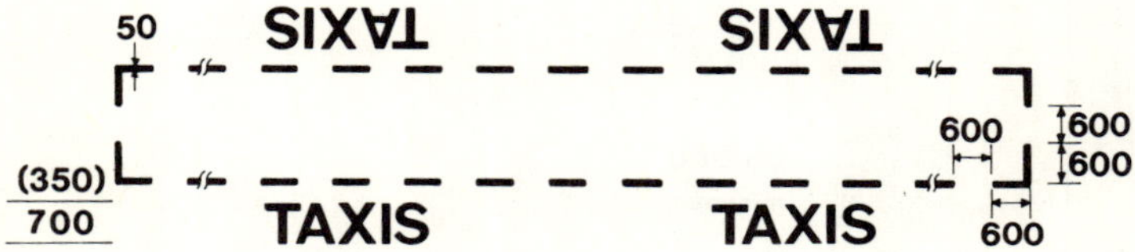

To indicate to vehicular traffic that part of a carriageway, at the side or in the middle of the road, which should be kept clear for use by hackney carriages

Permitted variants: "police", "doctor" or "ambulances" may be substituted for "taxis" to indicate an area for use by a police or doctor's vehicle or by ambulances, as appropriate. "loading bay" may be substituted for "taxis" to indicate the limits of places where vehicles may wait to load or unload. "solo motor cycles only", "solo motor cycles", "motor cycles" or "solo m/cs" may be substituted for "taxis" to indicate the limits of places at the side and in the middle of the road within a controlled parking zone where motor cycles and mopeds may stand. "large or slow vehs only" may be substituted for "taxis" at a lay-by or other part of the carriageway to indicate the limits of places where large or slow vehicles may wait. "Disabled" may be substituted for "taxis" to indicate an area for use by vehicles displaying a disabled person's orange badge. "Buses may be substituted for "taxis" to indicate an area where buses may wait and "coaches" may be substituted for "taxis" to indicate an area where coaches may wait

(See Direction 6)

1028.1

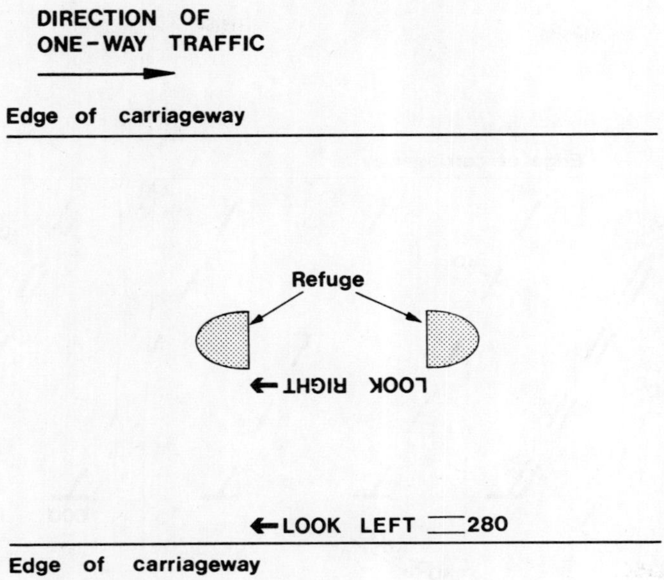

To warn pedestrians of the likely direction of approaching traffic

1029

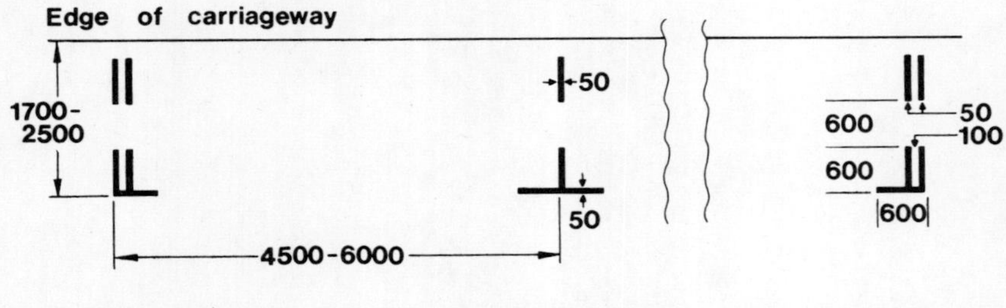

To indicate to vehicular traffic parking places, subject to such conditions, if any, as may be in force

Permitted variant: The lines between individual car parking spaces may be omitted

(See Direction 6)

1032

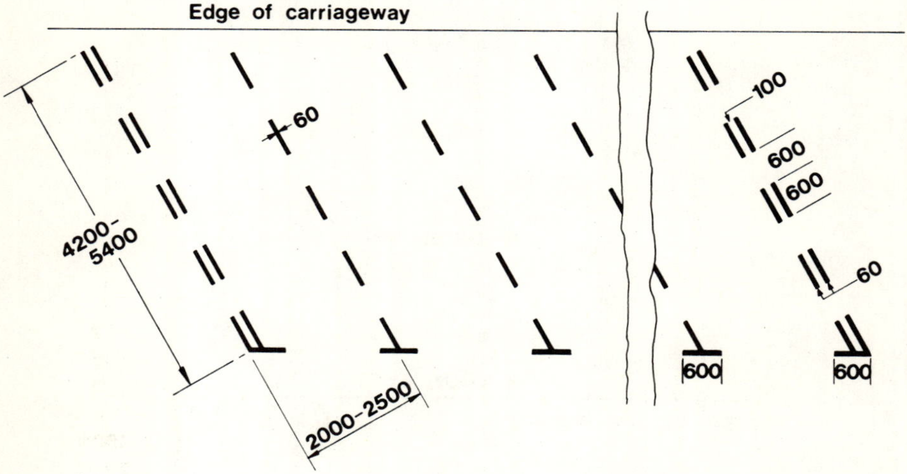

To indicate to vehicular traffic echelon parking places, subject to such conditions, if any, as may be in force

Permitted variant:

The angle between the spaces and the edge of the carriageway may be varied

(See Direction 6)

1033

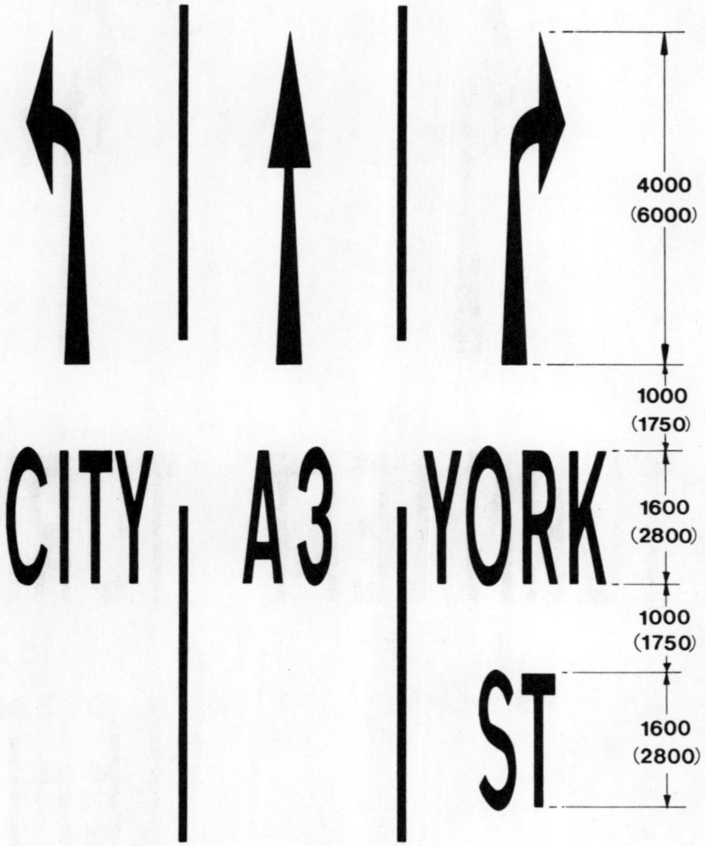

To indicate to vehicular traffic appropriate traffic lanes
Permitted variants: See Regulation 20(3)(*b*)
1035

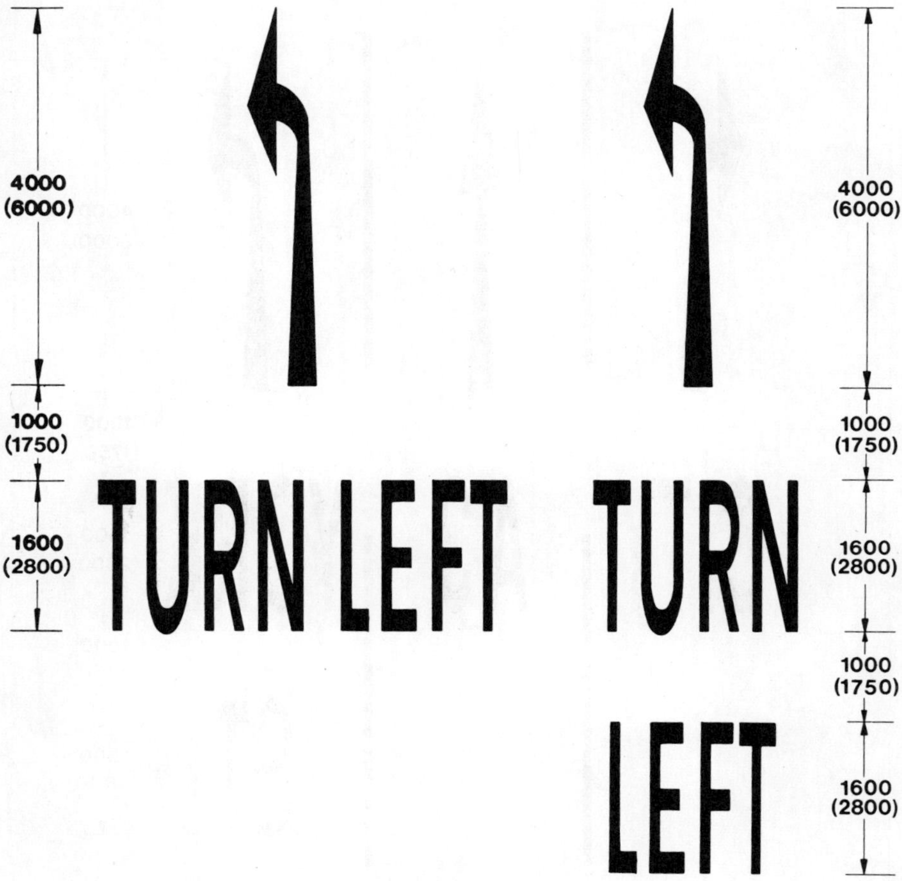

To indicate to vehicular traffic a compulsory left turn (alternative methods)
(See Direction 6)
1036.1

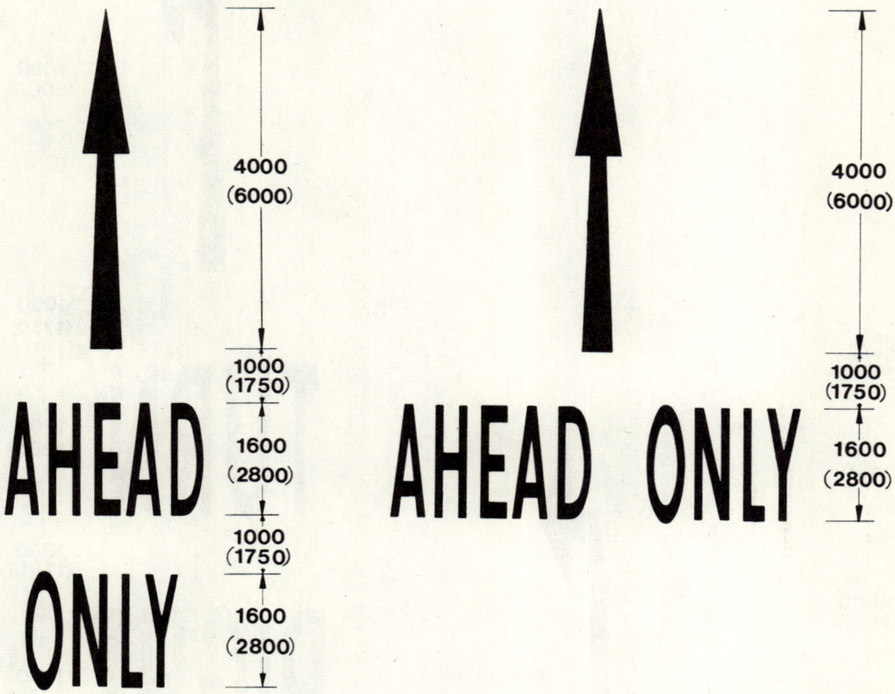

To indicate that vehicular traffic must only proceed in the direction of the arrow (alternative methods)
(See Direction 6)
1036.2

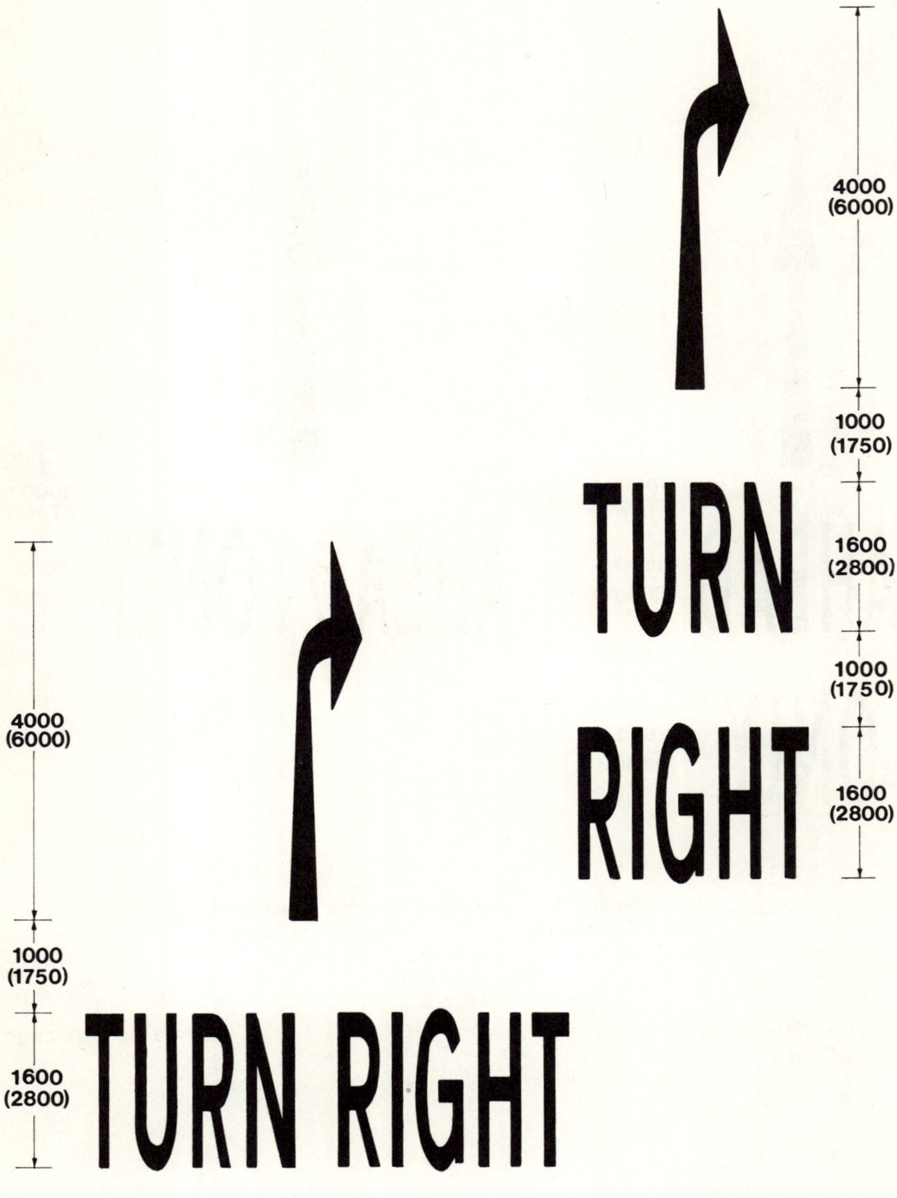

To indicate to vehicular traffic a compulsory right turn (alternative methods)
(See Direction 6)
1037.1

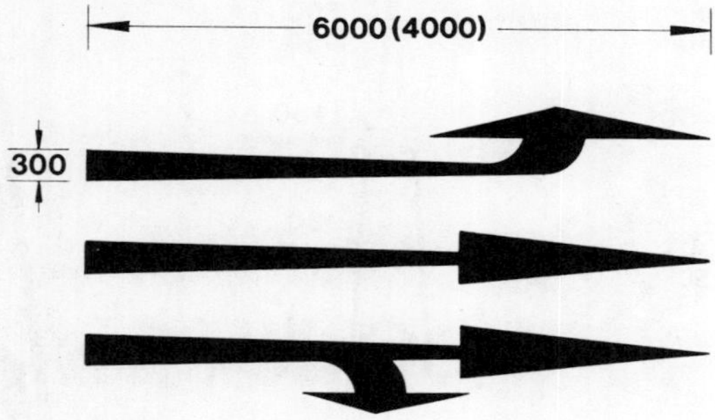

To indicate to vehicular traffic appropriate traffic lanes
Permitted variants: The direction of each arrow head may be varied to indicate left, ahead and right turns to suit the circumstances save that no arrow head may show more than two directions
1038

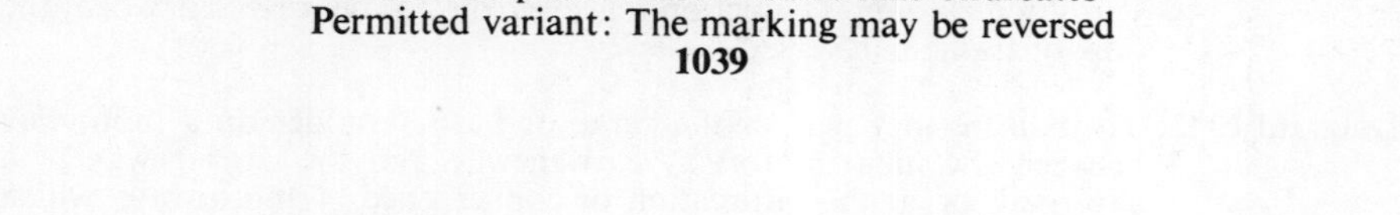

To indicate to vehicular traffic the entrance to a deceleration lane at a road junction or another place where a traffic lane bifurcates
Permitted variant: The marking may be reversed
1039

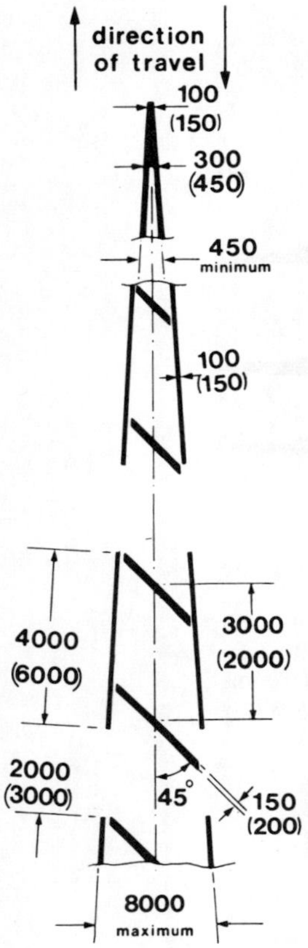

1040

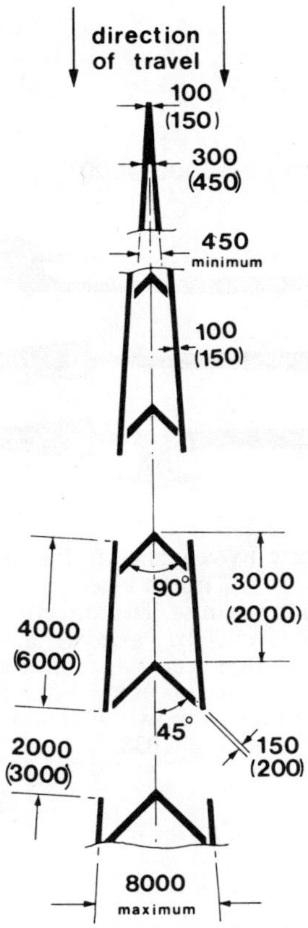

1041

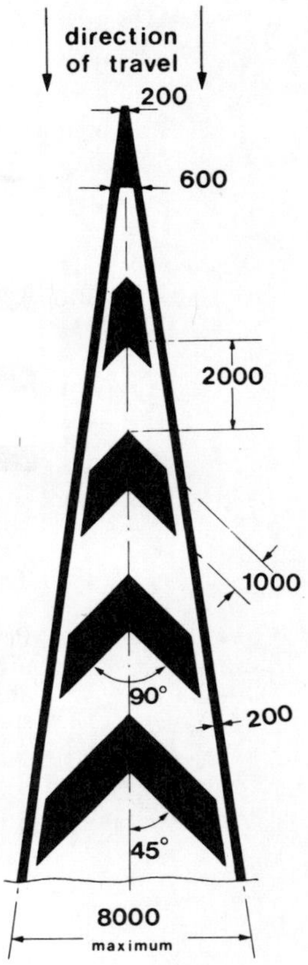

1042

Diagram 1040: To indicate that part of the carriageway which vehicular traffic should not enter unless it is seen by the driver of the vehicle to be safe to do so

Diagram 1040.1: See page 163

Diagram 1041: Same as 1040 where traffic passes in same direction on either side
Permitted variant: Direction of chevron to be reversed when the flow of traffic is reversed

Diagram 1042: To indicate that part of the verge or hard shoulder on a motorway between the main motorway carriageway and the carriageway of a slip road, or at the bifurcation or convergence of motorways which vehicular traffic must not enter except in an emergency
Permitted variant: Same as 1041

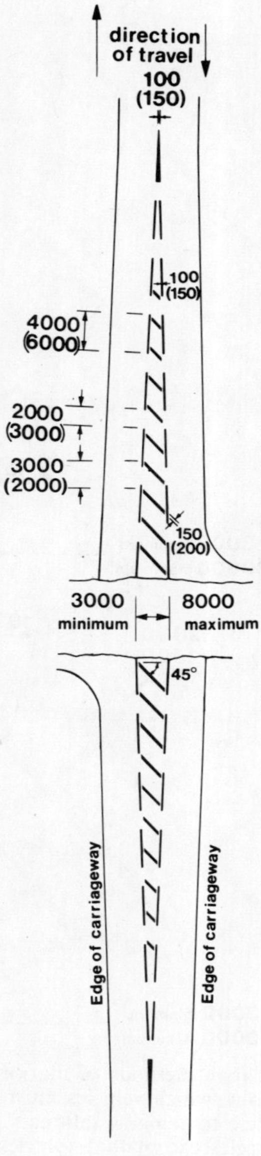

Same as 1040 where marking is not adjacent
to either edge of the carriageway
1040.1

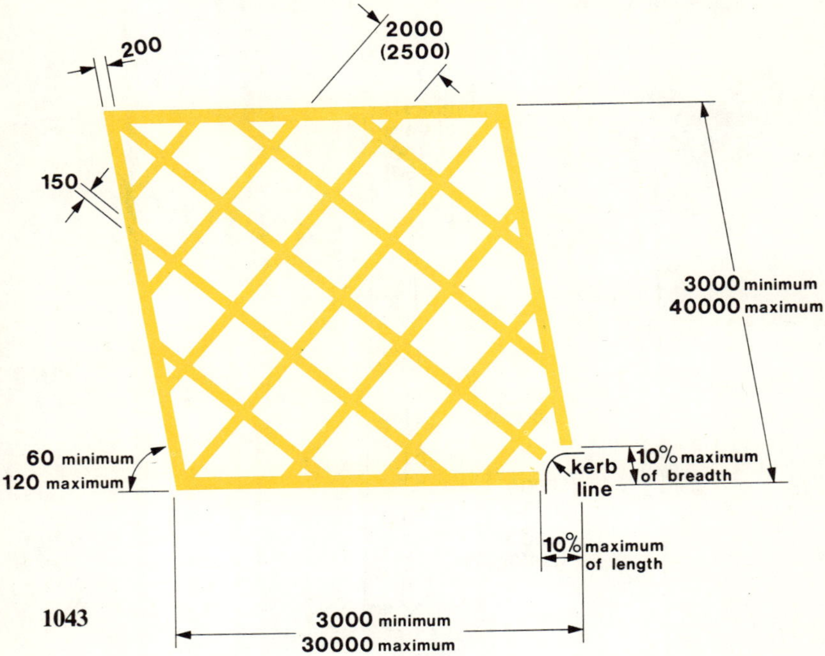

1043

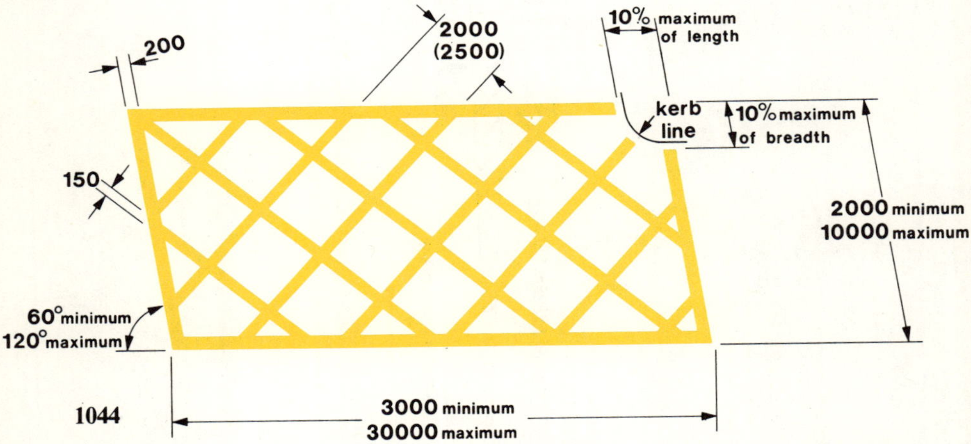

1044

Diagrams 1043 and 1044: Alternative methods of marking an area of carriageway at a junction, other than a roundabout, which vehicles must not enter in a manner which then causes any part of the vehicle to remain stationary within the marked area due to the presence of stationary vehicles except that vehicles waiting to complete a right turn may remain stationary within the area for so long as prevented from completing that turn by reason either of oncoming vehicles or of the presence of other stationary vehicles waiting in or near that area to complete a right turn

Permitted variant: Any corner may be cut away in the manner shown in the bottom right hand corner of diagram 1043 and in the top right hand corner of diagram 1044 to a maximum of 10% of the length of the side affected to accommodate a corner kerb. Any corner shown as cut away may be completed in the manner of the other corners shown as not cut away

(See Direction 6)

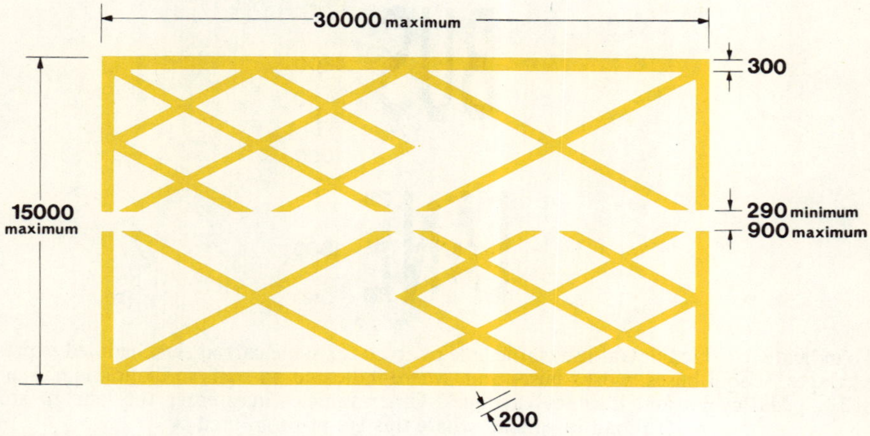

An area of the carriageway at a level crossing which vehicles must not enter in a manner which then causes any part of the vehicle to remain at rest within the marked area due to the presence of stationary vehicles

(See Direction 6)

1045

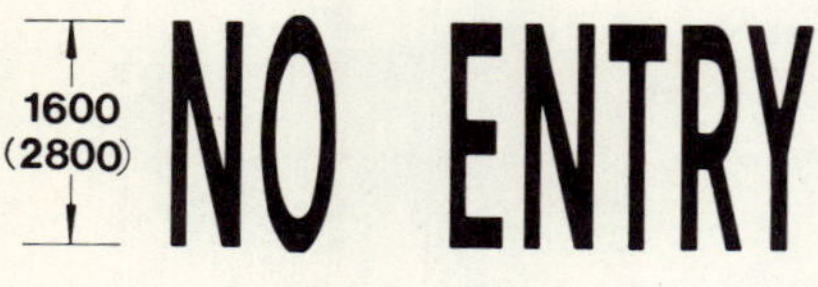

1046

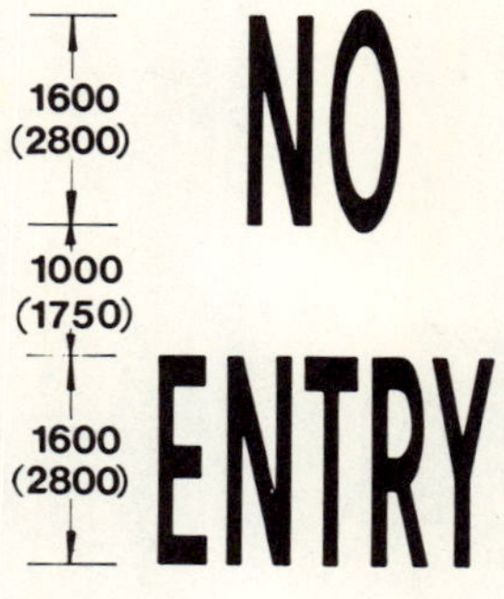

1047

Diagrams 1046 and 1047: Alternative methods of indicating "no entry" for vehicular traffic

Permitted variant: "play street" may be substituted for "no entry" to indicate play street restrictions on vehicular street

(See Direction 6)

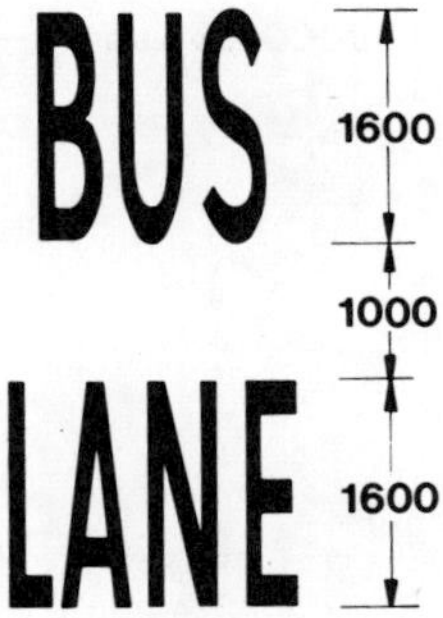

To indicate to vehicular traffic a traffic lane reserved for stage carriages, scheduled express carriages, school buses, works buses and, where indicated on signs in diagrams 654 and 812.1, pedal cycles and hackney carriages. Other vehicles may enter the lane to stop to load or unload where this is not prohibited

Permitted variant: The words "& Coach" may be added between "Bus" and "Lane" where the legend "& Coaches" is indicated on signs in diagrams 654 and 812.1

Note: Where the permitted variant is adopted there must be a gap of 1000 mm between each separate line of legend

(See Directions 6 and 30)

1048

Longitudinal line to indicate to vehicular traffic the boundary of a traffic lane reserved for stage carriages, scheduled express carriages, school buses, works buses and, where indicated on signs in diagrams 654 and 812.1, pedal cycles, hackney carriages and all vehicles constructed or adapted to carry 12 or more passengers. Other vehicles may cross the line to stop to load or unload where this is not prohibited

(See Directions 6 and 30)

1049

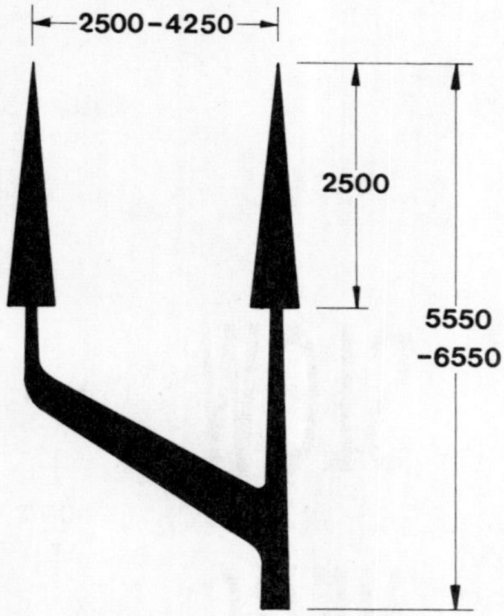

To advise vehicular traffic of possible movements at the end of a traffic lane marked by signs shown in diagram 1048 and bounded by the line shown in diagram 1049. Permitted variant: The left hand arrow may indicate a left hand turn as shown in the road marking in diagram 1036.1

(See Direction 6)

1050

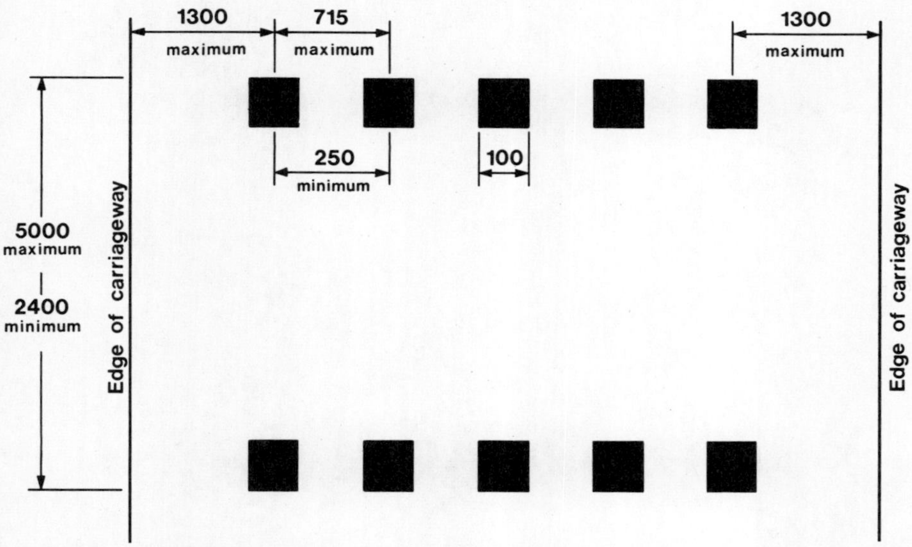

To indicate police controlled crossings at which traffic is subject to control by a police constable in uniform or a traffic warden, being control which is normally in operation during periods amounting in the aggregate to not less than 20 hours in any week or to indicate the most suitable place for pedestrians to cross a carriageway within 10 metres of light signals conforming to Regulation 31 or 31 taken with 35

Permitted variant: The square marks may be varied to circular marks of 100 mm diameter. The number of marks may be increased or reduced according to the width of the carriageway

1055

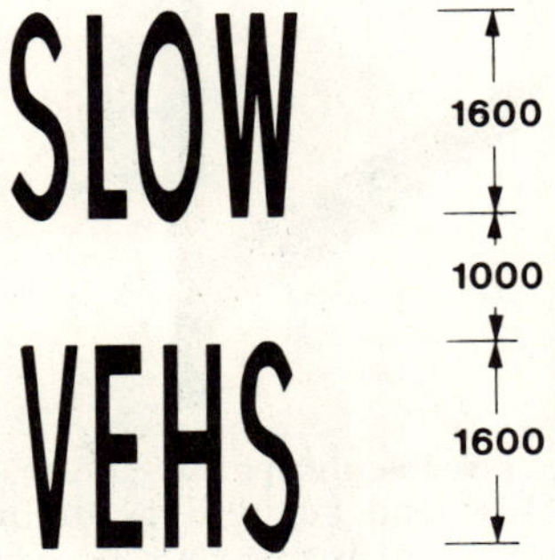

To indicate a crawler lane provided for the use of slow moving vehicles
1056

SCHEDULE 3 (See Regulation 32 and Direction 34)

Size and colour of arrow in light signals for control of vehicular traffic and methods of incorporation of the arrow in those signals

Dimensions in any diagram shown in this Schedule are expressed in millimetres unless otherwise specified

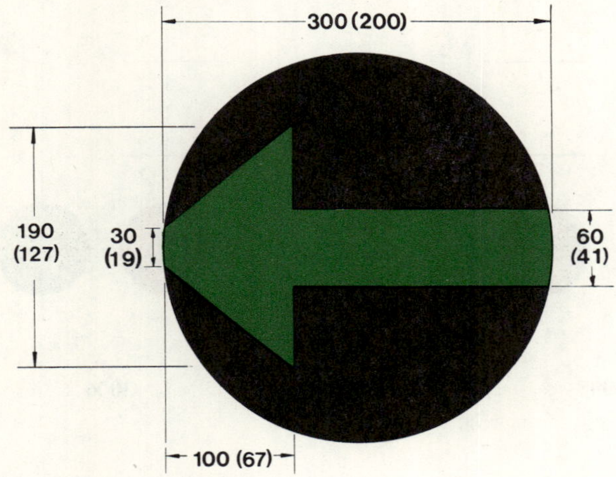

Details of lens showing green arrow
3001

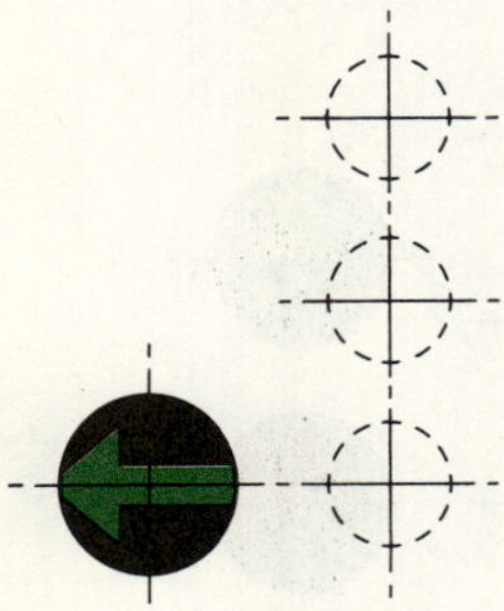

3002

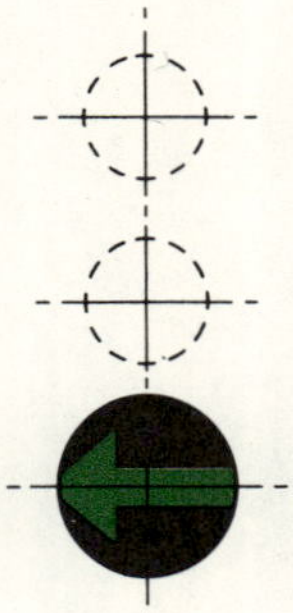

3003

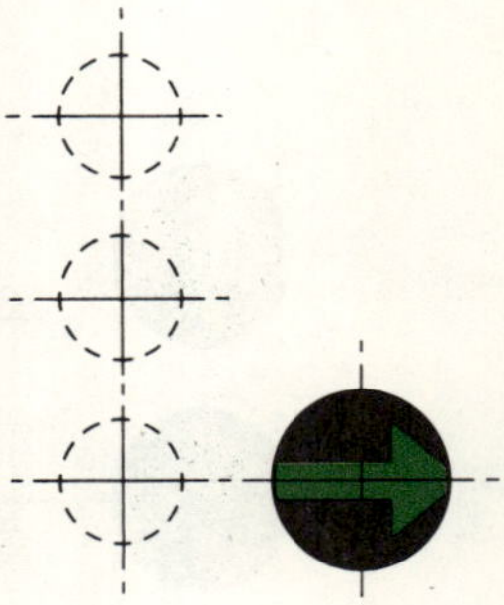

3004

Diagrams 3002 to 3011: Methods of fitting green arrows to traffic light signals

SCHEDULE 3

Size and colour of arrow in light signals for vehicular traffic and methods of incorporation of the arrow in those signals (contd.)

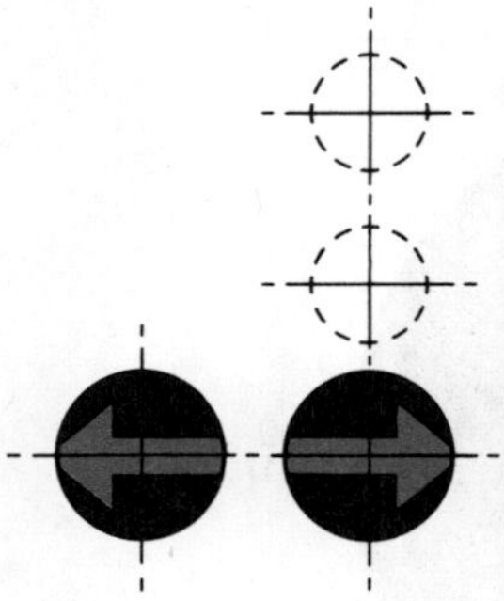

3005

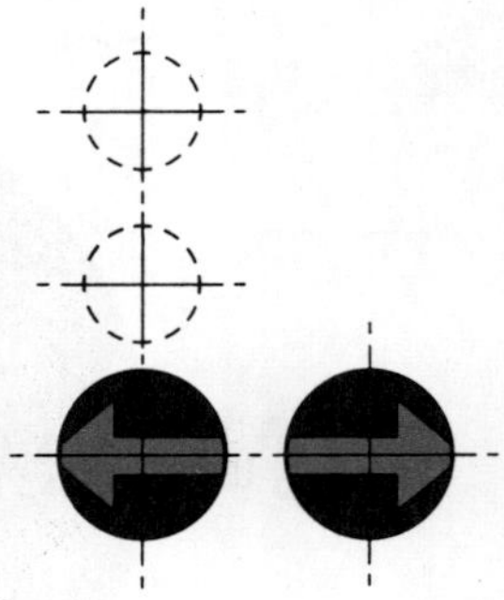

3006

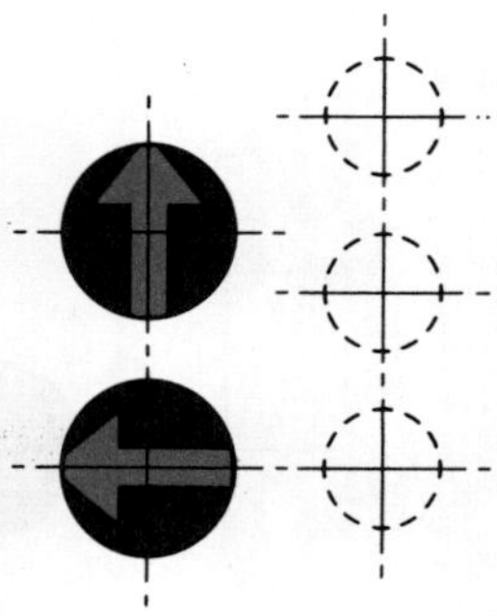

3007

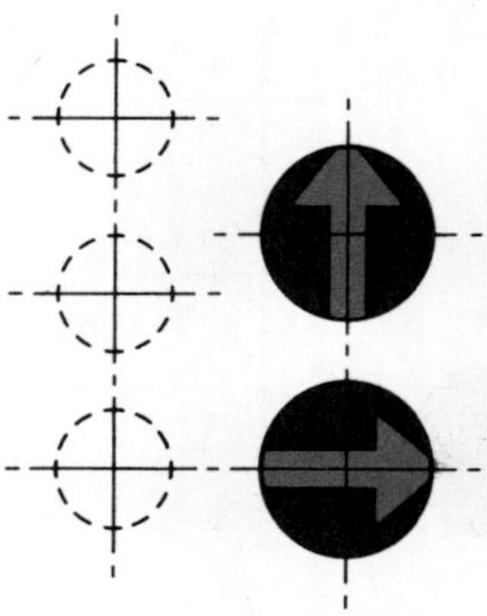

3008

SCHEDULE 3

Size and colour of arrow in light signals for vehicular traffic and methods of incorporation of the arrow in those signals (contd.)

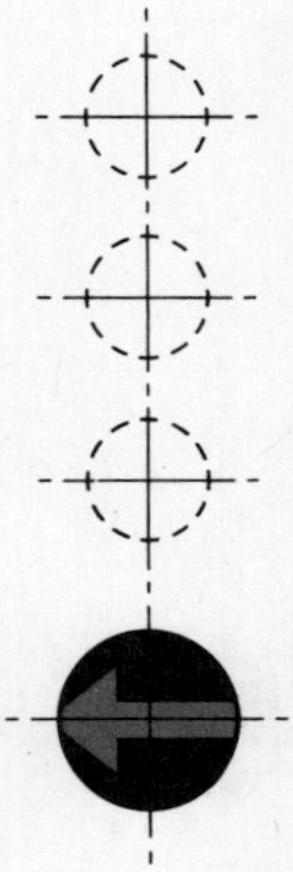

3009

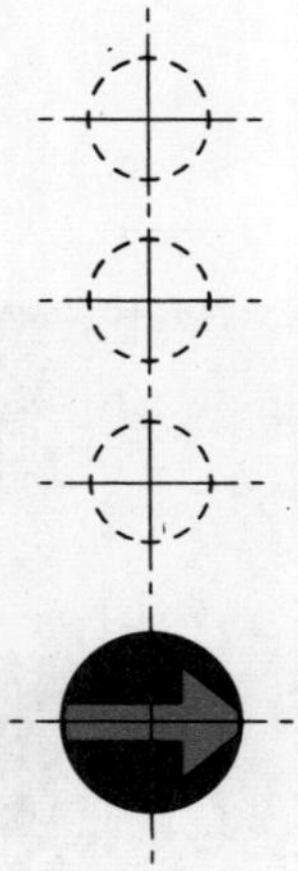

3010

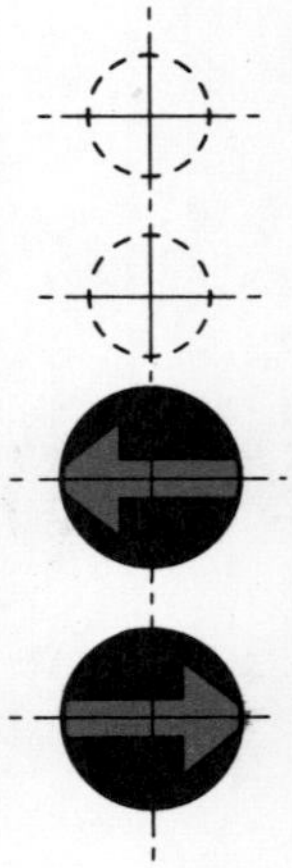

3011

SCHEDULE 4 (See Regulation 35)

Size, colour and type of light signals for pedestrians

Dimensions in any diagram shown in this Schedule are expressed in millimetres unless otherwise specified

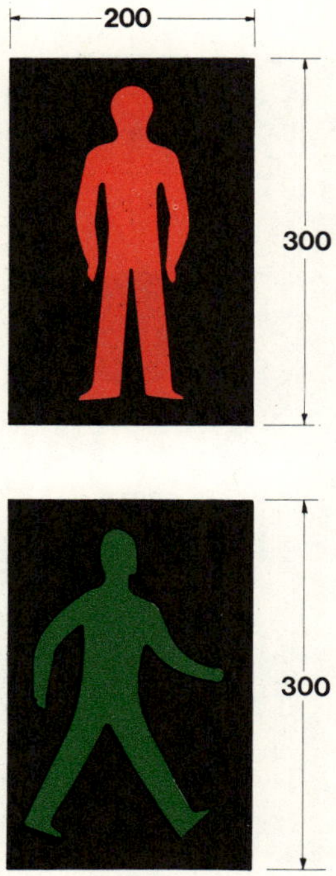

4001

SCHEDULE 4 (See Regulation 35)

Size, colour and type of light signals for pedestrians (contd.)

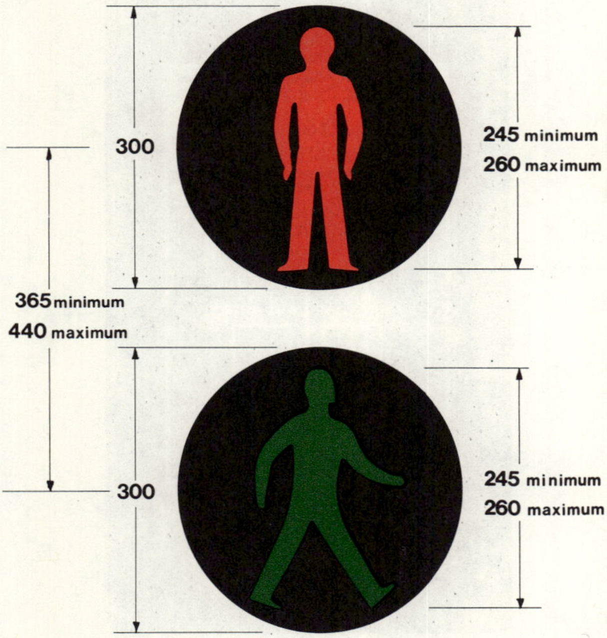

4002

SCHEDULE 4 (See Regulation 35)

Size, colour and type of light signals for pedestrians (contd.)

Instructions to pedestrians above the push button control for calling up pedestrian phases at traffic signals

4003

SCHEDULE 5 (See Regulation 36)

Size, colour and type of light signals for lane control of vehicular traffic

Dimensions in any diagram shown in this Schedule are expressed in millimetres unless otherwise specified

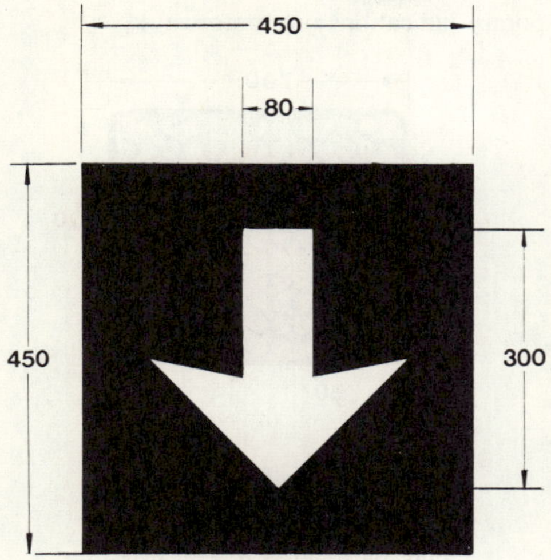

Lane open to vehicular traffic facing the signal
(See Direction 6)
5001

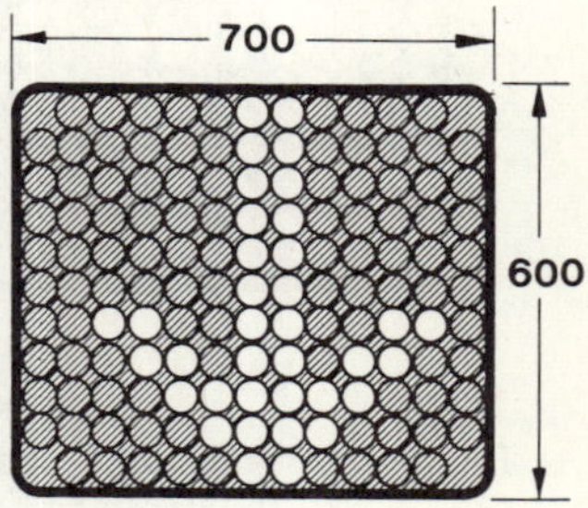

Lane of a carriageway open to vehicular traffic facing the signal
(See Direction 6)
5002

Lane closed to vehicular traffic facing the signal
(See Direction 6)
5003

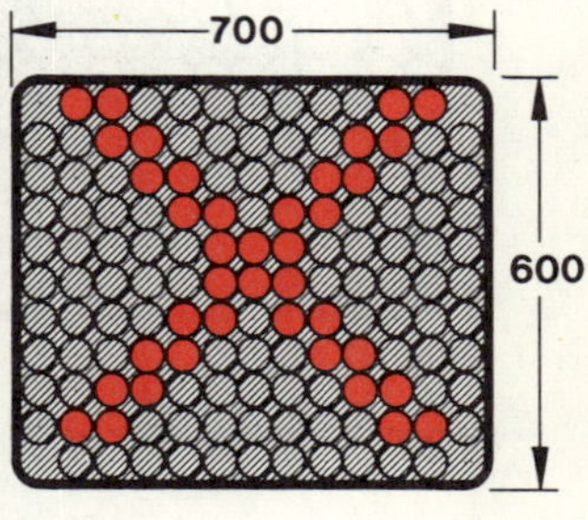

Lane of a carriageway closed to vehicular traffic facing the signal
(See Direction 6)
5004

SCHEDULE 6 (See Regulation 39 (1))

Dimensions in any diagram shown in this Schedule are expressed in millimetres unless otherwise specified

PART I

Size, colour and type of temporary indications on motorways

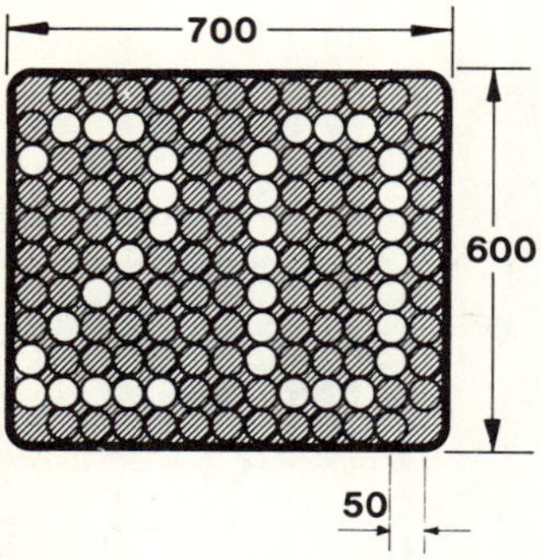

Temporary maximum speed (mph)
Permitted variant: The legend may be moved 50 mm to the right
(See Direction 39)
6001

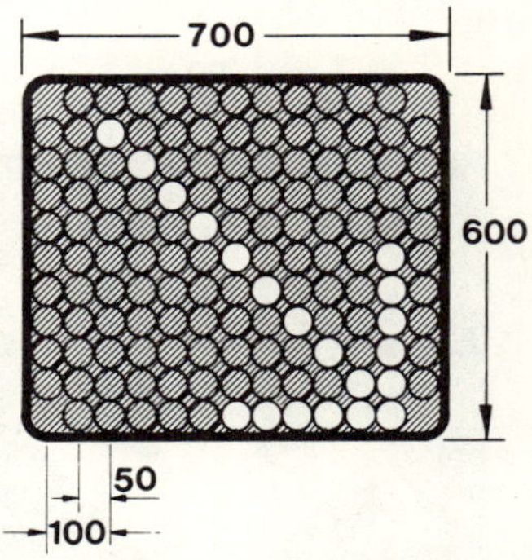

Move to the traffic lane on your right
Permitted variant: The arrow may be pointed downwards to the left to indicate change to lane on left
(See Directions 39 and 40)
6002

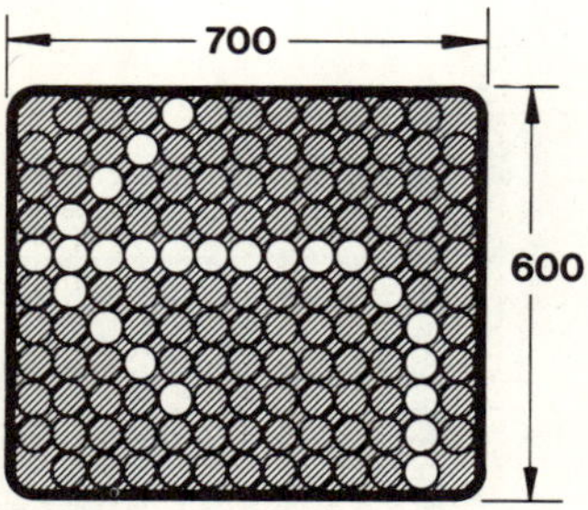

Leave motorway at next exit ahead
(See Direction 39)
6003

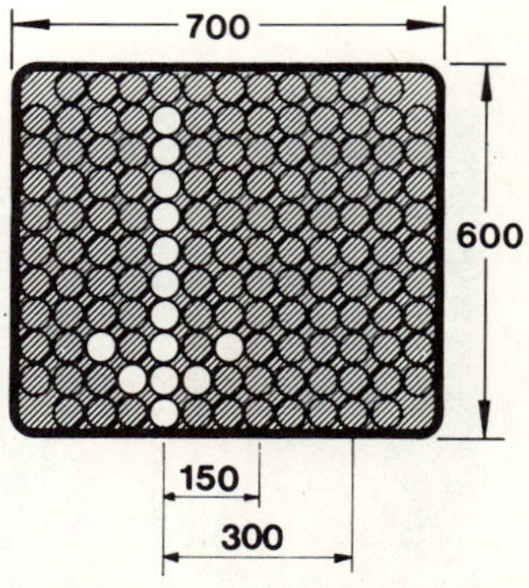

Lane available to vehicular traffic
Permitted variants: The arrow may be moved 150 or 300 mm to the right
(See Directions 39 and 40)
6004

SCHEDULE 6 *PART I*

Size, colour and type of temporary indications on motorways (contd.)

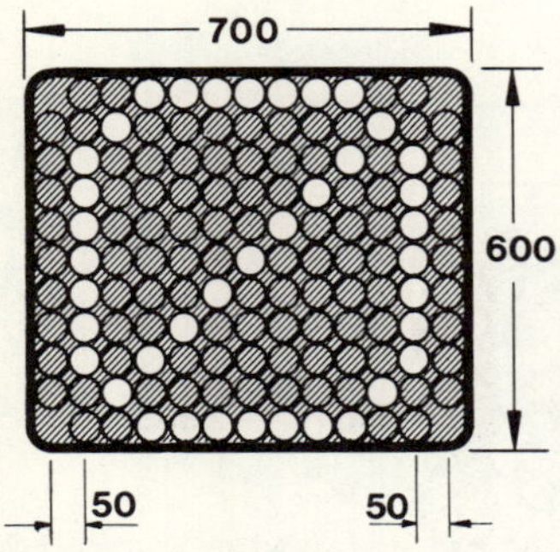

End of temporary indications
Permitted variant: The symbol may be moved 50 mm to the right or the left
(See Direction 39)
6005

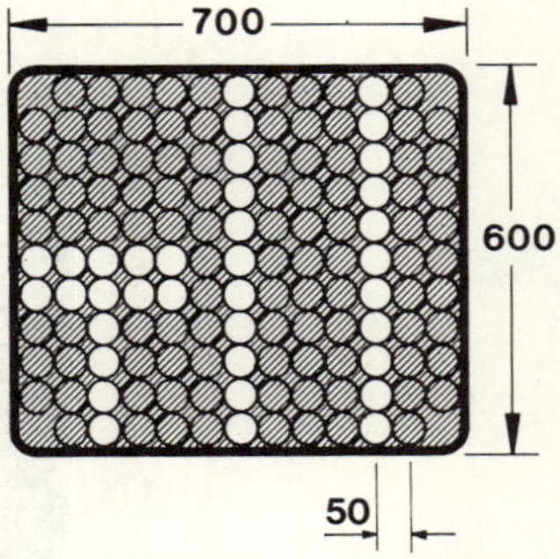

Left hand land of three lane carriageway closed to vehicular traffic ahead
Permitted variants:
The symbols may be varied to accord with the circumstances to indicate that the left hand lane and centre lane are both closed to vehicular traffic. The complete symbol may be moved 50mm to the right
(See Direction 40)
6006

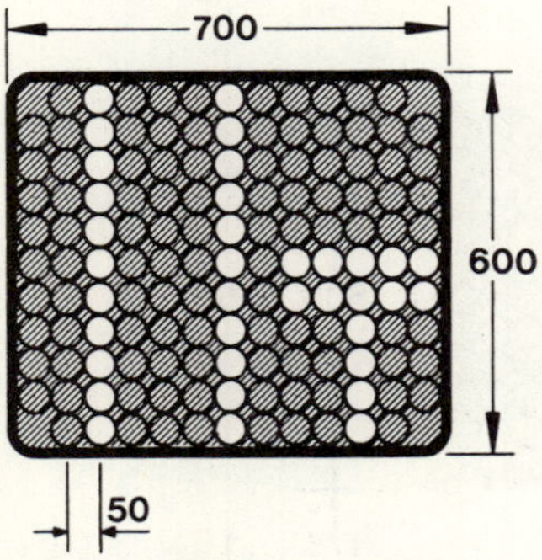

Right hand lane of three lane carriageway closed to vehicular traffic ahead
Permitted variants:
The symbols may be varied to indicate that the right hand lane and centre lane are both closed to vehicular traffic. The complete symbol may be moved 50mm to the left
(See Direction 40)
6007

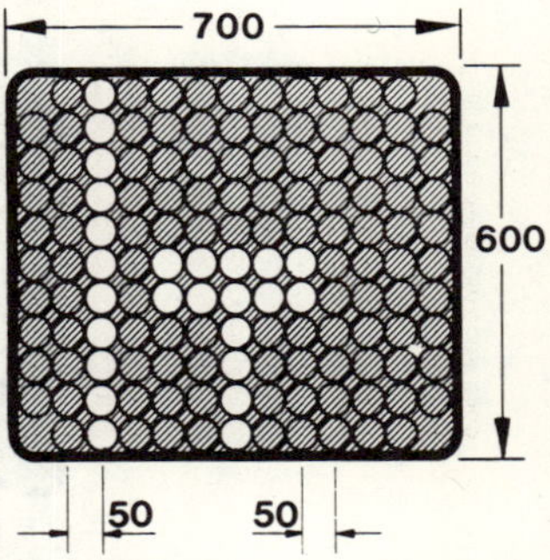

Right hand lane of two lane carriageway closed to vehicular traffic ahead
Permitted variant:
The symbols may be reversed to indicate left hand lane closed to vehicular traffic
(See Direction 40)
6008

SCHEDULE 6 (See Regulation 39 (2))

PART II

Diagrams showing the relationship between flashing amber lights prescribed in Regulation 39(3) and matrix capable of displaying signs shown in Part 1 of this Schedule

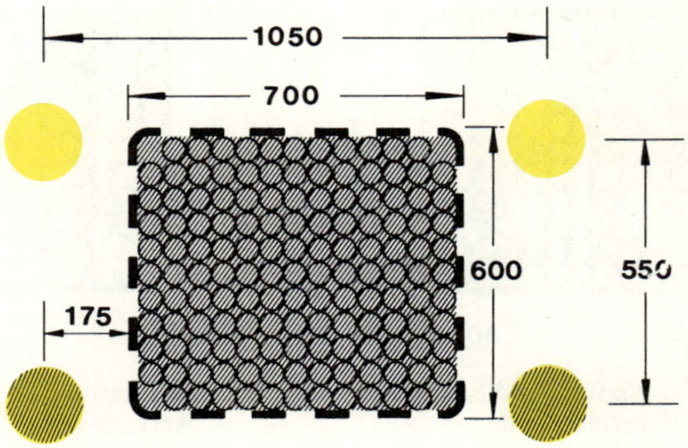

6021

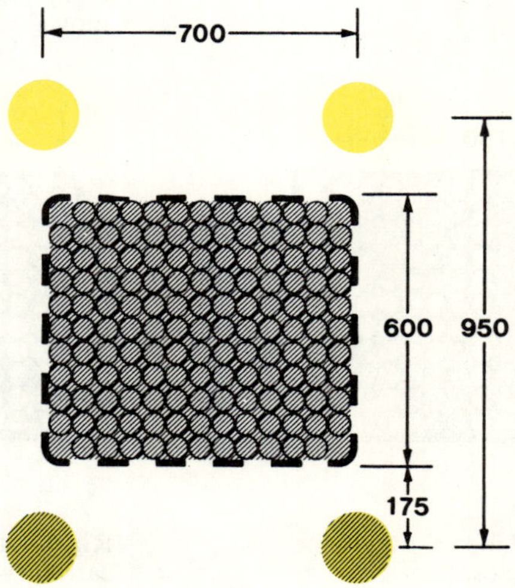

6022

SCHEDULE 6 (See Regulation 31 (3))

PART III

The relative positions of the lamps comprising the light signals prescribed by Regulation 31 (3)

6031

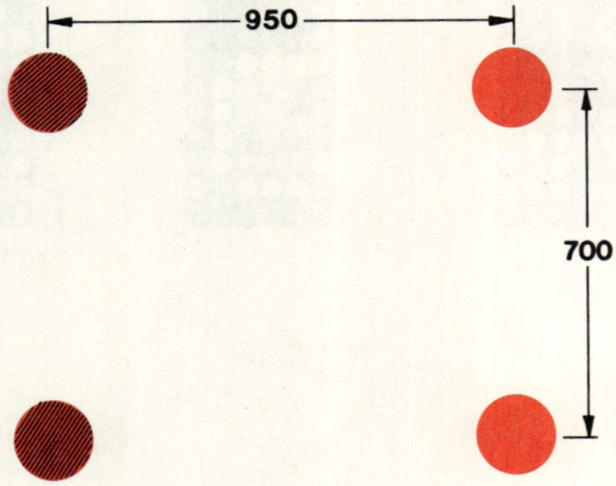

6032

SCHEDULE 6 (See Regulation 39 (5))

PART IV

Numerals for use in the sign shown at diagram 6001

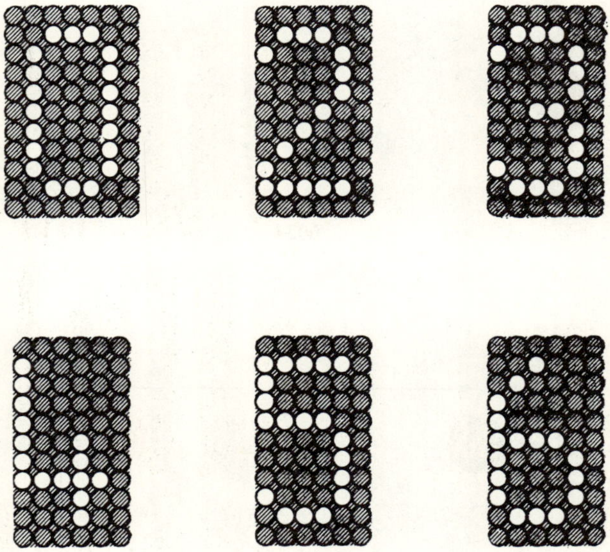

SCHEDULE 7 (See Regulation 14)
Proportion and form of letters, numerals and other characters

PART I
Transport Medium capital alphabet for use on signs with a red, blue or green background

SCHEDULE 7
Proportion and form of letters, numerals and other characters (contd.)

PART II

Transport Medium lower-case alphabet for use on signs with a red, blue or green background

SCHEDULE 7

Proportion and form of letters, numerals and other characters (contd.)

PART III

Transport Medium numerals for use on signs with a red, blue or green background

SCHEDULE 7

Proportion and form of letters, numerals and other characters (contd.)

PART IV

Transport Medium other characters for use on signs with a red, blue or green background, also on the grey or black background of a gantry

SCHEDULE 7

Proportion and form of letters, numerals and other characters (contd.)

PART V

Transport Heavy capital alphabet for use on signs with a white or yellow background

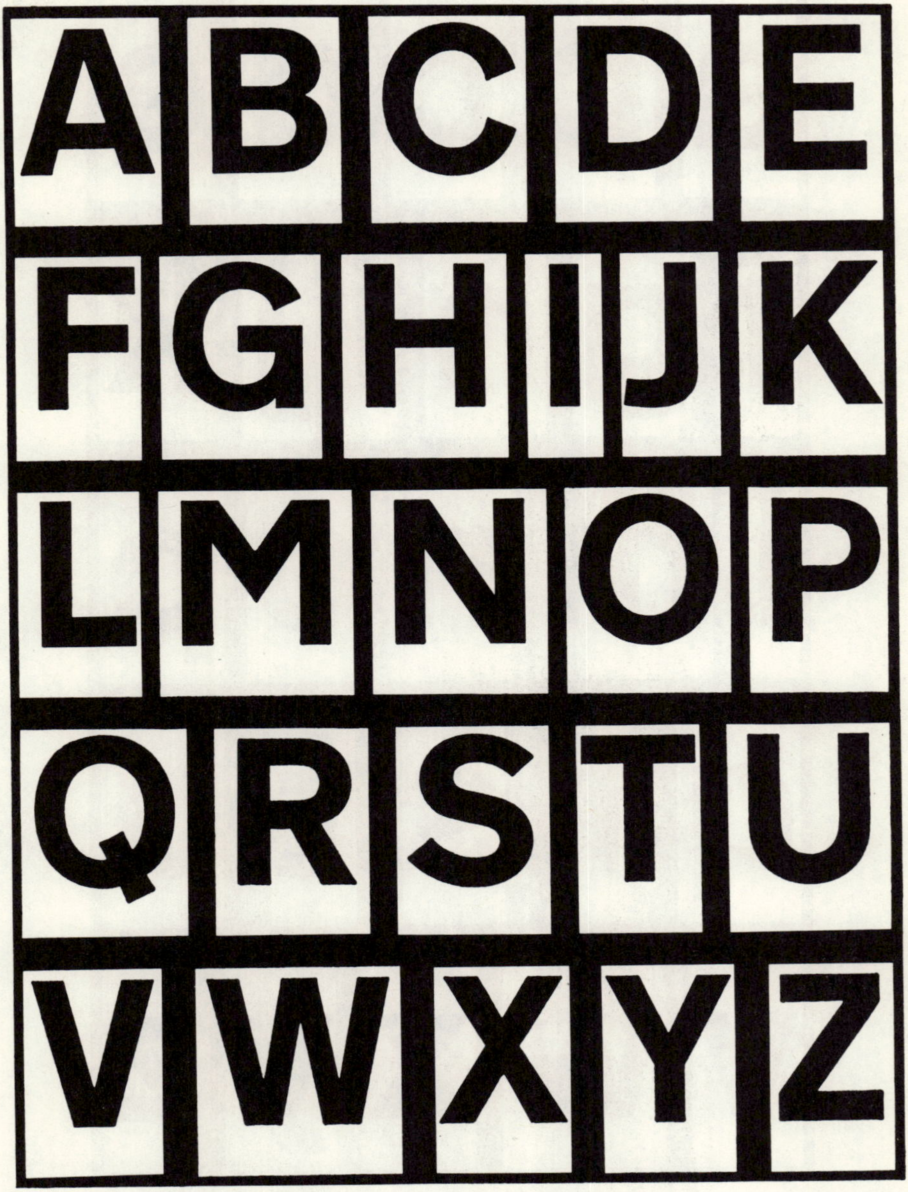

SCHEDULE 7

Proportion and form of letters, numerals and other characters (contd.)

PART VI

Transport Heavy lower-case alphabet for use on signs with a white or yellow background

SCHEDULE 7

Proportion and form of letters, numerals and other characters (contd.)

PART VII

Transport Heavy numerals for use on signs with a white or yellow background

SCHEDULE 7

Proportion and form of letters, numerals and other characters (contd.)

PART VIII

Transport Heavy other characters for use on signs with a white or yellow background

SCHEDULE 7

Proportion and form of letters, numerals and other characters (contd.)

PART IX

Letters and numerals for use in route numbers on the sign shown in diagram 757 and on any sign shown in Schedule I Part V

SCHEDULE 7

Proportion and form of letters, numerals and other characters (contd.)

PART X

Road marking alphabet and numerals with a height of 1.6 metres.
Colour to be white.

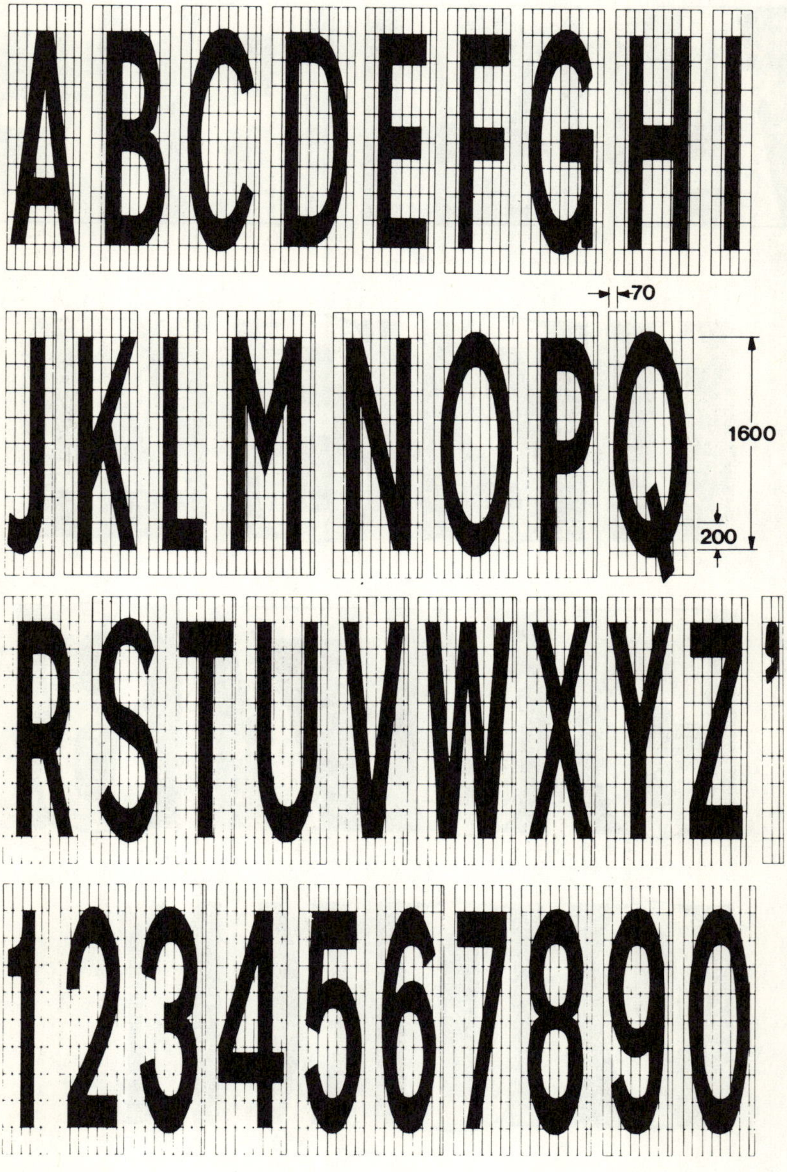

SCHEDULE 7
Proportion and form of letters, numerals and other characters (contd.)

PART XI

Road marking alphabet and numerals with a height of 2.8 metres.
Colour to be white.

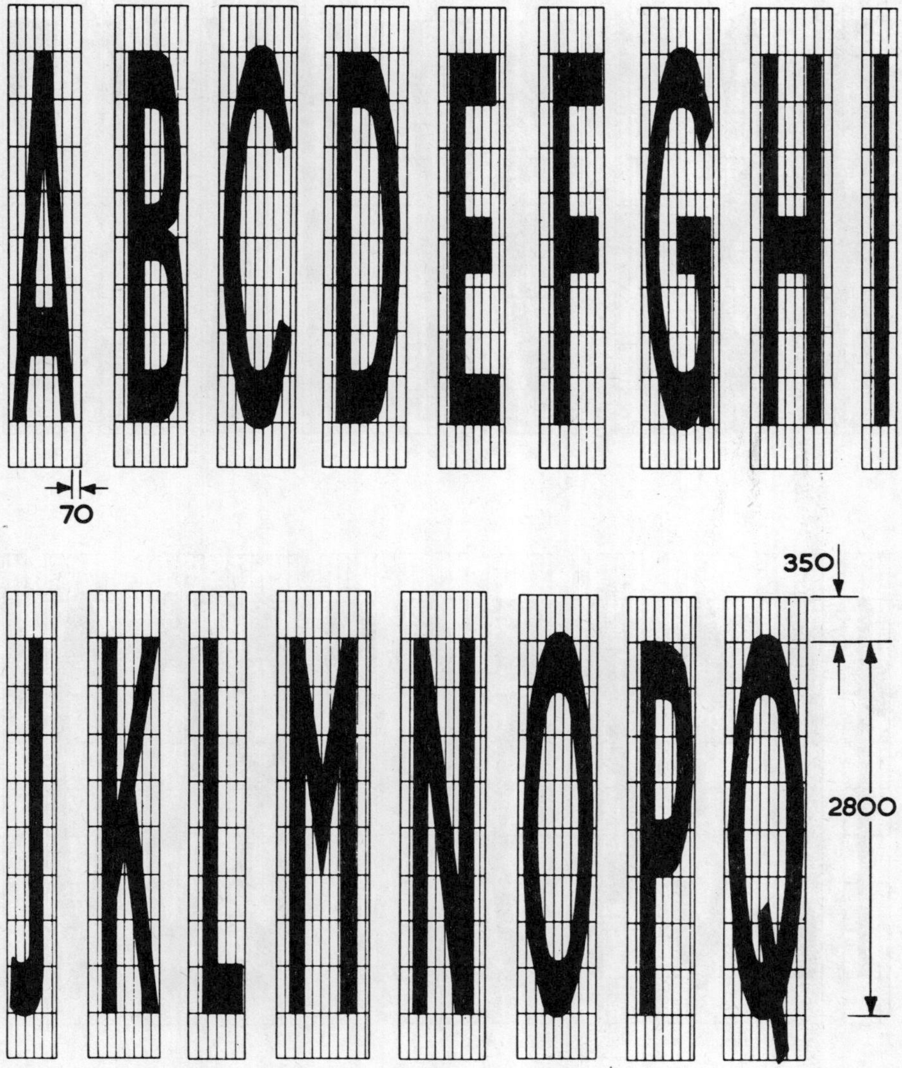

SCHEDULE 7

Proportion and form of letters, numerals and other characters (contd.)

PART XI (contd.)

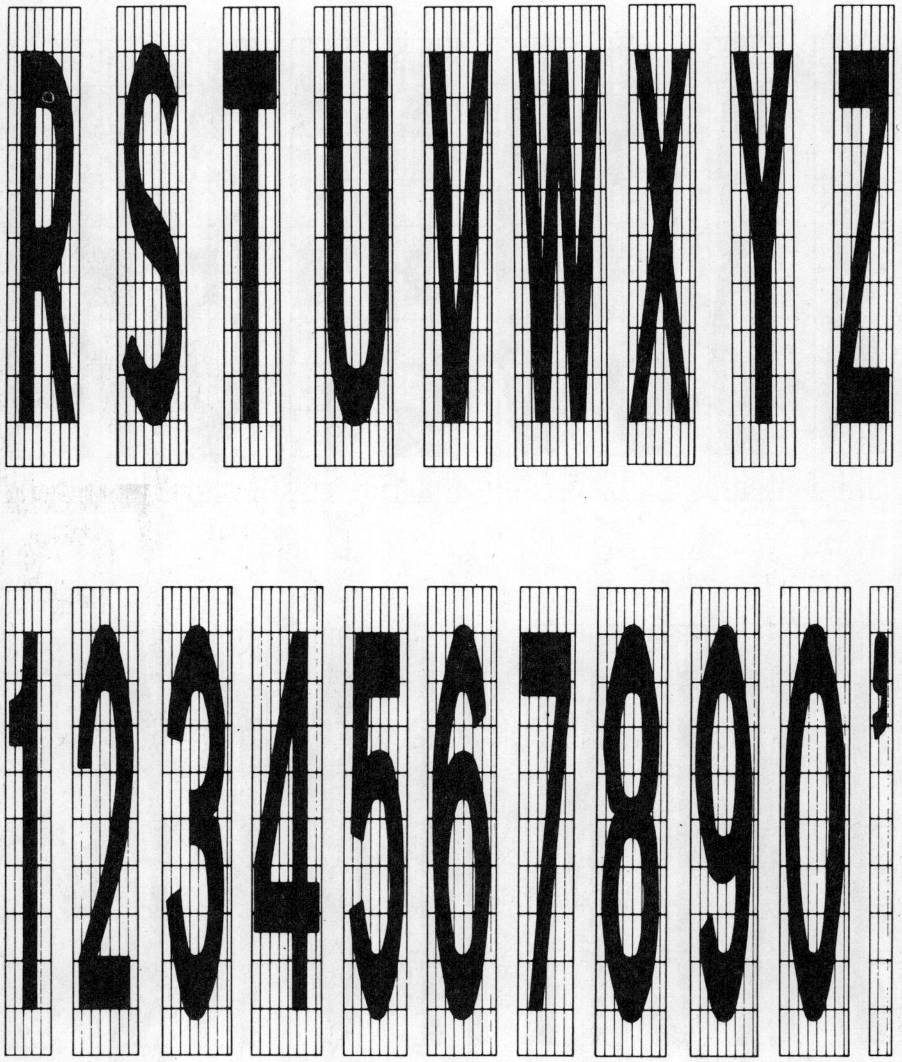

SCHEDULE 7

Proportion and form of letters, numerals and other characters (contd.)

PART XII

Road marking alphabet for use in the markings shown in diagrams 1027.1 and 1028.1
Colour of the alphabet to be white or yellow appropriate to the colours prescribed for the road marking by Regulation 24

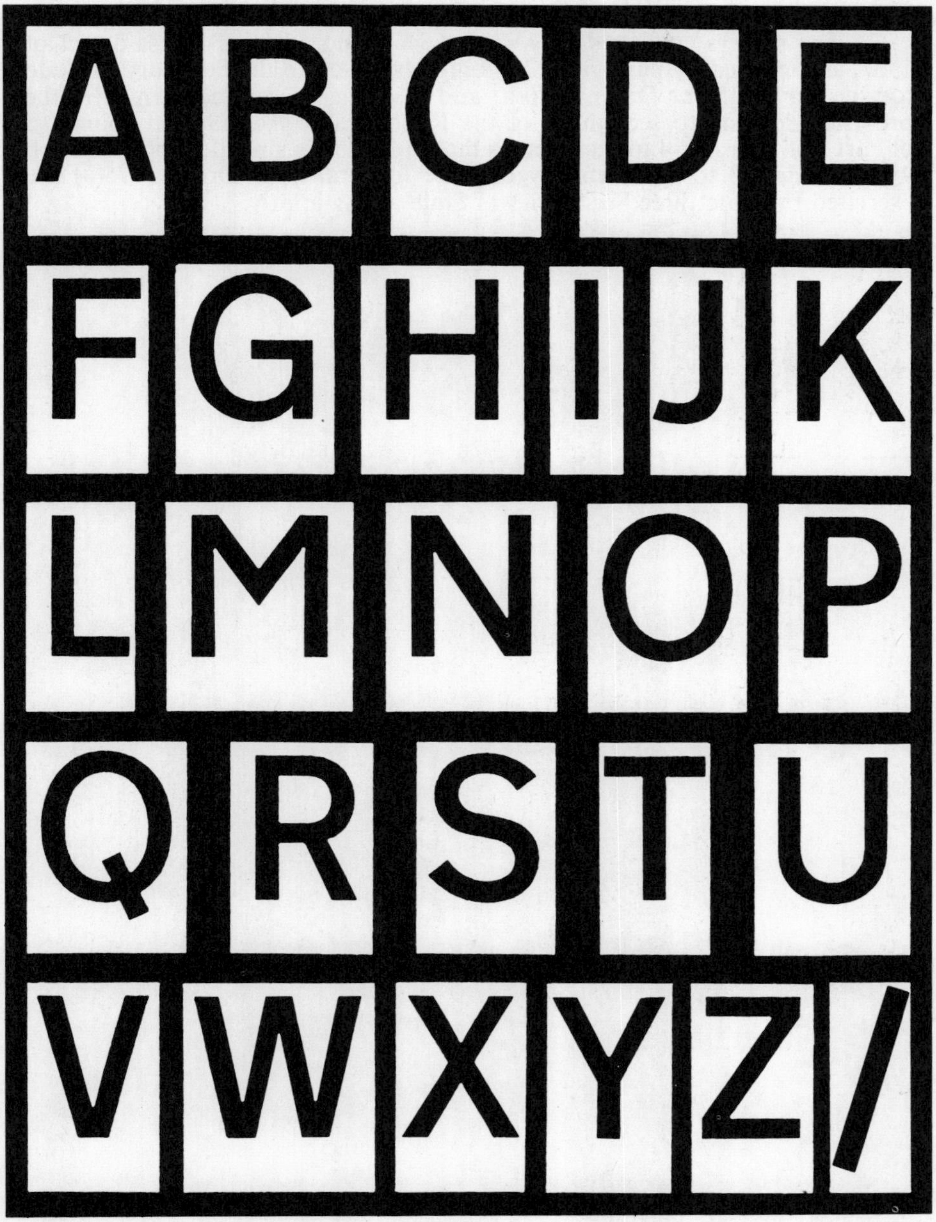

SCHEDULE 8

Exercise of powers

(1) The power conferred by section 25 of the Road Traffic Regulation Act 1967 is exercised by the Secretary of State for Transport as respects England, by the Secretary of State for Scotland as respects Scotland and the Secretary of State for Wales as respects Wales (see the definition of 'the appropriate Minister' in section 104(1) as read subject to section 108 of that Act).

(2) The powers conferred by sections 54(1) and 55(1) of the said Act of 1967, as amended by paragraph 24(*b*) of Schedule 3 to the Secretary of State for the Environment Order 1970(**a**) and also the powers conferred by the provision relating to section 22 of the Road Traffic Act 1972 in column 5 of Part I of Schedule 4 to that Act, as that provision is amended by paragraph 9 of Schedule 3 to the Secretary of State for Transport Order 1976(**b**) are exercised by those three Secretaries of State acting jointly.

(**a**) S.I. 1970/1681.
(**b**) S.I. 1976/1775.

Part II

General Directions

1. These Directions may be cited as "The Traffic Signs General Directions 1981".

2. The Traffic Signs General Directions 1975(**a**) are hereby revoked.

3. In these Directions the expressions "hours of darkness", "motorway", "primary route", "non-primary route", "road marking", "stud", "the Regulations of 1964" and "temporary statutory provision" have the same meanings as they have in the Traffic Signs Regulations 1981 (hereinafter in these Directions referred to as "the Regulations") and the expression "principal road" has the meaning assigned to it by section 84B(8) of the Road Traffic Regulation Act 1967.

4.—(1) Any reference in these Directions to a diagram by a number is a reference to the diagram of that number in any of the Schedules to the Regulations.

(2) Any reference in these Directions to any sign shown in a diagram being a diagram in any of the Schedules to the Regulations shall be construed as including a reference to any such sign varied in accordance with the provisions of the Regulations.

5. Without prejudice to section 64 of the Road Traffic Regulation Act 1967—

(1) whenever a sign shown in diagram 734.7 or in any of the diagrams 837.1 to 838.2 is to be placed for the first time at any given site on or near a primary route, that sign shall not be so placed unless the site shall have first been approved in writing by or on behalf of the Secretary of State; and

(2) whenever the sign shown in diagram 601.1 is to be placed for the first time at any given site on or near any road whatsoever, that sign shall not be so placed unless the site shall have first been so approved as aforesaid, except that if the said site shall already have been duly so approved for placing the sign shown in diagram 601 in Schedule 1 to the Regulations of 1964, its replacement by the sign shown in diagram 601.1 shall be treated as a placing otherwise than for the first time for the purposes of this sub-paragraph.

6.—(1) Except as provided by the next following sub-paragraph, signs shown in diagrams 606, 607, 609, 612 to 614, 616, 617 to 622.2, 622.4 to 625.1, 626.1 to 632, 636 to 640, 640.2A, 640.3 to 640.5, 641 to 644, 646, 647, 650 to 656.1, 660 to 662, 712, 712.1, 719.2, 719.3A, 729.1, 729.2, 760, 761, 801.3 to 801.5, 806 to 808.3, 810, 810.1, 812.1 to 812.4, 818.2 to 819.3, 1016.1 to 1021, 1025.1, 1025.3, 1028.1, 1032, 1033, 1036.1, 1036.2, 1037.1, 1043 to 1050, 5001 to 5004 may be placed on or near a road only to indicate the effect of an Act of Parliament, Order, Regulation, Bye-law or Notice which prohibits or restricts the use of the road by traffic.

(**a**) S.I.1975/1536.

(2) As exceptions to the provisions of the preceding sub-paragraph, the signs shown—

(*a*) in diagram 606 when erected on the central island of a roundabout or when used in combination with a plate of the type shown in diagram 608,

(*b*) in diagram 609 when used in the said combination or when placed on a road approaching its junction with a dual-carriageway road,

(*c*) in diagrams 616, 1046 and 1047 when placed at a site which has been approved in writing by or on behalf of the Secretary of State, and

(*d*) in diagrams 712.1, 719.3A and 729.2 when including a symbol represented in any of the diagrams in Part I, and no symbol so represented in Part II of Schedule 1 to the Regulations,

may be placed on or near a road in the circumstances prescribed respectively at (*a*) to (*d*) above for those signs notwithstanding that they do not in those circumstances so indicate as aforesaid.

In this paragraph "dual carriageway road" means a length of road on which one part of the carriageway is separated from another part by a central reservation, and "central reservation" means works, not consisting in a street refuge, provided in a road for separating one part of the carriageway of that road from another part for the safety or guidance of vehicular traffic using that road.

7. The signs shown in diagrams 701 to 717 may be placed only on or near a primary route and the signs shown in diagrams 718 to 726 may be placed only on or near a non-primary route, except that the signs shown in diagrams 718.2 and 718.3 may be placed on or near any road when varied to include a blue border.

8. The signs shown in diagrams 823 to 825 when the colour of the background is blue may be placed only on or near a motorway, when the colour of the background is green may be placed only on or near a primary route and when the colour of the background is white may be placed only on or near a non-primary route; and the signs shown in diagrams 837.1 to 838.2 may be placed only on or near a primary route or a motorway.

9. The signs shown in diagrams 901.1 to 925 may be placed only on or near a motorway.

10. The traffic signs shown in the diagrams whose numbers appear in column 1 of the table set out in this paragraph shall not be used on a road unless so used in conjunction with the road markings shown in the diagrams whose numbers appear in column 2 of that table opposite to the number in column 1 to which they relate:

Provided that the provisions of this paragraph requiring the use of the signs shown in diagrams 601.1, 602, 611.1 and 650 in conjunction with a road marking shall not apply during the execution of works on a road in the vicinity of the place where any of those signs is erected, if those works necessitate the temporary removal of that marking, and shall not apply if any of those signs is erected only temporarily in connection with the execution of works on a road.

TABLE

Column 1 Sign diagram number	*Column 2* Road marking diagram number
601.1	both 1002.1 and 1022
602	both 1003 and 1023
611.1	both 1003.3 and 1003.4
650	either 1025.1 or 1025.3
653	both 1048 and 1049
654	both 1048 and 1049

Any reference in this paragraph and in the next following paragraph to a traffic sign shown in diagram 601.1 and to the number of that diagram in the said table shall be treated as a reference until the 31st December 1981 inclusive of that date to any sign which can be treated as if prescribed by the Regulations until that date if it is a sign of the type shown in the diagram numbered 601 in Schedule 1 to the Traffic Signs Regulations 1964.

References in this paragraph to the road marking shown in diagram number 1002.1 specified in column 2 of the table above include, until the 31st December 1983 inclusive of that date, references to any road marking which can be treated until that date as if prescribed by the Regulations if it is a sign of the type shown in diagram 1002 in Schedule 2 to the Regulations of 1975.

11.—(1) The sign shown in diagram 501 shall not be used unless used either in combination with a plate of the type shown in diagram 502 and in conjunction with the sign shown in diagram 601.1 or in combination with a plate of the type shown in diagram 503 and in conjunction with the sign shown in diagram 602.

(2) The sign shown in diagram 545 shall not be used unless used in combination with any one of the following, that is to say, with a plate of the type shown in diagram 546 to 547.3, or the traffic sign (warning lights) prescribed by Regulation 37(2) of the Regulations.

(3) The traffic signs shown in the diagrams whose numbers appear in column 1 of the table set out at the end of this paragraph shall not be used unless used in combination with a plate of the type shown in the diagrams whose numbers appear in column 2 of that table opposite to the number in column 1 to which they relate.

(4) Where the indications given by any of the signs shown in diagrams 530, 532.1 and 629 to 629.2 are varied in accordance with Regulation 12(1)(*a*) of the Regulations, the sign whose indications shall have been so varied shall

not be used displaying the permitted variant unless used in combination with another sign of the same type whose indications have not been so varied as aforesaid and which gives the indications prescribed in the relevant diagram without the permitted variant.

TABLE

Column 1 Sign diagram number	*Column 2* Plate diagram number
533	either 534.1 or 534.2 or 535.1
544.2	547.4
562	either 537.3 or 563
617	either 618 or 618.1
632	either 570 or 645

12. A plate of the type shown in diagrams 502, 503, 511, 518, 519, 519.1, 525 to 527, 534.1, 534.2, 535.1, 537.1 to 537.4, 546, 547.1 to 547.4, 553, 556.3, 556.4, 563, 564.1, 570 to 573, 575, 579, 602.1, 607, 608, 618, 618.1, 619.3, 619.4, 620, 620.1, 622.3, 625.2, 627, 636.1, 642.1, 643 to 645, 656, 656.1, 660.2, 662, 802.1 to 805, 807, 812.3, 812.4 and 817.1 shall not be used unless used in combination with the signs which are specified beneath the diagrams showing the plate.

13. A plate of the type shown in diagrams 637, 639, 640, 641 or 646 may be placed on or near the side of a road only if there is placed in conjunction with that plate and on the same side of the road a road marking shown in diagrams 1016.1, 1017 or 1018, except that this paragraph shall not apply where any such plate is so placed for the purposes of a temporary statutory provision.

14. A plate of the type shown in diagram 638 or 640 may be placed on or near the side of a road only if there is placed in conjunction with that plate and on the same side of the road a road marking shown in diagram 1019, 1020 and 1021, except that this paragraph shall not apply where any such plate is so placed for the purpose of a temporary statutory provision.

15. The sign shown in diagram 545 when used in combination with the plate shown in diagram 547.1 or with the sign (amber flashing lights) prescribed by Regulation 37(2) of the Regulations may be placed only on a road on which, in the vicinity of the site of the sign, there is a place patrolled from time to time by a school crossing patrol or otherwise in use by children under supervision as provided by Regulation 37(2)(*b*).

16. The traffic sign shown in diagram 574 may be placed on a site on or near a road only where that site lies either in a place or area which is an infected place or area or part thereof for the purposes of the Diseases of Animals Act 1950(**a**), as extended by the Rabies Act 1974(**b**), or outside but near the boundaries of such a place or area, and shall not be retained there after that place or area or part thereof ceases to be or to be in such an infected place or area or part thereof.

17. The signs shown in diagrams 564, 564.1, 564.5 to 569.1, 754 to 756.1 and the signs shown in diagrams 858 to 858.2 when those last-mentioned signs are displayed on the yellow but not on the blue permitted backgrounds may be placed on or near a road only in connection with the execution of works thereon, or a temporary obstruction thereon, and any such sign so placed and any other sign shown in a diagram in Schedule 1 to the Regulations so placed as aforesaid shall not be retained on or near the road after the completion of the works or the removal of the obstruction, as the case may be, unless—

(i) it is a sign of the type shown in diagram 565.1 and if so, that sign may be retained on or near a road after the completion of the works for so long as the highway authority concerned sees fit, or

(ii) it is a sign of the type shown in diagram 565.2 bearing the words "Give way markings erased", or "stop markings erased" and if so, that sign shall have been removed as soon as the road markings have been replaced and in any event not later than 28 days from the date of completion of the works.

18.—(1) Signs shown in diagrams 603 and 604 may be used only where one-way working is necessary owing to a temporary closure to vehicular traffic of a width of the carriageway of a road.

(2) The signs shown in diagrams 615 and 811 shall not be used unless used in conjunction with one another and shall not be used at all in conjunction with the signs shown in diagrams 603 or 604.

(3) The signs shown in diagrams 634 and 635 may be used only by a constable in uniform or a person acting under the instructions or authority of the chief officer of police for the police area in which the signs are to be placed.

19. The sign shown in diagram 569.2 or 569.3 may be placed on or near a road only in connection with works involving an alteration in the layout of the carriageway or involving the removal of or change in the road markings or other traffic signs placed on or near a road at cross roads or other junctions (including in the case of the sign shown in the diagram 569.3 an automatic railway level crossing within the meaning of Regulation 25(1) of the Regulations), and shall be retained for not more than 3 months from the date of the completion of those works.

20. Signs shown in diagrams 830, 830.1, 831 and 832 (except when varied to contain the words "weight check") may be used only in connection with a traffic census the taking of which on a road has been approved by the highway authority for that road, by the chief officer of police of the police area in which the road is situate, and by or on behalf of the Secretary of State.

21. The signs shown in diagrams 833 to 836 may be used only to regulate the movement of vehicular traffic into and out of premises with more than one access to a road.

(**a**) 1950 c. 36.
(**b**) 1974 c. 17.

22. The sign shown in diagram 536 shall be mounted on two posts and so much of each post as extends above ground level shall be coloured black and white in alternate horizontal bands, each band being not less than 250 nor more than 335 millimetres in depth.

23.—(1) The sign shown in diagram 560 or diagram 561 shall be so placed that the top of the sign is not less than 550 millimetres nor more than one metre above the surface of the carriageway in the immediate vicinity.

(2) Where the sign shown in diagram 560 or diagram 561 is mounted on a post specially provided for the purpose, that part of the post which extends above ground level shall be coloured black and white in alternate horizontal bands, each band being not less than 225 nor more than 350 millimetres in depth.

(3) The signs shown in diagrams 560 and 561 shall be so erected as to display the colour red on the left-hand edge of the carriageway viewed by the drivers of approaching vehicles and the colour white on the right-hand edge of that carriageway so viewed as aforesaid unless the said right-hand edge is the edge of the central reservation of a dual carriageway when the said signs shall be so erected as to display the colour amber on the said right-hand edge viewed by those drivers instead of the colour white.

24.—(1) The road marking shown in diagram 1001 shall not be placed on a road unless it is so placed for use in conjunction with the light signals prescribed by paragraph (2) or paragraph (4) of Regulation 31 of the Regulations or with the light signals prescribed by the said paragraph (2) as varied in accordance with Regulation 32 of the Regulations or unless it is so placed at a site where vehicular traffic is from time to time controlled by the police.

(2) Where both primary and secondary signals within the meaning of Regulation 34(6) of the Regulations have been erected, the reference in sub-paragraph (1) above to light signals prescribed by the said paragraph (2) or paragraph (4) of Regulation 31 or by the said paragraph 2 as so varied as aforesaid shall be construed as a reference to both the primary and the secondary signals or if either the primary or secondary signals are not operating, to the primary signals operating alone or to the secondary signals operating alone as the case may be.

25. The road markings shown in diagrams 1002.1 and 1022 shall not be placed on a road unless they are so placed for use in conjunction with the sign shown in diagram 601.1 or until the 31st December 1981 inclusive of that date, with any sign which can be treated as if prescribed by the Regulations until that date if it is a sign of the type shown in the diagram numbered 601 in Schedule 1 to the Traffic Signs Regulations 1964; and the road marking shown in diagram 1003.4 shall not be so placed as aforesaid unless it is placed for use in conjunction with the sign shown in diagram 611.1.

26.—(1) Subject to sub-paragraph (4) of this paragraph, the road marking shown in diagram 1017 may be placed on a side of a road only for the purpose of indicating a statutory prohibition or restriction on the waiting of vehicles which applies on that side for at least eight hours during the period from 7 a.m. to 7 p.m. on at least four days other than a Sunday in any week.

(2) Subject as aforesaid, the road marking shown in diagram 1018 may be placed on a side of a road only for the purpose of indicating a statutory prohibition or restriction on the waiting of vehicles which applies on that

side for at least eight hours during the period from 7 a.m. to 7 p.m. on at least four days other than a Sunday in any week and at some other times other than those during the period from 7 a.m. to 7 p.m.

(3) Subject to sub-paragraph (5) of this paragraph, the road marking shown in diagram 1016.1 may be placed on a side of a road only for the purpose of indicating a statutory prohibition or restriction on the waiting of vehicles which does not fall to be indicated by the road markings mentioned in sub-paragraphs (1) and (2) of this paragraph.

(4) In sub-paragraphs (1) and (2) of this paragraph the references to a statutory prohibition or restriction on the waiting of vehicles shall be construed as excluding references to any such prohibition or restriction as aforesaid imposed—

(*a*) on waiting for the purpose of loading or unloading a vehicle,

(*b*) so as expressly to limit the duration of waiting of vehicles within a particular period,

(*c*) on waiting where the provisions of such prohibition or restriction exempt the waiting of a vehicle in respect of which a certificate of such exemption has been granted to the owner thereof as being one of a class of persons who qualify for the grant of such a certificate solely on the ground that they are all persons whose usual place of abode is at premises situated beside a road specified in relation to the prohibition or restriction, or

(*d*) on waiting of a goods vehicle (as defined by section 196(1) of the Road Traffic Act 1972 (**a**)) but of no other vehicle.

(5) In sub-paragraph (3) of this paragraph the reference to a statutory prohibition or restriction on the waiting of vehicles shall be construed as excluding references to any such prohibition or restriction imposed on waiting such as is described in sub-paragraph (4)(*a*), (*c*) or (*d*) of this paragraph.

27.—(1) The road marking shown in diagram 1020 may be placed on a side of a road only for the purpose of indicating a statutory prohibition or restriction on the waiting of vehicles for the purpose of their being loaded or unloaded (but not for indicating a statutory prohibition or restriction which expressly limits the duration of waiting by vehicles within a particular period for the purpose of their being loaded or unloaded) which applies on that side for at least eight hours during the period from 7 a.m. to 7 p.m. on at least four days other than a Sunday in any week.

(2) The road marking shown in diagram 1021 may be placed on a side of a road only for the purpose of indicating a statutory prohibition or restriction on the waiting of vehicles for the purpose of their being loaded or unloaded (but not for indicating a statutory prohibition or restriction which expressly limits the duration of waiting by vehicles within a particular period for the purpose of their being loaded or unloaded) which applies on that side for at least eight hours during the period from 7 a.m. to 7 p.m. on at least four days other than a Sunday in any week and at some other times other than those during the period from 7 a.m. to 7 p.m.

(3) The road marking shown in diagram 1019 may be placed on a side of a road only for the purpose of indicating a statutory prohibition or restriction on the waiting of vehicles for the purpose of their being loaded or unloaded (but not for indicating a statutory prohibition or restriction which

(**a**) 1972 c. 20.

expressly limits the duration of waiting by vehicles within a particular period for the purpose of their being loaded or unloaded) which applies otherwise than is specified in sub-paragraphs (1) and (2) of this paragraph.

28. A road marking shown in diagrams 1016.1, 1017 or 1018 shall not be used unless used in conjunction with at least one plate of the type shown in diagrams 637, 639, 640, 641 or 642.1 (used as directed in paragraph 12 of these Directions) which plate shall be placed on the same side of the road as that on which is placed that marking, except that this paragraph shall not apply where any such marking is placed within a controlled parking zone.

In this and the next succeeding paragraph the expression "controlled parking zone" means an area in which all roads have been marked, except where parking places have been designated, with one or more of the road markings shown in diagrams 1016.1 to 1021, the entrances for vehicular traffic into the area being indicated by a sign shown in diagram 806 or 806.1.

29. A road marking shown in diagrams 1019, 1020 or 1021 shall not be used unless used in conjunction with at least one plate of the type shown in diagrams 638, 640 or 642.1 which plate shall be placed on the same side of the road as that on which is placed that marking and such a marking shall be placed on the footway as near as practicable to the edge of the carriageway or, if there is no footway, on the carriageway as near as is practicable to its edge, except that nothing in this paragraph shall require the provision of a plate in conjunction with any such marking if the marking is placed within a controlled parking zone.

30.—(1) The road markings shown in diagram 1023 shall not be placed on a road unless so placed for use in conjunction with the road marking shown in diagram 1003.

(2) The road markings shown in diagrams 1025.1 and 1025.3 shall not be placed on a road unless so placed for use in conjunction with at least one sign of the type shown in diagram 650 which shall have been erected on or near the same side of the road as that on which the marking is placed.

(3) The road marking shown in diagram 1048 shall not be placed on a road unless so placed for use in conjunction with the marking shown in diagram 1049 and either the traffic sign shown in diagram 653 or that shown in diagram 654; and the marking shown in diagram 1049 shall not be placed on a road unless so placed for use in conjunction with the marking shown in diagram 1048 and either the sign shown in diagram 653 or that shown in diagram 654.

31. Studs incorporating reflectors may be placed on a road only if such studs are of a type which has first been approved in writing by or on behalf of the Secretary of State.

32. No sign, used in accordance with the provisions of Regulation 27 of the Regulations may be retained at any place on or near a principal road after the expiration of six months from the date on which the sign was erected at that place, or such longer time as may be approved in writing by or on behalf of the Secretary of State, or be retained in any case after the termination of the need for such a sign.

33. Where the lamp mentioned in Regulation 30 of the Regulations is mounted on a post specially provided for the purpose—

(1) if that post is a post placed on a street refuge or central reservation on a zebra crossing and yellow globes also are attached to, or mounted on that post, then the provisions of paragraph 2(4) of Part II of Schedule 2 to the 'Zebra' Pedestrian Crossings Regulations 1971(**a**) shall have effect and apply to the colouring of that post in so far as it extends above ground level up to the point where the yellow globes are mounted or attached and beyond that point any remaining part of the post shall be coloured in accordance with sub-paragraph (2) of this paragraph; and

(2) if that post is a post so placed as aforesaid but yellow globes are not also attached to, or mounted on it or if the post is placed elsewhere than on a zebra crossing, then that post shall be coloured grey but with two white bands, each band being not less than 275 nor more than 335 millimetres in depth, being so arranged that at least 275 but not more than 335 millimetres extend between the nearest edges of the two bands, and the upper edge of the uppermost band being at least 275 but not more than 335 millimetres below the lowest part of the lamp:

Provided that where such a post is constructed of concrete it shall not be coloured in either manner as aforesaid but shall remain in its natural colour.

In this paragraph "zebra crossing" has the same meaning as in the said Regulations of 1971 and "yellow globes" means globes in relation to which the provisions of Part II of Schedule 2 to the said Regulations of 1971 are complied with.

34.—(1) Light signals such as are prescribed in Regulations 31 to 33, 35, 36, 37(2), 38 and 39 of the Regulations may be placed on or near a road only if the following conditions are satisfied, that is to say—

(*a*) the said signals are so placed that they face the stream of traffic to which they are intended to convey respectively the warning, information, requirements, restrictions or prohibitions prescribed by the Regulations;

(*b*) the apparatus (including the content of all instructions stored in, or executable by it) used in connection with the said signals is of a type which has been approved in writing by or on behalf of the Secretary of State; and

(*c*) if the light signals are light signals prescribed by Regulation 31(4) of the Regulations and are to be erected at or near a level crossing (where a road is crossed by a railway) otherwise than in pursuance of an Order made by the Secretary of State under section 66 of the British Transport Commission Act 1957(**a**) (which empowers the Secretary of State to authorise special arrangements at public level crossings) or of an Order so made under section 124 of the Transport Act 1968(**b**) (British Railways Board's obligations at level crossings with roads other than public carriage roads), the site for, and the number and disposition of, those signals shall first have been approved in writing by or on behalf of the Secretary of State after consideration of such plans for the site and such other information as he may require for the purposes of his function in this condition.

(2) If, after any light signals such as are mentioned in sub-paragraph (1) of this paragraph have been placed on or near a road, the apparatus used

---

(**a**) 5 & 6 Eliz. 2 c. xxxiii. (**b**) 1968 c. 73.

in connection with the said signals is altered so as to enable any further instructions to be stored in, or made executable by, the apparatus, the said signals shall not be further used unless that alteration is of a type which has been approved in writing by or on behalf of the Secretary of State.

(3) The light signals prescribed by Regulation 31(2) and (4) of the Regulations or those light signals as varied in accordance with Regulation 32 thereof shall not be used unless used in conjunction with the road marking shown in diagram 1001, except that this sub-paragraph shall not apply while works which necessitate the temporary removal of that road marking are being executed on a road in the vicinity of the place where the said light signals are erected.

(4) The containers enclosing the lamps of each of the kinds of light signals mentioned in sub-paragraph (1) of this paragraph shall be coloured black, except that if those containers enclose lamps of the light signals prescribed by Regulation 31(3), 36, 37(2) or 39 of the Regulations, they may be coloured grey instead of black.

(5) Any of the kinds of light signals mentioned in sub-paragraph (1) of this paragraph other than the signals prescribed by Regulation 35 of the Regulations may be mounted with a backing board and if so mounted, the backing board shall be coloured black and may have a white border not less than 85 nor more than 95 millimetres in width in the case of signals prescribed by Regulation 31(4) of the Regulations and not less than 45 nor more than 55 millimetres in width in the case of the other kinds of light signals which may be so mounted.

(6) Without prejudice to the next following sub-paragraph, where light signals prescribed by any of the Regulations specified in sub-paragraph (1) of this paragraph are mounted on a post specially provided for the purpose, that part of the post which extends above ground level shall be coloured grey and may have one white band not less than 140 nor more than 160 millimetres in depth, the lower edge of the band being not less than 1·5 nor more than 1·7 metres above the level of the surface of the ground in the immediate vicinity.

(7) In the case of light signals prescribed by Regulation 33 of the Regulations, instead of being mounted on a post coloured in accordance with the provisions of the last preceding sub-paragraph, they may be mounted on either a post coloured yellow (but having no such white band as therein specified) or alternatively on a tripod coloured yellow.

35. Where a sign shown in a diagram in Schedule 1 other than a sign shown in diagram 569, 569.1, 603 to 605.1, 651, or 845 to 852 is mounted on a post specially provided for the purpose, that part of the post which extends above ground level shall be coloured grey except to the extent provided in sub-paragraphs (*a*) to (*d*) below—

(*a*) in a case where different provision as to the colouring of the post is made in the foregoing provisions of these Directions;

(*b*) in a case where the post is constructed of concrete, or is supporting a sign placed temporarily on the road in connection with the execution of works or any obstruction thereon and is constructed of timber, then the concrete post shall remain in its natural colour and the timber post supporting such a sign so placed may remain in its natural colour;

(*c*) in a case where the post is not likely to be readily visible to pedestrians, then one white band of not less than 140 nor more than 160 millimetres in depth may be provided, the lower edge of the band being between 1·5 and 1·7 metres above the level of the surface of the ground in the immediate vicinity; and

(*d*) the structure, if any, on which the beacons or the lamp respectively prescribed by Regulations 28(1), and 40 of the Regulations are supported shall be coloured either grey or yellow or in alternate bands of red and white or of black and white; and such a structure for supporting the beacons prescribed by Regulation 28(2) of the Regulations shall be coloured black and white in alternate bands.

36.—(1) The back of any sign shown in a diagram in Schedule 1, other than a sign shown in diagram 569.1, of any backing board or other fitting provided for the assembly of such a sign, including any container enclosing apparatus for the illumination of that sign, shall be coloured—

(*a*) black, if the sign is mounted on the same post as that on which light signals prescribed by Regulation 31(2) of the Regulations or those signals as varied by Regulation 32 thereof, or prescribed by Regulation 33 of the Regulations are mounted, and

(*b*) grey in any other case except that information about sites for placing the sign may be indicated on the back of the sign in characters not exceeding 15 millimetres in height.

(2) The back of a sign of the type shown in diagram 569.1 in Schedule 1 shall be coloured either grey or white.

37. The traffic signs shown in diagrams 806, 806.1, 807 and 808.1 may only be placed on or near a road if every road contained within the controlled parking zone indicated by the said signs so shown has been marked with a road marking of a kind shown in one of the diagrams 1016.1 to 1021 appropriate to the nature of the restriction in force except in so far as the parking places for vehicles have been designated and provided on that road.

In this paragraph the expression "controlled parking zone" has the same meaning as in paragraph 28 of these Directions.

38. The light signals prescribed by Regulations 31(3) and 38 of the Regulations and the light signals shown in any diagram in Parts I and II of Schedule 6 may be displayed only on or near a motorway.

39. The light signals prescribed by Regulation 31(3) of the Regulations shall not be displayed over or in relation to a traffic lane (as defined by Regulation 36(1) of the Regulations) at the same time as any sign shown in any of the diagrams 6001 to 6005 is also being displayed over or in relation to that same traffic lane and at the same place on that lane.

40. The traffic signs shown in diagrams 6002 and 6004 may be displayed only over a traffic lane as so defined and the signs shown in diagrams 6006, 6007 and 6008 may be displayed only at the side of the carriageway to which the indications given by those signs relate.

41.—(1) Without prejudice to the provisions of paragraph 34 of these Directions, this paragraph applies to all traffic signs which are not continuously in use over a period of 24 hours and are capable of being brought into and taken out of use for the time being by the operation of any electrical or other apparatus.

(2) The said electrical or other apparatus by which the traffic signs to which this paragraph applies are brought into and taken out of use and any other

apparatus (including the content of all instructions stored in, or executable by it) used to secure that the said traffic signs comply with the relevant provisions of the Regulations shall be of a type which has been approved in writing by or on behalf of the Secretary of State before the said traffic signs are placed on or near any road.

(3) If, after any traffic sign to which this paragraph applies has been placed on or near any road, the said electrical or other apparatus by which the sign is brought into and taken out of use, or which is used to secure that the sign complies with the relevant provisions of the Regulations, is altered so as to enable any further instruction to be stored in, or made executable by, the apparatus, the said sign shall not be further used unless that alteration is of a type which has been approved in writing by or on behalf of the Secretary of State.

42. At least one road marking of the kind shown in diagram 1014 shall be placed for use in conjunction with a road marking of the kind shown in diagram 1013.1 on the length of carriageway which extends backwards from the commencement of any continuous line marked on the carriageway as a part of the last mentioned road marking so shown, such commencement being viewed in the direction of travel of a vehicle driven so as to have and keep that continuous line on the right hand or offside thereof in accordance with Regulation 23(2)(*b*) of the Regulations, and if more than one road marking of the kind first above-mentioned is placed on the said length of carriageway then those road markings shall be so spaced apart that one follows in in line in front of the other.

43. Nothing in these Directions shall be taken to limit the power of the Secretary of State acting as the appropriate Minister by any special Direction to dispense with, add to or modify any of the requirements of these Directions in their application to any particular case.

PART III

GENERAL CITATION AND COMMENCEMENT

This Instrument may be cited as the Traffic Signs Regulations and General Directions 1981, and shall come into operation on 13th August 1981.

9*th June* 1981	Norman Fowler, Secretary of State for Transport.
10*th June* 1981	George Younger, Secretary of State for Scotland.
9*th June* 1981	Nicholas Edwards, Secretary of State for Wales.

EXPLANATORY NOTE

(*This Note is not part of the Instrument.*)

The Instrument in Part 1 re-enacts with amendments the Traffic Signs Regulations 1975 (S.I. 1975/1536). The principal changes are:

1. Regulation 9A prescribes the size, colour, type and significance of the sign shown in diagram 610 providing a special significance for emergency vehicles (Regulation 9A(3)).

2. Regulation 11(2), dealing with automatic railway level crossings, extends the significance of the traffic sign controlling certain vehicles approaching such crossings where the crossing is without barriers but is monitored remotely and automatically by the operation of light signals.
3. Regulation 12 extends the range of permitted variants for the indications given by many signs.
4. The provisions as to the illumination of signs by lighting and by the use of reflecting material have been rearranged and a number of requirements have been relaxed (Regulations 15 to 19).
5. Regulation 37 introduces new provisions enabling the flashing amber lights prescribed in sub-paragraph (2)(*c*) to be used when school children are crossing the road under the supervision of a teacher or other school officer, a traffic warden or a constable in uniform.
6. A number of new signs are introduced into Schedules 1 to 6 including a sign warning of the presence of blind, elderly or handicapped pedestrians, signs for controlling the movement of goods vehicles of specified maximum gross metric weight, signs indicating the closure of a lane or lanes of a carriageway and a road marking for use with the 'STOP' sign shown in diagram 601.1

Part II of the Instrument re-enacts with amendments The General Directions 1975. The principal changes are:

1. A reduction is made in the number of signs which are required to have their sites approved by the Secretary of State prior to their erection (Direction 5).
2. Direction 11(4) provides that where certain signs may be varied to display metric units the signs so varied must always be used in conjunction with signs of a similar type displaying imperial units.
3. Direction 32, dealing with the period of time temporary signs may continue to be displayed on site, ceases to apply to signs other than those used in accordance with the requirements of Regulation 27 (about certain temporary signs).
4. There is no longer any requirement for the siting of light signals to be approved by the Secretary of State (except in certain cases relating to the signals erected at railway level crossings) (Regulation 31(4)) (Direction 34(1)). Only light signal apparatus which conforms to a type which has been approved by the Secretary of State may be used (Direction 34(1)(*b*)).

Printed in England for Her Majesty's Stationery Office by Bemrose Specialist Print, Derby.
850/J54 C200 7/81

ISBN 0 11 016859 3